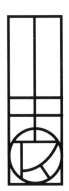

Elbert Hubbard, ca. 1912. Photographed by Moffett Studios, Chicago.
(Courtesy Elbert Hubbard-Roycroft Museum)

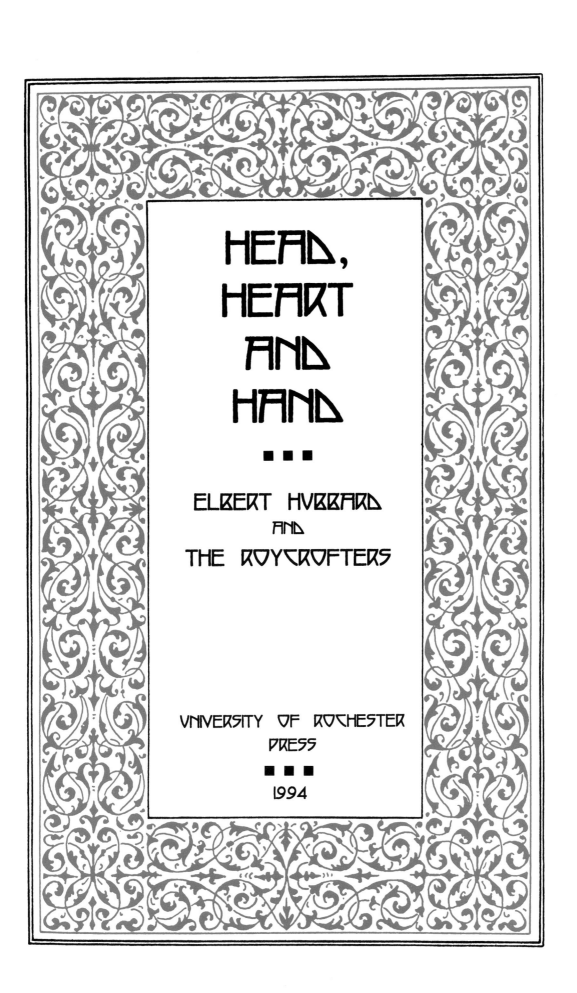

HEAD, HEART AND HAND

...

ELBERT HUBBARD
AND
THE ROYCROFTERS

UNIVERSITY OF ROCHESTER
PRESS
■■■
1994

First published 1994

University of Rochester Press
200 Administration Building, University of Rochester
Rochester, New York, 14627, USA
and at PO Box 9, Woodbridge, Suffolk IP12 3DF, UK

Library of Congress Cataloging-in-Publication Data
Head, heart, and hand : Elbert Hubbard and the Roycrofters / edited by
Marie Via and Marjorie Searl.
    p.   cm.
    Exhibition catalog.
    Includes bibliographical references and index.
    ISBN 1–878822–43–8 (acid-free paper) : — ISBN
1–878822–44–6 (pbk. : acid-free paper) :
    1. Hubbard, Elbert, 1856–1915—Exhibitions.   2. Roycroft Shop—
Exhibitions.   3. Arts and crafts movement—New York (State)—East
Aurora—Exhibitions.   I. Via, Marie, 1952– . II. Searl,
Marjorie, 1947– . III. University of Rochester. Memorial Art
Gallery.
   NK1149.R6H43   1994
  745′.09747′96—dc20   94–26743

British Library Cataloguing in Publication Data
Head, Heart and Hand: Elbert Hubbard and
the Roycrofters
   I. Via, Marie   II. Searl, Marjorie
   745.50973

    ISBN 1–878822–43–8
    ISBN 1–878822–44–6 pbk

Printed in Great Britain

Contents

Acknowledgements

The opportunity to express appreciation to those who have contributed to the success of *Head, Heart and Hand* is simultaneously satisfying and daunting, not unlike the task of organizing the exhibition itself. A full accounting of those who provided information, assistance, and encouragement during the past two years would constitute another chapter in this book, but a number of colleagues, friends, and collectors deserve special mention.

The entire staff of the Memorial Art Gallery rallied to the aid of the exhibition team, and we are truly grateful for Director Grant Holcomb's unswerving confidence in our ideas and abilities. In the curatorial department, particular thanks go to Dan Knerr, assistant registrar; Carol Acquilano, preparator; and Kathy Ertsgaard, curatorial secretary, all of whom willingly bit off more than anyone can comfortably chew to insure the success of *Head, Heart and Hand*. Susan Dodge Peters, assistant director for education; Patricia Rodewald, assistant curator of education; Delores Jackson Radney, community programmer; and Susan Daley, secretary for education, contributed time, energy, ideas, and spirit to this project. In addition, Chris Garland, assistant director for development; Lu Harper, librarian; Nancy Kelly, Gallery Store manager, John King, exhibition designer; Joel Roemer, assistant facilities manager; Deborah Rothman, public relations manager; Shirley Wersinger, public relations assistant; Judith Van Bramer, membership manager; and Paula Zahniser, events coordinator, shouldered the plethora of behind-the-scenes tasks required to complete an undertaking of this magnitude. In addition, an energetic group of interns and volunteers helped with everything from microfilm research to proofreading: Cindi Bartlett, Libby Clay, Jennifer Goyette, Marilyn Hamilton, Christina Matta, Karen Popernik, and Dan Strong.

At the American Federation of Arts, organization of the exhibition tour was orchestrated with skill and composure by Donna Gustafson. Bob Nisson and Jeannie Schweder led a dazzling creative team from Rumrill-Hoyt, which donated its design and promotion services to serve the Gallery. Jane Lytle and the staff of Muse Film and Television, together with Kevin Meyers and the crew at WXXI-TV, produced a revealing companion documentary about the Roycroft community. And a capable group of conservators—Michael Adams, Tom Branchick, Dan Clement, Malcolm Collum, Rick Sherin, Jonathan Thornton, and Ralph Wiegandt—revitalized objects that were feeling the effects of being used and enjoyed for nearly a century.

Robert Easton of the University of Rochester Press guided the catalogue to completion with perspicacity and good humor. The authors presented us with insights to engage novices and experts alike; we are indebted to Jean-François Vilain for his generous contribution of professional editorial review as well. James M. Via labored long hours under bright lights to make beautiful photographs that balance delicately between document and homage. And Stephen Easton, whose English cottage was connected to the Gallery by fax line and FedEx, designed a publication that evokes the spirit of the best material from the Roycroft Press itself.

To the lenders who so generously parted with their Roycroft treasures during the eighteen-month *Head, Heart and Hand* tour, we extend our warmest appreciation. They and a host of other collectors, Roycrofters, and scholars welcomed us into their homes, wrote letters of support, shared their research, identified faded photographs, transcribed the spidery handwriting in crumbling correspondence, introduced us to that friend of a friend whose mother was a Roycrofter. So to Susan Ahearn, Peg Ainsworth, Bruce Austin, Cathy Baker, Jackie Barcos, Andrew Bergman, Dick Blacher, Francis Bowen, Linda Brady, Ira and Ellen Current, Irene Wurtenberg DeMille, Joe Flaherty, Christopher Forbes, Viggo J. Frost, Bill Green, Charlie Hamilton, Betsy Heussler, Dr. and Mrs. Paul Kugler, Bill and Joann Hartung, Nancy Heussler, Jerry Hiller, Kari Horowitz, Dard Hunter III, Alfreda L. Irwin, Michael James, Rix and Sydney Jennings, Bruce Johnson, Marty Kingsley, Mary Kipp, Scott LaFrance, Boice Lydell, Tom Lunt, Henry McCartney, Dawn McGuire, Michele McNabb, Warren Moffett, Krista Wolf and Gary Nardo, David Pankow, Jack Quinan, David Rago, Len and Winnie Robinson, Mark and Sarah Roelofs, the members of the Roycrofters-at-Large Association, Dave and Debbie Rudd, Robert Rust and Kitty Turgeon-Rust, Jack Schang, Eleanor Jackson Searl, Jane Siebert, David Silver, Al Sipprell, Mary Spahn, Gen Steffan, Jack Stewart, David Tatham, Catherine Hoover Voorsanger, Evelyn Walker, Karin Wieder, Glenda Wiese, and Bill Young—thanks!

Two years of visits to East Aurora were made especially pleasant and productive by the "Wayside Lunch Club": Bruce Bland, co-curator of the Elbert Hubbard-Roycroft Museum, whose energy and enthusiasm were wildly contagious; Dr. Elbert Hubbard III, who provided a physical link with the Fra; Rita Hubbard, whose sunny disposition and words of encouragement worked magic from our very first encounter at the Scheide-Mantel House; and Ed Godfrey, "Mr. East Aurora," who shared his memories and will forever be part of ours.

Finally, we salute our husbands, James M. Via and Scott Searl, who cheerfully endured our erratic schedules, unselfishly encouraged our single-minded focus, and fully shared our fascination with the Roycroft phenomenon.

Marie Via
Assistant Curator

Marjorie B. Searl
Estelle B. Goldman Curator of Education

Directors' Forewords

SERENA RATTAZZI

Elbert Hubbard, the promotional genius and guiding force behind the Roycroft community in East Aurora, New York, is in many ways the quintessential American hero. After having made his fortune selling soap for the Larkin Company, Hubbard traveled to Europe to experience the wider world and to further his education. One of the most important events of his European sojourn was his visit to William Morris's Kelmscott Press in 1894. Inspired by Morris and his ideas, Hubbard initiated his own publishing venture, the Roycroft Press. Its success led to the founding of other Roycroft shops that produced furniture, metalwork, and leather goods. Like the finely printed books and monthly magazines of the Roycroft Press, these products were aimed at a largely middle-class public, who eagerly purchased them.

With the establishment of the Roycroft community Hubbard had fulfilled one of the dreams of the Arts and Crafts philosophers: a self-contained and self-supporting community of people living, working, and playing together. Thanks to Hubbard's tireless promotion, the community became as famous as the objects it produced. Tourists visited East Aurora, vacationed at the Roycroft Inn, and purchased souvenirs and mementos of their visits. Between 1895 and 1938 the Roycrofters played a large role in the popularization of the Arts and Crafts movement in America.

Nineteen ninety-five marks the 100th anniversary of the founding of the Roycroft community. The Memorial Art Gallery of the University of Rochester, located only eighty miles from the Roycroft campus, aptly observes the centenary of the Roycrofters by opening this exhibition, the first to survey both the extensive production of the Roycroft shops and the nature of the community.

Much of the credit for the successful realization of the project belongs to Marie Via, curator of the exhibition and general editor of the catalogue. Her interest in the Roycroft community and her research have brought the contributions of Elbert Hubbard and the Roycrofters to light. Both Marie and Grant Holcomb, director of the museum, have our sincere thanks.

We are also deeply indebted to many individuals and museums for their generous loans to the exhibition. Without their cooperation, this project would not have been possible.

At the American Federation of Arts, I wish to acknowledge the contributions of the following: Rachel Granholm, Curator of Education; Donna Gustafson, Curator of Exhibitions; Sarah Higby, Exhibitions Assistant; Evie Klein, Exhibitions Scheduler; Michaelyn Mitchell, Head of Publications; Gabriela Mizes, Registrar; Jillian S. Slonim, Director of Public Information; and Robert Workman, Director of Exhibitions.

While the history of the Roycrofters is inextricably linked to western New York, their influence was felt nationally. It is therefore gratifying that this tour will bring the exhibition to a wide audience and renew interest in the Roycroft legacy. For this we thank the museums participating in the tour: the Akron Art Museum; the Allentown Art Museum; the Frederick R. Weisman Museum of Art, Pepperdine University; the Virginia Museum of Fine Arts; and the New York State Museum.

Finally, our thanks are extended to the Lila Wallace-Reader's Digest Fund for their support of this exhibition through the AFA's ART ACCESS Program.

[signature]

Director
The American Federation of Arts

GRANT HOLCOMB

The excellence of the twentieth-century craft tradition in western New York is perhaps without equal in this country. *Head, Heart* and *Hand: Elbert Hubbard and the Roycrofters* explores the beginning of this extraordinary legacy.

It is appropriate that the Memorial Art Gallery organize this significant exhibition. As we approach a new century, upstate New York remains one of America's richest centers of fine craft production. This area's contemporary ceramists, glassblowers, metalworkers, weavers and furniture makers are linked to the Roycroft tradition and continue to foster an abiding appreciation for handmade objects. The Board and staff of the Memorial Art Gallery are proud to present an exhibition that pays tribute to a regional phenomenon that became a vital and significant part of this country's Arts and Crafts movement.

Many individuals and organizations, including the generous lenders who have shared their treasures with us, have enabled us to organize this important exhibition. Crucial early support came from the Gallery's Averell Council, headed by Council President Kathy D'Amanda. The National Endowment for the Arts, the New York State Council on the Arts, and the Henry Luce Foundation, Inc. have demonstrated, once again, their commitment to the study, interpretation, and understanding of the arts in America. We are extremely grateful for their support.

Our partnership with the American Federation of Arts has enabled us to share the legacy of the Roycrofters with other parts of the country. Instrumental in this collaboration were Serena Rattazzi, Director; Robert Workman, Director of Exhibitions; and Donna Gustafson, Curator of Exhibitions.

Finally, I extend our gratitude to the staff of the Memorial Art Gallery, especially Marie Via, Assistant Curator, and Marjorie Searl, Estelle B. Goldman Curator of Education. Through their many efforts, the Gallery is able to fulfill its primary educational missions, from scholarly research and interpretation to a fuller understanding and appreciation of art. Marie Via, who initiated the idea for the exhibition and has seen it through to completion, deserves special citation. I remain deeply grateful to this friend and colleague whose "head, heart and hand" have created this major exhibition.

Grant Holcomb

Director
Memorial Art Gallery of the University of Rochester

Roycroft Office Staff, ca. 1912.
(Courtesy Elbert Hubbard-Roycroft Museum)

Elbert Hubbard's Roycroft

JACK QUINAN

The Roycroft community was established in the village of East Aurora, New York, by Elbert Hubbard, a wealthy executive in a Buffalo soap and mail order company who had decided, at the age of thirty-six, to leave business in order to become a writer. What began as a modest printing establishment in 1895 soon evolved into a community of over five hundred artists, crafts-men, and other workers who were drawn together by Hubbard's charisma, by the congenial atmosphere, and by a loose allegiance to the social and artistic ideals of the English reformers John Ruskin and William Morris. Once fully developed, the Roycroft flourished for about a dozen years on the strength of Hubbard's energetic leadership, his wealth, and his ability to attract people of talent to the enterprise, but after the decade following his tragic death on the Lusitania in 1915, the institution went into a decline from which it never recovered.

The objects in this exhibition are tangible evidence of the once-thriving Roycroft community, chosen to demonstrate something of the variety and range of Roycroft production, and for their own artistic merit. As art objects, however, much of this work is relatively modest in comparison, say, to the virtuoso metalwork of a Benvenuto Cellini, or the furniture of a Thomas Chippendale. Roycroft work, like most American Arts and Crafts production, is simple in conception, com-mon in its use of materials, and literal in its execution. As such it appears to defy many of the most cherished values of the Western artistic tradition, values centered on classicism, richness of materials and technique, and the primacy of individual creativity. Thus the objects in this exhibition raise a number of questions about the Arts and Crafts movement in general and the Roycroft community in particular. What were the ideals of the movement? What was the relationship of the Roycroft to the larger picture of the Arts and Crafts? What was the history of the Roycroft, and what was its impact locally and nationally?

The Arts and Crafts movement came about in re-sponse to the deleterious effects of industrialism on society and on artistic production in nineteenth-century England. In the headlong scramble to establish successful manufacturing enterprises prior to labor and zoning laws and the building of an adequate infrastructure, English cities swiftly turned into quag-mires of social injustice, disease, and crime. At the same time, in a seemingly unrelated realm, such mechanized techniques as machine stamping and molding led to a proliferation of hideously overwrought interior furnishings—a pseudo-opulence that belied the seamy underside of the social reality.[1] A small group of writers, including Augustus Welby Pugin, Charles Dickens, Thomas Carlyle, and John Ruskin, attacked existing social conditions and called for a return to the spiritual values of the Middle Ages, when hand-craft, the camaraderie of the guilds, and a deep commitment to work constituted the ingredients of a purer and simpler way of life.[2] William Morris, one of John Ruskin's students at Oxford in the 1850s, was the first to put these reformist ideas to work by forming a guild-like Arts and Crafts organization. Morris was an inspired artist who produced timelessly beautiful, nature-inspired fabric and wallpaper patterns, wrote prolifically, painted, lectured, and enlisted other talented individuals to make and decorate furniture and architectural decor.[3] In the later stages of his career, Morris turned his tremendous intellect and energies to printing and produced some of the finest works in the history of that field, most notably the Kelmscott *Chaucer*, which would be of great significance to Elbert Hubbard. Both Ruskin and Morris, and many of their English followers, held a deep commitment to socialism and to social activism that was substan-tially diluted in the American movement in favor of a commercial emphasis.

Arts and Crafts ideas reached North America through a variety of channels. Ruskin, Morris, Dickens, and Carlyle were widely read by the American intelli-gentsia, and English periodicals such as the *Studio* and the *Builder*, which contained articles pertaining to aspects of Arts and Crafts design, were circulated in

American arts communities. The products of some of the English craftsmen were marketed in American stores and magazines, and some American architects, including H. H. Richardson, commissioned works by Morris and Company for some of their buildings.[4] In addition, a number of English practitioners, including Walter Crane, C. R. Ashbee, May Morris (William Morris's daughter), and Richard Le Gallienne, visited and lectured on the Arts and Crafts in America. Likewise, such Americans as Jane Addams, Ellen Gates Starr, Gustav Stickley, Elbert Hubbard, Frank Lloyd Wright, Charles Eliot Norton of Harvard University, and President Andrew White of Cornell University visited England and made personal contact with leading figures in the movement there.[5]

An American receptivity to the English Arts and Crafts ideas is not surprising in view of common language, parallel experiences with industrialism in the nineteenth century, and a widespread perception that American laws, civic institutions, and cultural values are derived from English models. Yet at a deeper level there are enormous differences between the two nations—differences of size, landscape, climate, history, social structure, and national character—which account, in part, for the distinctive nature of the Arts and Crafts movement in America and which raise additional questions. Why was America, by now established as a leading world power, so willing and eager to embrace a form of English medievalism? Indeed what *was* America like at the turn of the twentieth century?

Following the Civil War, America entered a period dominated by the so-called "robber barons," ruthlessly ambitious industrialists and bankers like John D. Rockefeller, Andrew Carnegie, Jay Gould, E. H. Harriman, J. P. Morgan, and Henry Clay Frick, who amassed huge fortunes and obtained monopolistic control of railroads, steel manufacturing, oil refining, mining, banking, and other aspects of industry. In little more than a generation America changed from a predominantly agricultural society to a predominantly industrial one. Older cities expanded rapidly and cities like Chicago, Pittsburgh, and Cleveland became industrial powers. Tenements proliferated, suburbs became a way of life for the middle class, the frontier was declared closed, and ambitious world's fairs celebrating the new industrial technology were staged in Philadelphia (1876), Chicago (1893), Buffalo (1901), and St. Louis (1904).

Alongside the conspicuous wealth of the few, the principal consequence of the industrial and economic revolution of the later nineteenth century was a hopeless tangle of urban social problems similar to those seen earlier in England—disease, crime, over-crowded tenement living, long work days for women and underage children in unsavory sweat-shop and factory condi-

tions, and the ruthless exploitation of immigrants. Around 1900 the mood of the American public began to shift toward social reform, favoring government intervention to break up the trusts and monopolies, to establish graduated income taxes, and to pass legislation that would protect and enhance the lives of the urban poor. This marked the beginning of the Progressive Era with which the life span of the Roycroft community coincided.

The relationship of the Arts and Crafts movement to the broad socio-political currents of American life at the turn of the century is neither simple nor obvious. Arts and Crafts societies were formed in numerous American cities during the 1890s and Arts and Crafts communities were established nationwide. Although only a small percentage of the total national population of around seventy-six million was directly involved, the impact of the movement, through the efforts of such popularizers as Gustav Stickley and Elbert Hubbard, would bring the ideas and products of the Arts and Crafts to the American public. The bungalow, perhaps the quintessential architectural expression of the movement, would become a common American house type, and many homes would include at least some token pieces of "mission" furniture and art pottery. It is important to acknowledge in this context that the Arts and Crafts movement was *not* the dominant theme in American life circa 1900, however. Mainstream America preferred classicism in the form of Colonial Revival architecture, realism in painting, and variations on historical themes in furniture. English Tudor and Gothic motifs provide a secondary theme, and there is occasional evidence of European Art Nouveau design in American life, for instance in the work of Louis Comfort Tiffany and Louis Sullivan.

Part of the difficulty in characterizing the Arts and Crafts movement in America lies in the varieties of its forms and its diffusion. It varied with regions, with individual interpretations, and with degrees of aspiration for commercial success among its practitioners. The extremes are represented by Jane Addams's Hull-House in Chicago, a settlement house established along English lines[6] at which the Arts and Crafts were taught as a way of elevating the lives of the poor in urban slums, and, on the other hand, operations like Charles Limbert's furniture manufacturing company in Grand Rapids and the Rookwood Pottery in Cincinnati, businesses that produced and marketed mission furniture and art pottery on a much larger scale.

New York State, a major center for all of the manifestations of Arts and Crafts activities, was a microcosm of the national scene.[7] On the commercial end of the spectrum were the furniture manufacturing enterprises of Gustav Stickley in Eastwood, New York, and his brothers Leopold and John George in nearby Fayetteville. Commencing in 1901, Gustav Stickley published the *Craftsman* magazine, which became the principal voice of Arts and Crafts ideas in America. Though less well-known, Joseph P. McHugh of New York City was one of the first to produce a mission style of furniture in America and received considerable acclaim at the Pan-American Exposition in Buffalo of 1901.[8] At the other end of the spectrum was Charles Rohlfs, who operated a small shop in Buffalo, producing unique, fanciful pieces in his own version of the Art Nouveau style.[9] Around 1905, the Larkin Company, the Buffalo soap and mail order firm of which Elbert Hubbard was a founding partner, developed its own line of mass-produced mission furniture (which was available by redeeming premium certificates obtained through the purchase of soap), as did other large-scale furniture manufactories such as Sears, Roebuck & Co.[10]

Producers of art pottery also abounded in New York State, among which two centers dominated—one, the New York State School of Clay-Working and Ceramics at Alfred University, founded by Charles Fergus Binns in 1900, and the other in the person of Syracuse-based Adelaide Alsop Robineau, the brilliant ceramist and editor/publisher of *Keramic Studio*, the principal organ of the Art Pottery movement in America. Other pottery producers included the Tiffany Studios in New York City, Frederick Walrath's pottery in Rochester and Charles Volkmar's in Corona, Durant Kilns in Bedford, Middle Lane in East Hampton, Jervis Pottery in Oyster Bay, and Van Der Meulen in Dunkirk. As Coy Ludwig has demonstrated in his fine catalogue and exhibition of 1983, *The Arts & Crafts Movement in New York State: 1890s-1920s*, additional manifestations of Arts and Crafts in the state included the Heintz Art Metal company in Buffalo, several art glass companies, a number of small presses, and the architectural work of Harvey Ellis and Claude Bragdon in Rochester and of Frank Lloyd Wright in Buffalo. The academic centers at Columbia University, Pratt Institute, Mechanics Institute (now Rochester Institute of Technology), and the Chautauqua Institution also fostered aspects of Arts and Crafts ideals and manual training.[11]

New York State boasted four Arts and Crafts communities, including the Roycroft, a relatively large representation of a phenomenon that was thinly scattered across the United States. The Elverhoj Colony near Poughkeepsie was founded in 1913 by two Danish-born Americans, Johannes Morton and A. H. Anderson. The colony was small, consisting of eight permanent members, and functioned as a combined school and workshop that focused upon the production of jewelry. Even smaller was the community that produced Briarcliff furniture in and around Ossining-on-Hudson. Byrdcliffe Colony was established at Woodstock in 1902 by Ralph Radcliffe Whitehead, a wealthy English-

man; his wife, Jane Byrd Whitehead; Hervey White, Harvard-trained socialist with experience at Hull-House; and Bolton Coit Brown, a Stanford University professor who was educated at Syracuse University. According to Ludwig, "Byrdcliffe was to be a place where the fusion of ideas and the teaching of crafts could take place among compatible, intelligent friends in an inspiring rural setting."[12] Under Whitehead's sponsorship thirty buildings were constructed at Byrdcliffe, crafts courses were offered, and production included furniture, pottery, textiles, and metalwork. The furniture proved too expensive to produce; Brown and White departed in the early years, leaving Whitehead and his wife to carry on with a focus on pottery and weaving. One senses an altruism about Byrdcliffe, reflected in its modest advertising, that differentiates it from the Roycroft enterprise in East Aurora.[13]

These communities came into existence with varying intentions of artistic purity and commercial purpose, but they belong to a venerable impulse in American history that can be traced back to the Puritan communities of seventeenth-century New England and include the Utopian communities—the Shakers, Brook Farm, New Harmony, and Oneida—that course through the nineteenth century.[14] The significant difference is that the Arts and Crafts communities were not grounded in traditional religious conviction.

The Roycroft and Elbert Hubbard

The history and individual nature of the Roycroft community is inextricably tied to the character and aspirations of its founder, Elbert Hubbard. Hubbard has been the subject of at least six full biographies and innumerable articles, most of which tend to be hagiographical and focus almost exclusively upon his life in the Roycroft years, 1895 to 1915. Yet considering that Hubbard spent the first twenty-three years of his working life in business and the final twenty years as a Roycrofter, it is the intention of this essay to give more weight to the significance of Hubbard's business experience to the nature of the Roycroft enterprise than has been done in the past.[15] This will shift the balance of our understanding of Hubbard and the Roycroft from the mythic level promoted by Hubbard and his admirers to a discussion based on the nature of Hubbard's actual formative experience.

Hubbard became involved in the soap business when, at the age of fifteen, he met John D. Larkin, a partner in the Chicago-based soap firm of Larkin and Weller, who was courting his sister. Hubbard, a handsome and garrulous young man, cheerfully signed on as a "slinger" to sell soap door-to-door throughout the Midwest.[16] Later, in his Roycroft days, Hubbard described himself in these terms:

Fig. 1: Elbert Hubbard, ca. 1870.
(Courtesy Elbert Hubbard-Roycroft Museum)

> I used to have a new vest every trip, and it was a miracle in chromatics that spoke for itself. But this was nothing to my smile—my smile was contagious, also infectious, as well as fetching. When I arrived in a town everybody smiled, and invited others to smile. The man who dealt out White Rock splits smiled, the 'bus driver glowed, the babies cooed, the dogs barked, and the dining-room girls giggled, when I came to town. I scattered smiles, lilac-tinted stories, patchouli persiflage, good cheer and small silver change all over the route . . . and I sold the goods . . .[17]

Hubbard's ability to laugh at himself was part of his charm. When, in 1875, John Larkin decided to establish his own soap manufacturing business in Buffalo, Hubbard was invited along as a junior partner.

The history and development of the Larkin soap company is a classic American success story. Beginning in a small, two-story brick building in Buffalo, rented for $500 for the year 1875, the business grew to national prominence by 1892, when it was incorporated and $500,000 in stock was made available to the public.[18] At the outset, John Larkin supervised the soap production and bookkeeping while Hubbard took care of sales and advertising, for which he had a special talent. Hubbard's product names (*Sweet Home*, *Artistic*,

Silken Windsor, and *Creme Oatmeal* soaps); his slogans ("Factory to Family—Save All Cost which Adds No Value"); and his advertising copy[19] captured the public imagination by appealing to fundamental social and economic values leavened with a touch of humor. The juxtaposition of the French "creme" with the homey "oatmeal" is already, in 1878, a foreshadowing of the irreverence of Hubbard the Roycrofter.

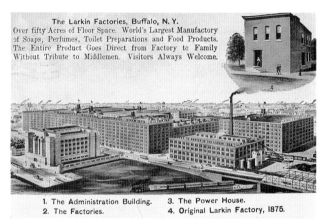

Fig. 2: The Larkin Company's original headquarters and its later buildings.
(Courtesy Jack Quinan)

Hubbard was equally a master of sales promotion and brought to it a boundless energy and almost restless willingness to experiment. Hubbard's promotional strategies operated on three fronts from 1875 until his departure from the company in 1893. First, he worked to eliminate salesmen; second, he employed premiums as incentives for customers to purchase soap; and third, he attempted to enlist customers in the effort to solicit other customers.

Hubbard began his effort to eliminate salesmen in 1881 by the direct mail solicitation of storekeepers. In 1883, when the United States postal rates dropped from three cents to two cents per half ounce, the Larkin Company began to solicit its customers directly through the mail, thereby eliminating salesmen altogether.[20] Hence the Larkin Company motto: "Factory to Family—Save All Cost which Adds No Value."

In the early 1880s Hubbard also began to experiment with premium items, wrapping a single bar of soap with a handkerchief or including chromolithographic pictures with an order.[21] These efforts led, in 1886, to Hubbard's greatest promotional invention, the "$6 Combination Box," later adjusted to the "$10 Combination Box." The "Combination Box" was a package of one hundred bars of soaps and toilet articles (representing a major outlay of funds for most families at that time) that included as a premium, or "gift," eleven silver-plated items; customers were given thirty days to pay for their purchases.[22] During the following few

See Page 3 for Prices of any Quantity of Products with any Premium.
109

Upright-Grand Piano.

Given for One hundred and ten Certificates; OR with $10.00 worth of Larkin Products for $115; OR given with $220 worth of Products.

A reliable Piano made throughout of high-grade material by the Empire Piano Co., 107 E. 128th St., New York City, whose five-year guarantee accompanies each instrument. We have sent several hundred of them to satisfied customers.

Choice of Oak or Mahogany, finely polished. Only the best piano-finishing varnish used. Case extra heavy double-veneered, and crossbanded to avoid warping or splitting. Only hardwood used in the pilasters, trusses and backs.

Full-extension music-desk with automatic brace-support. Boston fall-board, with continuous hinge. Fitted with muffler-attachment.

Seven and one-third octaves; three strings to each note. Highest grade German bushed tuning-pins and piano-strings. French capstan repeating action used, with nickel brackets. Finest felt hammers, Ivory keys. Castered.

Height, 4 ft. 7½ in.; length, 5 ft. 5 in.; depth, 2 ft. 3 in. Piano is carefully boxed and shipped from New York City. See page 127. Weight, 850 lbs.

Piano-Benches.

No. 205½. Given for Five-and-one-half Certificates. With Products, see page 3.

A well-designed, roomy bench, which will go with any style of piano. Seat, 15 x 38 in., 21 in. high; contains a compartment for music, 32 x 11 in., 2½ in. deep, accessible by raising seat. Octagon legs; scroll feet. Made of Quarter-sawed Oak in **choice** of Golden-Oak hand-pol-

No. 205½.

ished finish, Imitation-Mahogany with genuine-Mahogany veneered seat hand-polished finish or Weathered-Oak waxed finish.

No. 46. Given for Six Certificates.
Same design and measurements as No. 205½. Has genuine Circassian Walnut veneered seat; other parts of Bench are of selected Red Gum, satin-walnut rubbed finish.

Wood-Seat Piano-Stool No. 22.
Given for Two Certificates.
Polished revolving wood-seat, 14½ in. in diameter; can be raised or lowered as desired. Heavy turned-legs and -post; glass-ball feet. **Choice** of solid Oak, imitation-Ebony,- Mahogany,- Rosewood or - Burl Walnut finish.

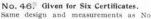

No. 22.

Piano Scarf No. 62.
Given for Two Certificates.
To mail, 6 cts. postage required.
Silk Piano Cover or Mantel Scarf in a handsome Oriental border pattern. Double-knotted 5-in. silk fringe.

No. 62.

Choice of Red, Dark Green or Olive-Green. Size, 31 x 92 in. including fringe.

Leather Music-Bag No. 81.
Given for One Certificate. To mail, 16 cts. postage required.

No. 81.

Especially constructed to carry sheet music or flexible-covered music-books. Better than roll, because it protects the ends of the music. Made of polished cowhide, with ends stitched in and two leather handles stitched on. Leather strap; nickel-plated buckle. **Choice** of Black or Tan. Size, 15 in. long, 6 in. wide.

No. 20.

Music-Roll No. 20.
Given for One-half Certificate. To mail, 9 cts. postage required.
Made of one piece of heavy, seal-grain Leather, with handle and strap. **Choice** of Black or Tan. All edges creased. Nickel-plated buckle. Length, 14½ in.

Fountain Pens.
ALL MAILED, POSTPAID.
Guaranteed to operate perfectly. If out of order at any time the makers will put in adjustment free of charge, if unbroken.
Every Pen is guaranteed solid 14-K. Gold with iridium point. Barrels made of finest quality of Para hard rubber, black, handsomely engraved and highly polished. Each in a box.

No. 0.
No. 0. Given for One-half Certificate.
Pen No. 4 size with short heel; size especially suitable for lady's use. Chased holder with tapered cap; complete with filler.

No. 601.
No. 601. Given for One Certificate.
Pen No. 6 size. The black, hard-rubber holder is turned, polished and chased; complete with filler.

No. 11.
No. 11. Autofiller. Given for One Certificate.
Pen No. 4 size. Combines all the advantages of the ordinary fountain-pen with the addition of self-filling and self-cleaning features. No inky joints to unscrew. Is filled instantly by a turn of the little stem. Ink flows evenly, perfectly and to the last drop.

No. 22.
No. 22. Autofiller. Given for Two Certificates.
Same as No. 11 Pen, but much larger size. Holder is ½ in. in diameter, with large ink-sack. Has size-No.-8 Pen, (Bank-size), a much easier writer than a smaller pen.

No. 801.
No. 801. Non-Leakable. Given for One Certificate.
Pen No. 4 size. The ink-tight joint at base of pen-section prevents pen from leaking no matter in what position it may be placed. Has screw cap.
Complete with filler. Convenient for woman's shopping-bag or man's vest-pocket. Length closed, 4 in.

No. 11.

Inkstand No. 11.
Given for One Certificate. To mail, 45 cts. postage required.
Combination of postal scale, (will weigh 8 oz.) two stamp drawers, pen rack, and two glass ink-wells with nickel tops. Enameled black with aluminum stripe. Base, 6½ in. square. Height, 7 in.

Bagster Self-Pronouncing Teacher's Bible No. 22.

Given for Two Certificates. To mail, 26 cts. postage required.
Contains the Old and New Testaments according to the Authorized Version.
Printed on Bagster white opaque Bible-paper; red-under-gold edges; round corners; bound in substantial Seal-grain black Leather with durable joints; flexible covers; opens flat.

Printed in Long Primer type. Contains new and revised Helps to Bible Study, new Concordance, Harmony of the Gospels, twelve colored Maps, alphabetical index of the Holy Scriptures, index of Proper Names with their meanings, index to Parables, 16 full-page plates that illustrate Scriptural subjects of the works of famous artists, Tables of Measures, Weights and Coins, marginal references and other valuable helps to students. Linen-lined covers with divinity circuit edges. Size, 9 x 6 x 1½ in.

No. 22.

Webster's Collegiate Dictionary No. 43.

Given for Three Certificates. To mail, 18 cts. postage required.
Edition de Luxe, printed on thin Bible paper. Bound in limp dark-brown seal; covers gold-tooled; full-gilt edges; round corners; indexed. 1136 pages. Opens flat. Over 1100 illustrations. Appendix contains vocabulary of Rhymes, Proper Names and English Christian Names; an account of the Chief Deities, Heroes, etc., in Classical Mythology; a table of Classical and Foreign quotations, Abbreviations, contractions and Arbitrary Signs used in writing and printing; Glossary of Scottish words and phrases.

No. 43.

Comprehensive vocabulary, full definitions, very complete etymologies. Pronunciation indicated by familiar diacritical marks and respelling. Size, 8½ x 5½ x 1½ in.

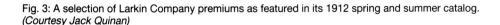

Fig. 3: A selection of Larkin Company premiums as featured in its 1912 spring and summer catalog.
(Courtesy Jack Quinan)

years Hubbard experimented with various premium enticements, including one—a set advertised as "silver spoons" that were actually of an alloy known as "German silver"—that brought considerable public embarrassment to the Larkin Company.[23]

In 1886 Hubbard tried inducing clients to solicit additional customers by allowing them to substitute six new customer names for payment on the $6 box. To his surprise, the newly solicited customers *also* solicited new customers, thereby creating an exponential rise in business, a strategy that would reappear in Hubbard's Roycroft days.

In 1891 Hubbard adjusted the "Combination Box" to $10 for one hundred bars of soap plus a "Chautauqua piano lamp," which he advertised as a $10 retail value.[24] The result was a $20 value for the customer—the soaps plus the lamp—at a cost of only $10, but since the Larkin Company had purchased ten thousand piano lamps for less than $4 apiece, a handsome profit was made on each unit sold.[25] The response to the "$10 Combination Box" in 1892 was so strong that thereafter the Larkin Company continually added new premium items; in a matter of a few years the business had become a catalogue sales operation.[26] By 1920 the Larkin Company was worth $30 million.[27]

Elbert Hubbard's motives for leaving the Larkin Company at the threshold of its meteoric rise to national prominence were twofold: first, he had decided, at the age of thirty-six, to become a writer, and second, he had fallen in love—notwithstanding that he was married with three children—with Alice Moore, an intel-lectually stimulating young school teacher whom he had met through the East Aurora chapter of the Chautauqua Literary and Scientific Circle.[28] These two motivations proved to be mutually reinforcing and together can be identified as the fundamental impetus (fueled by Hubbard's considerable egocentricity) for the formation of the entire Roycroft enterprise. Hubbard had begun to write his first book, *The Man: A Story of Today*, in 1890, and worked on a second book, *One Day: A Tale of the Prairies*,[29] in 1891 and 1892, with Alice's help, while he was still employed by the Larkin Company.

In September 1892 Hubbard informed John Larkin that he would be resigning from the company early in January 1893 in order to study writing at Harvard College.[30] He was unable to enter Harvard until September 1893 but in the interim he worked on his third and fourth books, *No Enemy (But Himself)* and *Forbes of Harvard*, sought out publishers, and continued to see Alice Moore, who had relocated to the Boston area.[31] Hubbard's interest in Harvard waned after a matter of months, but the experience fueled many years of anti-academic sentiment that he would express through the vehicle of the *Philistine* and in other writings. Hubbard's continued relationship with Alice precipitated a roman-tic saga of epic proportions that was protracted over the following decade. The details lie beyond the scope of this essay, but suffice it to say that Hubbard and Alice had a daughter in 1894, after which he returned to his family and life in East Aurora, had a fourth child by his wife, Bertha, in 1896, was divorced by Bertha in 1903, and married Alice in 1904.

Fig. 4: The Hubbard family at home in 1898. Left to right: Sanford, Elbert II (Bert), Katherine, Elbert, Bertha, Ralph.
(Courtesy Elbert Hubbard-Roycroft Museum)

The vicissitudes of Hubbard's personal life coincide with the development of the Roycroft community and undoubtedly have some continued bearing upon it, but the driving and defining force, once Hubbard was free from the Larkin Company, was his desire to write and to be published. Even Alice seems to have been swept aside, at least temporarily, in favor of that ambition.[32] The realization of these desires was facilitated by the settlement of about $65,000 Hubbard made upon leaving the Larkin Company—a substantial sum when one considers that Darwin Martin, his successor, was making $1,500 per year. In view of the wealth that he brought to the Roycroft enterprise, Hubbard might be compared to Ralph Radcliffe Whitehead of Byrdcliffe or Henry Chapman Mercer, the founder-owner of the Moravian Pottery and Tile Works in Doylestown, Pennsylvania (and a cousin of Jane Byrd Whitehead), but Hubbard's drive to write and to promote both himself and his enterprise with the full powers of his long experience in industry lends to the Roycroft the tincture of commercialism that distinguishes it from the more subdued activities in Woodstock and Doylestown.

The Formation of the Roycroft Community
In the absence of primary documentation it appears that the Roycroft community was not initially the result of a grand, unified scheme on Elbert Hubbard's part, but instead came into existence incrementally (as the other essays in this catalogue describe more fully), commencing with the Roycroft Press. Hubbard apparently resented having had to subject his early book manuscripts to largely unsympathetic commercial publishers, and in 1894 began a collaboration with Harry Taber, a former Denver newspaperman who operated a small press in East Aurora,[33] on his third book, *No Enemy (But Himself)*. In May of 1894 Hubbard made a two-month journey to England and Ireland, during which he visited William Morris's celebrated Kelmscott Press at Hammersmith and was inspired by the work produced there and by the Arts and Crafts philosophy behind it. There is a strong likelihood that Hubbard had some familiarity with the ideas of Ruskin and Morris through his association with Taber, through his long membership in the Chautauqua Literary and Scientific Circle, and by way of his voracious passion for books.[34] Hubbard must have recognized the parallel between Morris's rejection of nineteenth-century industrialism in England and his own departure from the Larkin business.

Hubbard and Taber published the first issue of *The Philistine: A Periodical of Protest* in June 1895. Soon thereafter Taber established the Roycroft Press for publishing the *Philistine* and within a matter of months Hubbard bought him out. The *Philistine* soon became very successful: according to Roycroft printing authority Bruce White, the circulation figures rose from 2,500

to 100,000 following the publication of "A Message to Garcia" in 1899. Subscriptions grew to 126,000 in 1906 and did not fall below 100,000 until after Hubbard's death in 1915.[35] Hubbard also began to publish, through G. P. Putnam's, the first of his popular monthly *Little Journeys* to the homes of the famous in 1894.

The first Roycroft book, *The Song of Songs*, was published early in 1896 with illuminations by Bertha Hubbard, but Hubbard had already begun to build up a work force by drawing upon the local labor pool, chiefly comprised of young women,[36] and by inviting

Fig. 5: Roycroft bookbinders at work.
(Courtesy Turgeon-Rust Collection)

talented printers and graphic artists to East Aurora to work and teach; Samuel Warner (graphic artist) came in 1895 and Cy Rosen (master printer) in 1896. That same year, Hubbard began a correspondence with W. W. Denslow, who would be sporadically involved in Roycroft graphic design. The *East Aurora Advertiser* cites a dinner attended by forty-seven Roycrofters in 1898—a rough approximation of the size of the work force at that time.[37]

Fig. 6: The first Print Shop, built 1897–1898, and Phalanstery, built 1899.
(Courtesy Turgeon-Rust Collection)

Hubbard's funds were substantial, but limited nevertheless, and it was only as he began to realize additional ways of generating new funds that the greatest Roycroft development took place. The success of some of his publications, especially the *Philistine*, certainly helped, but commencing in 1897 Hubbard began to lecture nation-wide and earned a handsome income doing so.[38] Frequent notices in the *East Aurora Advertiser* give some indication of Hubbard's lecture activities. For instance, on 20 October 1897 Hubbard left East Aurora on a tour of the eastern states; he gave thirty-one presentations in one month, six engagements being in Portland, Maine, and another six in Boston. He returned on 22 November and was off the following day for another engagement in Indianapolis. Similar entries can be found in the *Advertiser* throughout the remainder of Hubbard's life. It is said that whenever Hubbard needed money for a Roycroft project he went on the road lecturing.[39]

An indication of Hubbard's earning power has recently come to light in a letter of 24 January 1901 from William Martin of Oak Park, Illinois, to his brother, Darwin Martin: "I heard Hubbard lecture Sunday eve. 13th Central Music Hall—good audience—a man told

me that Hubbard's secretary told him that Hubbard made $30,000.00 last year clear, subscriptions coming in 1000 per day—or per week—forget which."[40]

The first physical evidence of the success of the fledgling Roycroft Press occurred on 14 October 1897, when Hubbard broke ground for a Print Shop (extant) about seventy-five feet north of his own house on Grove Street.[41] Not long after the Print Shop was completed in January 1898,[42] plans were begun for a three-story addition, known as the Phalanstery (extant), completed early in 1899. On 30 March 1899, ground was broken for a "massive stone building"—the Roycroft Chapel (extant)—on Grove Street at Main.[43] The pace

Fig. 7: The Roycroft Chapel, built 1899.
(Courtesy Turgeon-Rust Collection)

of developments at the Roycroft accelerated dramatically in 1899 and 1900. Buoyed by his successes as a writer ("A Message to Garcia," Hubbard's most famous and successful writing, was published in 1899 and would sell nine million copies before his death), as a nationally prominent public speaker, and by the sanction of an honorary degree from Tufts University in 1899,[44] Hubbard began to create an attractive environment for both established artists and fledgling craftsmen (see Laurene Buckley's accompanying essay).

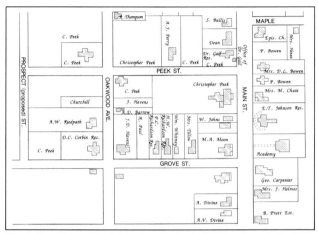

Fig. 8: The Roycroft neighborhood prior to Hubbard's arrival, 1880. Redrawn by Patrick A. Mahoney, RA, from *Illustrated Historical Atlas of Erie County, New York*, vol. 2 (New York: F. W. Beers & Co., 1880), 118–119.

If Hubbard began with modest aspirations in 1895, there is good evidence that by 1900 he had begun to formulate a plan whereby he would carve out the fourteen-building complex identified as the Roycroft campus from the several acres of occupied house lots at the junction of Grove and Main streets in East Aurora. Such an ambition was extraordinary in a village of about two thousand people, but it was routine in the Larkin Company, which had grown from three thousand square feet in 1875 to a total of three million square feet in 1912. Late in December 1899, Hubbard embarked upon a locally-unprecedented campaign of real estate acquisition, the moving of houses, and new construction that extended over the succeeding decade and that still serves as concrete evidence of the success of the whole enterprise. Between 1899 and 1902, Hubbard bought and relocated five homes, demolished a barn and remodeled a building on two other newly-purchased lots, and built two new houses and a workers' dormitory on Oakwood and Walnut Streets.[45] Thereafter, having cleared much of the space that is now occupied by the principal Roycroft buildings, Hubbard's real estate purchases diminished.

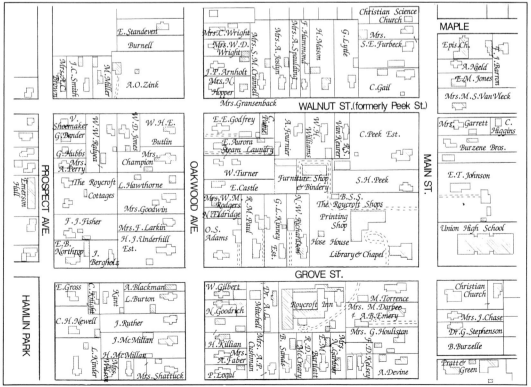

Fig. 9: The Roycroft neighborhood in 1909. Redrawn by Patrick A. Mahoney from *New Century Atlas of Erie County, New York* (Philadelphia: The Century Map Company, 1909), 32.

Hubbard used many of the houses that he bought, moved, or built to help attract some of the better-known artists and craftsmen to East Aurora. According to the *East Aurora Advertiser*, he provided houses for Cy Rosen, typesetter (1900), Louis Kinder, master bookbinder (1902), Lyle Hawthorne, Superintendent of Roycroft (1899), Louis Schell, a Roycroft pressman (1902), and M. J. Wheeler, gardener (1906). Emerson Hall on Prospect Street (extant) was fitted out as a dormitory with twenty sleeping rooms, five bathrooms, a dance hall, a bowling alley, and other amenities for Roycroft visitors and personnel in 1907.[46]

Fig. 10: Emerson Hall, built 1907.
(Courtesy Turgeon-Rust Collection)

Fig. 11: The new Print Shop, built 1899–1901.
(Courtesy Turgeon-Rust Collection)

Fig. 12: The Blacksmith Shop, later the Copper Shop, built ca. 1902.
(Courtesy Turgeon-Rust Collection)

Fig. 13: The Furniture Shop, built 1904.
(As published in *The Book of the Roycrofters*)

Fig. 14: The veranda, known as "The Peristyle," built 1905 to connect the first Print Shop with the Roycroft Inn.
(Courtesy Turgeon-Rust Collection)

As houses were moved away, buildings for new craft production were built. In 1899, Hubbard forged ahead with the two-story fieldstone building just southwest of the Roycroft Chapel.[47] According to the *East Aurora Advertiser*, this was intended to be a new Phalanstery and studio, but when it was completed early in 1901, with its L-shaped plan and stone tower, it was identified as the new Roycroft Print Shop (extant).[48] In 1903 Hubbard's own Victorian-style house on Grove Street was partially demolished to make way for the construction of the Roycroft Inn.[49] The stone Blacksmith Shop (extant) was constructed around 1902, and the Furniture Shop, a three-story wood frame building (extant) measuring forty by ninety feet, was erected in 1904.[50] Between 1899 and 1906, numerous additions to the first Print Shop, including its long veranda (extant), finally connected it to the Roycroft Inn some seventy-five feet away.[51] The Inn itself was also expanded several times between 1903 and 1914.[52]

In addition to the comfortable housing Hubbard provided, these handsome new working environments helped to attract and hold some of the leading artists to East Aurora, as this notice from the *East Aurora Advertiser* suggests: "Dard Hunter is now permanently located on the third floor in the tower [in the new Print Shop]. Dard's studio will be the envy of all art lovers before so many days."[53] The total Roycroft work force increased from 47 in 1898 to 175 in 1900 and eventually reached over 500 in the peak years.[54]

The marketing skills that Hubbard had honed in the Larkin Company played a vital role in the expansion and development of the Roycroft enterprise. His periodicals, the *Philistine*, the *Little Journeys*, and the *Fra*, carried numerous advertisements for Roycroft products and were supplemented from time to time by individual catalogues, mailed directly to customers. Hubbard did not hesitate to use the language and techniques of the mail order business to promote Roycroft books and handcrafted objects. Copies of new Roycroft publications were sent out "on suspicion" with letters from Hubbard inviting customers to purchase the books or return them[55]—the same principle under which Hubbard had "slung" soap in the 1870s. This tack also reflected the spirit of Larkin Company circulars of the 1880s that stated: "We ask permission to ship you a Box of this soap and if after 30 days' trial you are not satisfied with the bargain, will take the goods away and make no charge for what you have used."[56] Just as the Larkin "$6 Combination Box" of 1886 encouraged the customer to buy Larkin soap in bulk, Hubbard also offered special deals to bulk purchasers of Roycroft literature, as an advertisement in the *Philistine* indicates: "To Banks, Trust Companies, Railroads, Factories, Department Stores—We can supply you the following booklets by Elbert Hubbard by the thousand, your advertisement on front or back pages of the cover, all in deluxe form . . ."[57]

Taken as a whole, Larkin products and product promotions were suffused with an "artiness" and literary pretension that distinguish them from competitors in the mainstream of American business. Larkin soaps carried such names as *Artistic* and, in honor of a well-known actress, Helena Modjeska, *Modjeska Toilet Soap*. Hubbard's literary aspirations are foreshadowed in special offers of Larkin "$6 Combination Boxes" to readers of *Demorest's Family Magazine* and other selected magazines, and in "$6 Christmas Box" offers that included as premiums the complete works of Charles Dickens in one instance, and those of Sir Walter Scott in another. Many Larkin circulars are extended essays that begin with a narrative on the subject of a popular figure (such as John Howard Payne, the author of the ballad, *Home, Sweet Home*) or an issue of national interest (such as Prohibition) as leads into the subject of Larkin soap. In circulars featuring famous men, such as Napoleon and General Von Moltke, one senses the origins of Hubbard's *Little Journeys to the Homes of Great Men*. The 1889 text on Napoleon begins:

> After the terrific assault and wonderful victory of Napoleon at the bridge of Lodi, one of the Austrian generals said: "This beardless boy ought to have been beaten over and over again; for whoever saw such tactics? The blockhead knows nothing of the rules of war. To-day he is in our rear, to-morrow on our flank, and the next day again in our front. Such gross violations of the established principles of war are insufferable."
>
> Napoleon's reply was, "He was fighting to win battles, not for tactics."
>
> Our departure from the usual methods and plans of selling soap astonishes everybody; the prescribed rule being that soap must reach families through the different drug and retail stores, with all the colossal expenses attached thereto. Now we have cut right from all this legerdemain and sell direct from the factory to the families who use our soap, giving them all the profits and savings which are usually lost or expended in selling through the wholesale and retail stores. We are just as ready to trust the family as we are the grocery . . .[58]

A circular from 1 November 1892, shortly before Hubbard announced that he was leaving the Larkin Company, is chiefly concerned with the promotion of a new premium, but near the end of the text Hubbard slides into language that would characterize so many of his Roycroft publications: "In the commercial world we believe there is such a thing as wise liberality, perhaps the thought is best expressed in the words 'There is that scattereth and yet increaseth and there is that witholdeth yet tendeth to poverty.'"[59] It comes as no surprise, then, that many years later Elbert Hubbard the Roycrofter would deliver a talk entitled *Advertising as a Fine Art*.[60]

Among the many activities employed by Hubbard to generate enthusiasm for the Roycroft among a wider public were several conventions: the annual Roycroft Convention (sometimes called the Philistine Convention) in July, the New Thought or Science-of-Success Convention in August, a mid-winter convention in 1905 and 1906 called A Little Roycroft Revival, and the mid-winter Philistine Convention.[61] Such conventions, which began in 1902 or 1903,[62] quickly grew in size and constituted one of the principal reasons for the enlargement of the Roycroft Inn in 1905.[63] The New Thought convention of August 1905 was described in the *East Aurora Advertiser* as follows:

This week the New-Thought or Science-of-Success convention is in progress at the Roycroft shops. Though the July convention was great, this one is greater; crowds of people arrive on every train and the Roycroft Inn is taxed to its utmost capacity.

[Speakers will include] Elbert Hubbard; Ernest Crosby; Thomas Harned of Philadelphia, literary executor of Walt Whitman; Fred Burry, Editor of Burry's Journal of Toronto; Wilson Fritch, Bolton Hall; Ernest Loomis; Col. Marshall P. Wilder; G. E. [sic] Littlefield; Lyman Chandler; Alice Hubbard and Beulah Hood.[64]

Such activities have a parallel in Hubbard's earlier attempts, in business, to develop personal connections between Larkin customers and the Larkin Company headquarters. Larkin circulars of the 1880s often include the invitation: "When you are in Buffalo we will be much pleased to have you call and inspect our manufactory."[65] Hubbard's early efforts to entice customers to enlist new customers led to the designation of successful customer recruiters as "Larkin Club Secretaries," who were invited to the Larkin Company for an annual convention and tour of the factories.[66] While some of these developments post-dated Hubbard's tenure in the Larkin Company, Hubbard kept abreast of Larkin activities through Darwin Martin, with whom he corresponded and even visited with some regularity in the decade after he left the company.[67] The genesis of the idea of the conventions probably goes back to Hubbard's ten-year experience in the Chautauqua Literary and Scientific Circle, the popular four-year, college-equivalent, correspondence school program centered at the Methodist Sunday School teachers' institute on Chautauqua Lake, about fifty miles south of Buffalo. The CLSC was instituted in 1878 and by 1891 had

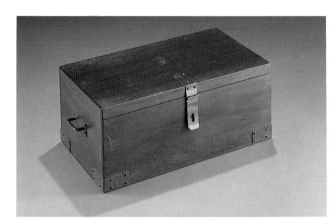

Plate 2: *Goodie Box.* Gumwood and copper, 9½ × 23 × 12½ in. *Elbert Hubbard-Roycroft Museum.*

180,000 mail-order subscribers. The Larkin Company's first "$10 Combination Box" premiums, the Chautauqua lamp and the Chautauqua desk, were named deliberately to associate the premiums with the popular correspondence school program to which both Hubbard and Martin had belonged.

Other parallels between Larkin and Roycroft abound. Each was run on a paternalistic model and was generally progressive in nature. There were marching bands, gymnasia, and baseball teams at each institution. Each had a bank and loan service, and each sponsored picnics for the workers.

Certain Roycroft promotional strategies were comparable to those employed at the Larkin Company, especially in the realm of "bulk savings." The Roycrofters' Goodie Box, a wooden trunk filled with sausage, nuts, honey, home-made pecan patties and other wholesome foodstuffs from the Roycroft farms, was doubtless the offspring of the Larkin "Combination

Plate 1: *Photograph of Roycroft Concert Band in Roycroft Frame.* Gelatin silver print in oak frame, 15½ × 18½ in. *Collection of Bruce A. Austin.*

Plate 3: *Roycroft Concert Band Drum.* Wood, metal, and painted skin, 37½ × 18 in. *Elbert Hubbard-Roycroft Museum.*

Plate 4: *Roycroft Softball*, ca. 1910. Leather, 3¾ in. diam.
Collection of Kitty Turgeon-Rust and Robert Rust, Roycroft Shops.

Plate 5: *Roycroft Bank Calendar*, 1912. Paper and ribbon, 10¾ × 8 in.
Collection of Richard Blacher.

Fig. 15: The Roycroft baseball team, including Bert Hubbard in the first row, third from left.
(Courtesy Elbert Hubbard-Roycroft Museum)

Box." Even the slogan used to advertise it, "From Farm to Family," echoes the Larkin Company's "Factory to Family" motto.

There are also close parallels between the types of manufacturing activities—furniture, leather, pottery—at the Larkin Company and those at the Roycroft. The Larkin Company's Buffalo Pottery subsidiary was started in 1901, just after the Roycroft Pottery was begun. The Larkin Company's Buffalo Leather company was purchased in 1904; the Roycroft Leather Department was established in 1905. Roycroft furniture production began around 1898 and required the construction of its manufacturing building in 1904; the Larkin Company purchased its furniture manufacturing subsidiary in Memphis, Tennessee, in 1907. Divergences occurred owing to the differences in the two enterprises: the Larkin Company purchased a glass company in Greensburg, Pennsylvania, while the Roycrofters established a metal shop.

Plate 6: *Roycroft Bank Check*. Paper, 3½ × 8¹³⁄₁₆ in.
Collection of Charles F. Hamilton.

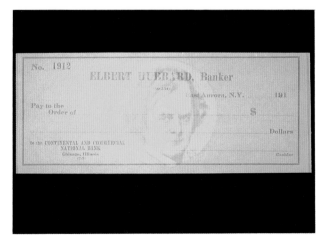

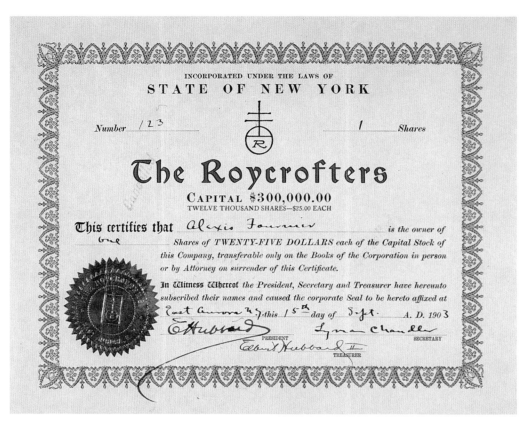

Plate 7: *Roycroft Stock Certificate*, 1903. Paper with foil seal, 10⅛ × 11½ in.
Collection of Kitty Turgeon Rust and Robert Rust, Roycroft Shops.

Both enterprises featured regular lectures, concerts, and presentations by creative and intellectual people from both America and Europe. Such individuals were brought into the Larkin Company weekly as a noon-time break from the intense business activities surrounding the mail order operation.[68] At the Roycroft, where such activities were more essential to the spirit of the community, there was a constant array of musical events, dances, exhibitions, and lectures on literature, travel, religion, notable artists in history, temperance, vaccination, the suffragette movement, and the "progress of the Negro." Hubbard lectured regularly at the Roycroft on a wide variety of topics, as did many other prominent national and international figures.[69]

If Hubbard's Roycroft enterprise exhibits patterns and habits of thought that were developed during his more than twenty years in the Larkin Company, the Roycroft was also driven by an element of competitiveness between Hubbard and his former partner, John D. Larkin. Their relationship was strained when, upon leaving, Hubbard demanded his share of the business in cash at a time when the American economy was severely depressed. Larkin felt that the extraction of Hubbard's share would cripple the business; Hubbard threatened to sue; a settlement was reached, but matters worsened as the story of Hubbard's child with Alice

and his divorce from Bertha unfolded. Both John Larkin and his wife Frances, Elbert's sister, sided with Bertha in the matter, as did his other sister, Mary Hubbard Heath. Consequently, there is little evidence of any contact between Hubbard and the Larkins after 1895 but, again, his relationship with his successor, Darwin Martin, enabled him to keep abreast of activities in the Larkin Company.

The Roycroft Arts and Crafts community, then, was the result of a complex swarm of forces and motives operating within and around Elbert Hubbard—his passion for books; his facility with language; the inspiration of William Morris and the Arts and Crafts ideals established in England; a certain rivalry, from Hubbard's point of view, with John Larkin; the habits of years in business; an antagonism for such institutions as marriage, the church, the university, the medical profession, and the established world of publishing; a desire to preside over his own establishment; and a substantial ego. The Roycroft was both an attempt at a social experiment, a creative use of his wealth and talent, and a weapon with which to strike back at those persons and institutions who had offended his sense of pride and social justice. Owing to the complexity of his motives and the fullness of his domination over the institution, Elbert Hubbard must bear the weight of responsibility for both its successes and its failures.

Roycroft Products and the Question of Quality

The question that remains unanswered concerns quality. How *good* were the Roycroft products? The answer is not simple. They varied considerably in quality because, in part, there was no unifying artistic vision at the Roycroft. Elbert Hubbard was primarily interested in writing. He began the Roycroft as a means to get his work published and to foster fine printing, but it is worth noting that while he encouraged leatherwork, metalwork, pottery, painting, furniture-making and music, he did not do much to encourage writers other than his wife Alice. The *Philistine* and Hubbard's other writings succeeded at a popular level and were complemented by the work in the Print Shop and the Bindery, but did not serve as a nucleus for a coherent body of artistic production as Gustav Stickley's furniture and Frank Lloyd Wright's architecture did in their respective centers. As a result, some of the designs of W. W. Denslow, Dard Hunter, and Karl Kipp attained a high degree of quality, while in other areas, such as the eclectic Roycroft buildings, much of the metalwork, the furniture, and some of the printing, the work was modest or undistinguished.

The challenge of staging an exhibition of Roycroft artworks involves not only decisions about quality (which is inherent in the object), but also decisions about whether to, and how to, present the more mundane objects, because an integral part of the Arts and Crafts philosophy as it was established at the outset in England centered upon the involvement of ordinary, unskilled people in the production—that is, the premise that the work itself, the process of *making*, was as important as the finished product.

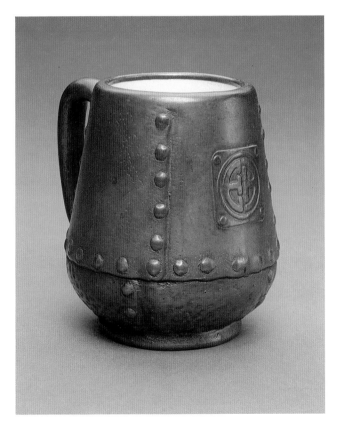

Plate 8: *Elbert Hubbard's Mug* ca. 1908. Manufactured by Clewell. Copper over porcelain, 4½ × 4 in.
Private collection.

Plate 9: *Two Stamps with Roycroft Perfin.* Paper, $^{15}/_{16}$ × $^{13}/_{16}$ in. (each).
Collection of Charles F. Hamilton.

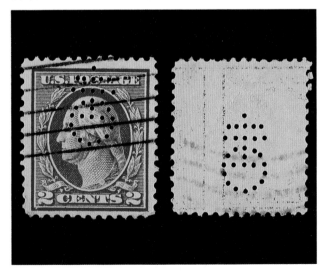

Postscript

How then can we assess the impact of the Roycroft? What was its place in the scheme of things at the turn of the century and in America since that time? What is its place in the Arts and Crafts movement as a whole? These questions inevitably bring us back to Hubbard. The Roycroft was in several significant respects close to the ideals and model of William Morris. It fostered a thoughtful atmosphere devoted to handcraft and brotherhood. Many people who would have spent their lives doing ordinary farm labor and house work were given an opportunity to learn printing, leathercrafting, and metalworking skills that were intellectually connected to the European medieval past by way of Victorian England. John Ruskin's belief that thinking persons should do some work with their hands and workers should be engaged in thinking was made a reality at the Roycroft. On the other hand, everything about the Roycroft—and nothing made at the Roycroft could escape the association—was tainted by Hubbard's pointed jibes and strident literary voice, a voice that too often represented his own pet peeves about society, was selfishly motivated, and lacked the single-minded commitment to human good that drove Morris, Ruskin, and many of the English originators of the movement.

The legacy of Elbert Hubbard's Roycroft is twofold. Hubbard did raise the intellectual consciousness of Americans a notch, especially in the areas of literature and fine printing. But his principal legacy, in this writer's opinion, is the *idea* of the Roycroft, the creation of the community and the transformation of the village of East Aurora into a center, however brief its existence, of real intellectual ferment—a place where things were going on that don't often occur in most American towns and villages, where people as varied as Clarence Darrow, the Mohawk Princess Viroqua, Richard Le Galliene, Henry Ford, Captain Jack Crawford, and Evelyn Crompton held forth on such subjects as feminism, Judaism, the ideas of Robert Owen, poetry, and business. There was even a lecture, in French, by M. Guy de Lestard, according to the *East Aurora Advertiser* of 25 August 1904, on "France as the Home of Art."

While East Aurora today retains the physical legacy of the Roycroft community and has struggled heroically with the restoration of the Roycroft Inn, it has not yet realized the value and potential of the Roycroft, not only as a historic landmark site but also as a place where Elbert Hubbard's belief in the free exchange of ideas through intellectual discourse could flourish once again. The Arts and Crafts movement has passed, but good ideas never do.

This essay is dedicated to Bruce Bland, whose enthusiasm for Elbert Hubbard has been an inspiration and whose efforts on behalf of the Elbert Hubbard-Roycroft Museum have benefitted and enlightened the public. The author would also like to express his gratitude to Diane Hayes for her careful research into the *East Aurora Advertiser*. The manuscript also benefitted considerably from information provided by Robert Rust.

Plate 10: *Elbert Hubbard's Hat*. Felt, ribbon, and leather, 5¾ x 15¾ × 16¾ in.
Elbert Hubbard-Roycroft Museum.

ENDNOTES

[1] For a brief discussion of the Arts and Crafts movement in England in the context of the development of modernism, see Nikolaus Pevsner, *Pioneers of Modern Design, from William Morris to Walter Gropius* (New York: Metropolitan Museum of Art, 1949).

[2] Thomas Carlyle was the first author to call attention in print to the evils of industry in "Sign of the Times" in the *Edinburgh Review* in 1829; Augustus Welby Pugin, an architect, wrote *Contrasts* in 1839, a book that compared life in England in 1840 to life in 1440 through a series of comparative plates; John Ruskin's most eloquent writing about medieval values is "The Nature of Gothic" in *The Stones of Venice* of 1851, but also persuasive is his *Seven Lamps of Architecture* of 1849; Dickens's writings are always about the underclass, but his *Hard Times* is specifically set in a fictional industrial city, "Coketown," modeled upon Manchester.

[3] Among the best of many biographies of William Morris is E. P. Thompson's *William Morris: Romantic Rebel* (London: Lawrence and Wishart, 1955).

[4] Richardson commissioned windows from William Morris's firm for Trinity Church in Boston, completed in 1877, and for the Glessner House in Chicago in 1885.

[5] Andrew White and Charles Eliot Norton were each acquainted with John Ruskin; Frank Lloyd Wright met C. R. Ashbee in 1900 and they visited each other and corresponded for many years; Mrs. Ashbee visited the Roycroft in December 1900, according to Alan Crawford in *C. R. Ashbee: Architect, Designer & Romantic Socialist* (New Haven: Yale University Press, 1985), 96–97. No one is quite certain whether Hubbard met William Morris or not; Hubbard's *Little Journeys* (to the homes of many famous individuals whom he couldn't have met, because they were deceased) have undermined his credibility regarding Morris.

[6] Addams had visited Toynbee Hall, a meeting house situated in the London tenements, and modeled Hull-House directly upon it. Established in 1884 by Henrietta and Canon Barnett, Toynbee Hall provided a forum for important speakers of the day and was the site of C. R. Ashbee's influential lecture on the work of John Ruskin.

[7] See Coy L. Ludwig, *The Arts & Crafts Movement in New York State, 1890s–1920s* (Hamilton: Gallery Association of New York State, 1983).

[8] On Joseph McHugh, see Anna Tobin D'Ambrosio, "The Distinction of Being Different": Joseph P. McHugh and the American Arts and Crafts Movement* (Utica: Munson-Williams-Proctor Institute, 1993).

[9] On Charles Rohlfs, see Michael James, *Drama in Design: The Life and Craft of Charles Rohlfs* (Buffalo: Burchfield Art Center, 1994).

[10] According to the Larkin Company catalogues collection in the Harry H. Larkin Jr. Collection of the Buffalo and Erie County Historical Society (BECHS), the Larkin Company offered a "mission clock" in 1905, and between 1906 and 1910 added a variety of mission-style tables, rocking chairs, and other pieces.

[11] See Ludwig, *The Arts & Crafts Movement in New York State*.

[12] Ibid., 45, 47.

[13] See Ludwig for a good description of all four Arts & Crafts communities. He also discusses a fourth colony, the Glen Eirie Workers, which issued a prospectus in 1902 but which seems to have never materialized.

[14] On Utopian communities of the nineteenth century, see Dolores Hayden, *Seven American Utopias: The Architecture of Communitarian Socialism, 1790–1975* (Cambridge, Mass.: MIT Press, 1976).

[15] Hubbard worked for Larkin and Weller for four or five years and the Larkin Company for eighteen years, hence his twenty-three years in the soap business.

[16] "Soap slingers" were salesmen who passed through neighborhoods distributing printed circulars about their products, returned to sling packages of soap onto the porches of potential customers, and came back about a week later to collect either the money owed or the soap. Slingers traveled throughout the country working assigned territories, and lived in hotels and boarding houses on company expense accounts.

[17] *Philistine* 16, no. 4 (March 1903): 117.

[18] According to Daniel I. Larkin (grandson of John D. Larkin), who has had access to the Larkin Company account books, the firm was recapitalized in 1920, at which time its stock value was increased from $1 million to $30 million. Total sales in 1920 amounted to $31 million.

[19] Much of the information included here regarding Larkin advertising was derived from a Larkin Company scrapbook in the Harry H. Larkin Jr. Collection at the BECHS. I am indebted to Daniel I. Larkin for calling my attention to this material.

[20] This discussion of Larkin sales techniques is based upon Mildred Schlei, "The Larkin Company—A History" (master's thesis, University of Buffalo, 1932); Darwin Martin, *The First to Make a Card Ledger* (Buffalo, 1932); and "Our Pioneers," *Ourselves* 13 (May 1921).

[21] The Larkin Company was not the first to employ premiums; the Babbitt Soap Company, an Ohio firm, did so in the 1870s.

[22] The offer of the "$6.00 Combination Box" on thirty days' time was unprecedented in those days, but is a logical extension of the soap slinger's practice of leaving a package of soap with a customer and returning a week later to collect on it.

[23] Hubbard's willingness to try something fundamentally unethical is noteworthy. Paul McKenna states: "In summation, the question is one of integrity. Throughout this history there has been one instance after another of Elbert Hubbard's unethical treatment of others." (*A History and Bibliography of the Roycroft Printing Shop* [North Tonawanda, N.Y.: Tona Graphics, 1986], 86)

[24] A variety of full page advertisements for the "Chautauqua piano lamp" are preserved in the Larkin Company advertising scrapbook in the Harry H. Larkin Jr. Collection.

[25] *The Larkin Idea* (May–November 1901): 57.

[26] According to *Ourselves*, a Larkin Company workers' publication, of 5 February 1906, nearly 1,000 premiums were available in the Larkin catalogue at that time.

[27] See endnote 17.

[28] For a complete account of Hubbard's affair with Alice Moore, see Charles F. Hamilton, *As Bees in Honey Drown* (South Brunswick and New York: A. S. Barnes and Co., 1973).

[29] Both *The Man* and *One Day* were published, the former by J. S. Ogilvie, New York, the latter by the Arena Publishing Company in Boston.

[30] Darwin D. Martin, "Autobiography," Darwin D. Martin Family Papers, Archives of the State University of New York at Buffalo.

[31] According to Hamilton, Hubbard enrolled in the Emerson College of Oratory as a special student while waiting to enter Harvard in the fall. (Hamilton, *As Bees in Honey Drown*, 62) Letters from Hubbard to Darwin D. Martin, his successor at the Larkin company, indicate that he was in East Aurora in March, in Chicago for the World's Columbian Exposition in April or May, in East Aurora at the end of May, and back in Chicago (and Hudson, Ill.) visiting the fair in June. (Martin Family Papers)

[32] During the spring and summer of 1894, Hubbard was forced to make a choice between staying with Alice in Boston or returning to live permanently with his wife and children in East Aurora. He chose East Aurora. That Bertha illuminated some of the first Roycroft books suggests that they had come to some kind of understanding whereby she would be involved with him in his new life as a writer and publisher.

[33] According to "Local and Personal," *East Aurora Advertiser*, 24 March 1893: "Harry P. Taber, lately a reporter on one of the Denver, Colorado papers, is visiting his parents, William K. Taber and wife." Taber was born and raised in East Aurora.

[34] That Hubbard had amassed a substantial personal library is evident

from his request of Darwin Martin in 1885 that Martin catalogue the library for him. (Darwin Martin diary entry, 15 August 1885, Martin Family Papers) According to "Local and Personal," *East Aurora Advertiser*, 20 June 1901, Elbert Hubbard's maternal uncle, George Read, operated a bookbinding shop in Buffalo for many years. Read may have whetted Hubbard's appetite for book design. McKenna suggests that Taber proposed to Hubbard "a journal recording the lives of famous European authors. He noted [Hubbard's European] trip in his column of the Pendennis Press's *Citizen* as a 'little journey to the homes of great men.'" (McKenna, *A History and Bibliography*, 35)

[35] For a thorough discussion of the *Philistine*, see Bruce A. White, *Elbert Hubbard's The Philistine, A Periodical of Protest, 1895–1915: A Major American "Little Magazine"* (Lanham, Md., and London: University Press of America, 1989).

[36] Whether conscious or not, Hubbard's use of young women (and men) from East Aurora and its environs takes its precedent in the "Lowell System," a method of drawing female textile mill labor for the mills of Lowell, Massachusetts, from local farms in the 1820s. In the Lowell system, young women (considered supernumerary in large farm families) were provided supervised housing and five-year contracts to work in the mills for wages that were usually sent back to the farm.

[37] "Local and Personal," *East Aurora Advertiser*, 1 December 1898.

[38] According to "Notes from the Shop: Timely Topics Concerning the Busy Workers at the Roycroft," *East Aurora Advertiser*, 25 April 1907: "Mr. Hubbard spoke in the Academy of Music, Philadelphia, on the 18 inst. to an audience of 3,000. The rent is $275 a night." On 21 March 1907, the *Advertiser* reported: "Another packed house in New York greeted Mr. Hubbard at Carnegie Hall last Sunday evening. Upwards of $1,200.00 were the receipts . . ." If these reports can be trusted, they suggest that Hubbard could earn twice as much in one lecture as the average employee earned in a year at that time.

[39] Daniel I. Larkin, conversation with author, 12 February 1994.

[40] William E. Martin to Darwin D. Martin, 24 January 1901, Martin Family Papers.

[41] "Local and Personal," *East Aurora Advertiser*, 14 October 1897.

[42] Ibid., 20 January 1898.

[43] Ibid., 30 March 1899.

[44] Ibid., 22 June 1899.

[45] According to "Local and Personal," *East Aurora Advertiser*, 7 December 1899, J. I. Laney sold his home on Grove Street to Elbert Hubbard, who turned it over to Lyle Hawthorne, Superintendent of the Roycroft. On 14 December 1899, W. D. Jones sold the house west of the Roycroft library on Main Street, known as the Moon house, to Elbert Hubbard; Hubbard then moved it, on 26 April 1900, from the rear of the Roycroft library to the lot south of William Kelly's below Prospect Avenue. Hubbard also tore down the barn on the lot west of the library, recently purchased of H. W. Richardson, preparatory to erecting other buildings. On 3 May 1900, Hubbard gave the Main Street dwelling that had been occupied by Charles Raesch to N. Ess, who moved it to the second lot south of Hamlin Park. On 11 October 1900, Hubbard purchased Mrs. Elizabeth Whitney's house and lot opposite the Roycroft, and moved the house to the lot just east of Charles Hinaman's on Prospect Avenue. On 10 January 1901, Mrs. Horatio Castle sold to Elbert Hubbard her Grove Street house and lot, which he moved to Prospect Avenue. On 14 November 1901, Hubbard began erecting a new house on Oakwood Avenue, between Grove and Walnut Streets, which was completed on May 15, 1902; at the same time, he was building another house on Walnut Street. On 19 June 1902, John Jordan sold his lot to Elbert Hubbard and moved his house to the Brayton lot adjoining F. R. Whaley's. On 31 July 1902, Hubbard purchased the Doyle residence on Prospect Avenue in order to fit it up as a dormitory for Roycroft visitors.

[46] Hubbard may have provided housing for other Roycroft artists; the newspaper evidence is not definitive.

[47] "Local and Personal," *East Aurora Advertiser*, 30 March 1899.

[48] "Roycroft Ripples," *East Aurora Advertiser*, 14 February 1907. The original Print Shop became the Roycroft bank; the safe is still extant in the basement.

[49] According to advertisements in *Little Journeys* published from March through October 1903, an Inn or Phalanstery was then "just completed" with thirty-eight sleeping rooms, receptions rooms, and a dining room that could accommodate one hundred guests.

[50] "Our Building Boom," *East Aurora Advertiser*, 1 December 1904.

[51] A number of people have pointed out to me a certain resemblance between the veranda that connects the Inn with the bank and the long pergola that extended behind Frank Lloyd Wright's Darwin Martin House (1904–1906) in Buffalo. The evidence is strong that there must have been some contact between the two men. Hubbard worked for the Larkin Company for many years, was Martin's supervisor, and continued to maintain a relationship with him until 1915. Wright designed the Larkin Company's administration building as well as Martin's own house; a house for Martin's sister, Delta; a house for Martin's brother, William; and a house for William R. Heath, the vice president of the Larkin company (and Hubbard's brother-in-law)—all around 1905 and 1906, when the Inn was under construction. I have discussed this issue in an article, "Did Frank Lloyd Wright and Elbert Hubbard Know Each Other?" *Arts & Crafts Quarterly* 5 (1992): 24–27. There is good evidence that they were aware of one another, and it is possible that the Inn's veranda was influenced by Wright's penchant for pergolas, but I feel certain that Wright was not in any way involved in the design. The piers of the Roycroft Inn pergola come close to classical precedent, and their proportions are heavier than those designed by Wright. By 1906 Wright was well into his Prairie style, in which piers carried roofs and eaves with pronounced cantilevers quite different from those of the Inn's veranda.

[52] "Local and Personal," *East Aurora Advertiser*, 30 March 1905 states: "One of the most beautiful and modern buildings in this village will be the new structure on Grove Street owned by Mr. Elbert Hubbard and now in the course of reconstruction. The old building, 'The Alberta,' has been partially torn down, and is being replaced by a grand salon and about a dozen open air bedrooms, besides a mammoth veranda. About twenty carpenters are now at work on the building. From 'The Alberta' proper to the Roycroft bank, a spacious veranda will be constructed, thus forming a large court between the buildings. The grand salon will be furnished with Roycroft furniture and valuable oil paintings by Alex Fournier. It is expected that the work will be completed in time for the Roycroft convention." According to "Roycroft Tips: Meetings for Roycrofters which are Proving Instructive," *East Aurora Advertiser*, 18 April 1907: "Last week Bill Roth and his gang raised the roof of the back part of the Inn, thereby making ten rooms where before there were only five."

[53] "Notes from the Shop: Timely Topics Concerning the Busy Workers at the Roycroft," *East Aurora Advertiser*, 25 April 1907.

[54] "Local and Personal," *East Aurora Advertiser*, 1 December 1898; *A Love Letter to the Elect* (East Aurora: The Roycrofters, [pre-1915]).

[55] For example, a letter from Elbert Hubbard to Mr. DeShon, dated 4 November 1902 and placed inside a copy of *A Message to Garcia and Thirteen Other Things*, reads:
Dear Mr. DeShon:
    Possibly we are slightly prejudiced, but the volume we have sent you to-day we think quite a Book. Anyway we have woven a lot of loving care into its making. We know you will be glad to inspect it as you have the spirit that is able to appreciate these Choice Things. If not wanted simply return at your convenience. And believe us, ever
        Sincerely yours,
        Elbert Hubbard

[56] Circular, 1886, Larkin Company advertising scrapbook, Harry H. Larkin Jr. Collection. The hundreds of items in this scrapbook, including broadsides, advertisements clipped from a variety of publications, chromolithographs, and product labels, are dated in ink but are not arranged in any order.

[57] *Philistine* 22, no. 4 (March 1903).

[58] Circular, 1889, Larkin Company advertising scrapbook, Harry H. Larkin Jr. Collection.

[59] Circular, 1 November 1892 (signed by Elbert Hubbard), Harry H. Larkin Jr. Collection.

[60] "Local Brevities," *East Aurora Advertiser*, 21 June 1914.

[61] Early mentions of the various Roycroft conventions appear in the *East Aurora Advertiser* on 6 July 1905; 24 August 1905; 28 December 1905; 20 December 1906; 11 July 1907; 15 August 1907; and 22 August 1907.

[62] Roycroft annual picnics date back at least to 1897, according to "Philistine Picnic," *East Aurora Advertiser*, 5 August 1897: "Thursday was bright and hot—just the day for the Philistine picnic that was held at Hansenburg's Natural Park . . . They ate their lunch in the beautiful grove; they fished in the placid and shallow waters; they cooked their fish in primitive fashion, they sang songs, fell into the water, played games, romped, laughed, and in time did exactly what the sons and daughters of Philistia would naturally do. It was a great day, surpassing even the wonders of the recent picnic of the G.O.P. of Erie County, but there was no beer."

[63] "Philistine Conference: In session this week at the Roycroft Shops and Hamlin Park", *East Aurora Advertiser*, 4 August 1904: "At this early date, the phalansterie is crowded to its utmost capacity and by Saturday the day of the annual Philistine Dinner it is expected between 500 and 1,000 out of town guests will be at the shops."

[64] "New Thought Convention: Held at the Roycroft from Aug. 19 to 25th Inclusive," *East Aurora Advertiser*, 24 August 1905. Ernest Crosby was an author and social reformer and follower of the single tax theorist Henry George; Marshall Wilder was an entertainer who traveled around the world, spending much of his career from 1883 to 1899 in London and thereafter in America in vaudeville; G. W. Littlefield was a wealthy Texas rancher, cotton plantation owner, and founder of the American National Bank in Austin, who had established a fund for the study of Southern history at the University of Texas at Austin; Lyman Chandler, Alice Hubbard, and Beulah Hood were Roycrofters. The other convention speakers are unknown to this writer.

[65] Circular, 1 November 1892, Larkin Company advertising scrapbook, Harry H. Larkin Jr. Collection.

[66] Regarding Larkin "Clubs of Ten" and "Club Secretaries," see Schlei, "The Larkin Company," 22–34.

[67] There are twenty-eight letters from Elbert Hubbard to Darwin Martin between 1893 and 1912 in the Darwin Martin Family Papers. These letters indicate that Hubbard and Martin occasionally met in Buffalo and in East Aurora during those years.

[68] Visitors who entertained or lectured at the Larkin Company included Booker T. Washington; Jack and Irving Kaufman, recording stars; Francis MacMillen, America's greatest violinist; H. Otis Blaisdell, the American typewriter champion; Billy Sunday, a baseball player turned evangelist; David Bispham, a renowned baritone; and M. V. Terhune, who wrote on women's issues under the name Marion Harland.

[69] Some prominent visiting lecturers at the Roycroft were lawyer Clarence Darrow; Edward Bok, publisher of the *Ladies Home Journal*; M. St. Andre de Lignereaux, the French Representative to the World's Fair at St. Louis; the Honorable George Daniels, Secretary of the Navy; Thomas Harned, literary executor of Walt Whitman; Janet Ashbee, wife of English Arts and Crafts artist and architect C. R. Ashbee; author Bret Harte; poet Richard Le Gallienne; and industrialist Henry Ford.

Jack Quinan is Professor and Chairman of the Department of Art History at the State University of New York at Buffalo. He is author of *Frank Lloyd Wright's Larkin Building: Myth and Fact* and a forthcoming study titled *Frank Lloyd Wright and Darwin D. Martin: An Architect-Client Relationship*.

Plate 11: *Roycroft Cigar Box with Cigars*. Manufactured by John W. Merriam & Co., New York. Wood, metal fittings, paper, and cigars, 2⅜ × 10⅝ × 5½ in. *Elbert Hubbard-Roycroft Museum*.

A Little Journey to the Roycroft Shops

RIXFORD JENNINGS

Final bell sounds—school's out! A happy sound for one third-grader who always seemed to have many more interesting things to do outside, after school. But this was Thursday, the day there would be a bundle of *Saturday Evening Post*s on the doorstep, as there had been each Thursday for many months, all of which meant starting right out to deliver copies to regular East Aurora customers and then making the rounds to sell the extras. And the sales route led into some mighty interesting places. Besides all the village stores and shops, the railroad depot was a great place to visit and usually was good for a sale or two. The bank offices, barber shops, and hotels were regular stops, as were the saloons, whose regulars always seemed to have an extra nickel or two.

The best part of the entire route was through the Roycroft Shops. First, the climb up the creaking wooden stairs to the Furniture Shop, stopping at the bulletin board to see any new Ray Nott cartoons, or the "Every Knock is a Boost" poster and the ever-present warning, "No Gabbyjacking Allowed." Then into the shop with its wonderful aroma of freshly-cut oak and pine and chestnut, and all those clean-smelling wood shavings. A few minutes there to marvel at the ease with which old Grandpa Standeven could carve beautiful letters into the backs of oak chairs and benches. That pungent smell of oil and wax and hot glue in the finishing shop! Then a short hop down below, just to listen to Lester Heller's stories while he poked, pushed, and grunted, filling the huge Roycroft medicine balls or lacing the smaller leather hand balls—and to marvel at his capacity to talk and spit out a seemingly unlimited supply of tacks while upholstering a big chair or settee.

Sometimes it was fun to go way up to the top floor of the Bindery to peek into the Modeled Leather Department. It was so quiet he was almost afraid to step, for fear of treading on a creaky board and startling all the pretty girls working there. He enjoyed the wonderful aroma of fine leathers, beeswax, and chemical dyes and stains, plus the smell of hot irons where Mr. Schwartz was applying gold leaf to the marvelous designs on the leather-bound books. Sometimes Mr.

Plate 12: *Child's Chair*, ca. 1910. Oak, leather, and metal tacks, 24¾ × 13½ × 13¾ in.
Collection of Mr. and Mrs. Rixford Jennings.

ScheideMantel would stop and talk, and even buy a *Post*.

Across the way the route led into the Copper Shop, with its bedlam of hammering and the screeching of metal saws—no chance of a sales talk there, but it was great fun to watch the bubbling and hissing of the big pickling tanks for cleaning the copper pieces.

No trip was complete without a quick run through the awesome black void of the coal bunkers—past the gigantic furnaces and into the Power House generator room, slick and shiny and also a little scary with huge electric generators, steam turbines, pumps, and impressive-looking marble control panels full of mysterious dials and switches. After the usual remarks from Mr. Heim, the engineer, or from one of his crew—that the *Saturday Evening Post* came out too often or that they could not afford the five cents—the boy would make suitable comments expressing sympathy for their sad financial plight.

And then it was off to the Print Shop to watch the enormous presses with their big rollers and long arms moving great white sheets of paper, and to marvel at the way part of the page came out in colors until finally all the colors, photographs, and type ended up fitting together perfectly.

There was always the side trip to the composing room to watch those fellows reading everything upside down or backwards. A few more moments to pass the time of day with Emil or Axel Sahlin, including the inevitable delay each trip while Emil carefully went through the entire magazine to decide whether it was worth buying. He was always on the look-out for a pretty girl's picture—but somehow he never found one that warranted springing for a whole nickel—it always ended up by his saying the *Post* came to the house by subscription anyway.

After struggling with several tremendous oak doors and up long flights of stairs into the Print Shop tower, the reward was the Advertising and Art Department— the Holy of Holies to an eight-year-old who was forever

drawing and sketching. His visits were not always convenient for the staff and must have been a quite a problem at times because that is where he acquired the questionable title of Saturday Evening *Pest*. However, on one occasion, much to his surprise, he was greeted with a cheery "Hi there, sonny, today we have something for you!" With this he was handed a bundle of printed sheets and instructions to put one in each of his *Saturday Evening Post*s until they were all used up.

The sheets turned out out to be small handbills, designed by Milton Feesley, then head of the Advertising Department. Although unappreciated by the young boy, this was an original and typically Roycroftie sales idea, titled "Two Long-Haired Businessmen." It featured photos of Hubbard, with long hair, a flowing tie, and a big smile, and of the eight-year-old, also with long flowing hair and a big Roycroft tie, but no smile, an indication that he did not share his parents' enthusiasm for that particular Hubbard image. Along with these photos was a suggestion that the reader buy a copy of the *Post* because Hubbard said it was almost as good

TWO LONG-HAIRED
BUSINESSMEN

 AM the boy who delivers Elbert Hubbard's "Saturday Evening Post" every week.

❦ The Fra calls me the Saturday evening "pest." But I know he does n't mean it. This is just one of his jokes.

❦ The people in the Roycroft Shops are my best customers. Even though I am a competitor of Elbert

Hubbard in the magazine business, he lets me sell in his Shops. This is professional courtesy, my Dad says.

❦ I am eight years old and have long yellow hair. The Fra's hair is long and black — or was once. Also, I have an account in the Roycroft Bank, saved from "Saturday Evening Post" profits.

❦ And, by the way, I want you as my customer.

❦ My magazine is the best in the world — Elbert Hubbard says it is second best, but I know better.

❦ Just phone me, or my mother, and I 'll bring you a "Post" this week.

❦ Yours for "Big Business," and more of it.

RIXFORD JENNINGS
Bell Phone 26 R   ·   ·   ·   East Aurora, N. Y.

Fig. 16: Advertisement for "Two Long-Haired Businessmen," 1914.
(Courtesy Rixford Jennings)

as the Roycroft *Fra* magazine and he didn't mind the competition.

The following Sunday evening found the newly recognized "big businessman" with the entire family—Father, Mother, and two sisters—duly ensconced on a front-row bench in the Roycroft Salon, as was their regular custom, awaiting the beginning of another evening of music, lectures, and other cultural activities. The waiting period may have seemed endless to many of the young people sitting in that extremely quiet, sometimes very warm room, but it was no annoyance to the young *Post* salesman, who never tired of studying the enchanting Fournier murals that encircled the entire salon and spilled out into the entrance lobby and music room. It was great fun to dream of riding one of the gondolas in the Venice scene or of climbing the Great Pyramid at sunset; other times he imagined a visit to London and the Houses of Parliament or to the colossal tomb of Caesar on the Tiber.

Finally the time came. A slight stir among the grownups and the great Fra Elbertus made his appearance, took his place in the huge leather-upholstered Morris chair under Dard Hunter's green leaded-glass floor lamp. All became very quiet, and the program began. Following a brief announcement of the selection and its composer, Lillian Hawley Gearhart would favor the audience with one of the great classics on the Steinway. As beautiful as it must have been, the selection always

seemed endless, a musical judgment influenced more by the painfully uncomfortable oak benches than any knowledge of musical form.

At the end of the piano recital, a change in the usual order of the evening took place. Instead of walking over to the lectern to arrange his papers and notes, Mr. Hubbard came down from the platform and walked toward the first row of benches, motioning and beckoning to the family and particularly to the young boy, who was taken so completely by surprise that he turned around to see if someone behind him was being called. Not so: that big, soft, and kindly voice was saying, "Come up here with me, sonny." After an infinitely long walk and a climb up to the podium that he thought he'd never make, he was introduced by Mr. Hubbard as the other "Long-Haired Business Man"!

There were additional comments on our newly-formed partnership, thoughtfully worded so as not to require a reply. Polite applause followed, as well as the remaining part of the evening's program, none of which was heard by one surprised and excited third-grader.

Rixford Jennings, ex-*Saturday Evening Post* salesman, learned the art of metalsmithing from his father, Walter Jennings, who was one of the Roycroft's principal copper craftsmen. For the past seven decades he has worked as a painter, illustrator, and graphic designer from his studio in East Aurora.

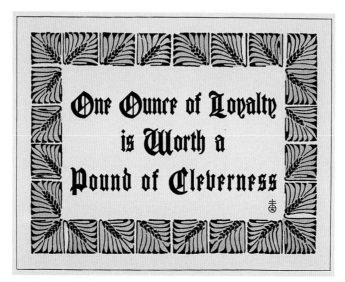

Plate 13: *Motto: One Ounce of Loyalty is Worth a Pound of Cleverness.*
Designed by Dard Hunter. Paper with ink and colors, 11½ × 15½ in.
Collection of Kitty Turgeon Rust and Robert Rust, Roycroft Shops.

The Roycroft Printing Shop:
Books, Magazines and Ephemera

JEAN-FRANÇOIS VILAIN

There is great irony in the renewed interest in Roycroft as part of the Arts and Crafts movement. Although Roycroft furniture and metalwork are today widely admired, relatively little attention is paid to the contributions that the Roycrofters made to the printing and graphic arts. The irony's source is twofold: it was through books and magazines that artists, designers, and craftsmen became aware of William Morris and the burgeoning movement in England; and Elbert Hubbard originally created Roycroft as a publishing venture for his own writing and some favorite works of other authors.

Hubbard's two periodicals, the wildly successful *Philistine* and the equally successful, and better designed, *Little Journeys*, brought an awareness of the ideals and aesthetics of the Arts and Crafts movement to thousands of homes outside the intellectual and artistic mainstream; the numerous advertisements in them for other Roycroft products, including the books, contributed to the continuing success of the enterprise. Many racks, stands, and bookcases were originally designed to showcase the magazines and books

published by Hubbard. Although these pieces are today collected to display pottery and metalwork, this attractive furniture is often curiously divorced from its intended purpose and stripped of its original contents.

There are many reasons for this apparent neglect: books, which are meant to be opened to be appreciated, do not have for today's Arts and Crafts enthusiasts the immediate visual appeal of other objects of the period, and they cannot be as easily displayed as ceramics or metalwork. Many collectors also fear that a knowledge of esoteric printing terms is necessary to understand or appreciate a well-made book. In addition, the Roycroft books have suffered, in the eyes of bibliophiles, from Hubbard's reputation as a huckster who mass-produced shoddy imitations, bound in poor-quality suede, of the elegant Kelmscott books published in England by William Morris. It is true that some Roycroft books were poorly conceived and imperfectly executed. And it is true that a row of book spines may not adorn a shelf quite as dramatically as an American Beauty vase. But it is also true that the printed products of the Roycroft Shop were vastly popular when they were created and this popularity contributed significantly to the renaissance of the printing and graphic arts in America.

Bookmaking in the 1890s

William Morris's "little typographical adventure,"[1] prompted in part by his dismay at the parlous state into which the art of the book had fallen, struck a responsive chord on both sides of the Atlantic. Faced with an ever-increasing demand for books from a rapidly growing reading public, publishers and printers embraced the sophisticated machines produced by the Industrial Revolution. The aesthetic aspects of the book were sacrificed on the altars of economy, speed, and mass production. Although a few well-made books were still produced, the idea that a book, carefully thought out, could delight the eyes and fingers, as well as the mind of the reader, had been largely abandoned by the

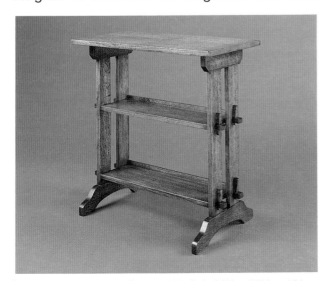

Plate 14: *Little Journeys Stand*, 1925. Oak, 26½ × 26⅛ × 15 in. Collection of Bruce A. Austin.

publishing world. Morris conceived the "ideal book"[2] as a unified whole involving page design, typeface, paper, ink, ornaments, and illustrations. A fervent admirer of things medieval, he strove to produce books that were "pocket cathedrals."[3] Although the books he made at his Kelmscott Press have been criticized for being intended to be looked at rather than read, Morris's precepts deeply influenced a new generation of eager, idealistic publishers, designers, and typographers.

At first Morris's revolution touched a limited public. A few private presses produced books, in limited editions, that reflect his ideals: the Ashendene and Eragny Presses, established in 1894 in England, and the publishing venture of Thomas B. Mosher, founded in 1891 in America. Commercial presses, such as the Bodley Head (1891) in London, Copeland and Day (1894) in Boston, Stone and Kimball, and Way and Williams (both 1895) in Chicago, also published elegant and well-designed books, in somewhat less limited print runs, that are direct heirs of Morris's views on bookmaking. It remained to Hubbard to "translate the great vision [of Morris] into terms of the vernacular and [bring] Beauty, in a relative degree but certainly, into the ken of literally thousands who never would have understood the message in any other form."[4]

The Beginnings of the Roycroft Printing Shop

It was through his membership in the Chautauqua Literary and Scientific Circle of East Aurora that Hubbard made two of the most important acquaintances of his life: Alice Moore and Harry P. Taber.[5] Alice became his writing partner, mistress, and, eventually, his second wife; Harry Taber gave a lecture to the Circle on printing that used examples from the early Venetian printers. This lecture introduced Hubbard to Aldus Manutius, the scholar-printer who published inexpensive but carefully crafted books, and to Nicolaus Jenson, whose beautiful Roman font has been a model for all subsequent type designers.[6] In 1893 Hubbard left his lucrative position at the Larkin Company in Buffalo to become a student at Harvard University and a full-time writer.[7] His brief stay at Harvard did not work out, but the modest success of his books—especially the fact that they were published—encouraged him to pursue a literary career.

When Hubbard visited England in 1894, Taber suggested that he write accounts of his visits to the homes of famous authors. Taber prepared a dummy of a sample *Little Journey* and, after many rejections, Hubbard persuaded George P. Putnam to publish a monthly series of booklets describing journeys to the homes of famous people. It was during his 1894 trip to England that Hubbard claimed to have visited William Morris at his home in Hammersmith, a suburb of London, and to have been struck by the beauty of the Kelmscott books; there is, however, no independent corroboration that such an encounter actually occurred.[8]

In 1894 Taber became associated with Newell White and Harry Wagoner at their small print shop in East Aurora, the Pendennis Press.[9] There he collaborated with Hubbard on the printing of the latter's *No Enemy (But Himself)*.[10] In June 1895, Taber, Hubbard, and William McIntosh, a fellow Chautauquan and managing editor of the *Buffalo Daily News*, published the first issue of *The Philistine: A Periodical of Protest*, to cash in on the public's appetite for alternatives to the stodgy magazines of the day, such as *Harper's Magazine* and *Atlantic Monthly*. Taber was the editor, with Hubbard and McIntosh as contributors. In September 1895 Taber established the Roycroft Printing Shop to publish the *Philistine* and the first Roycroft book, *The Song of Songs*, with a lengthy foreword by Hubbard.

By the time *The Song of Songs* was printed, on 20 January 1896, Taber, unable to keep on financing the slow-selling *Philistine*, had sold his interest in Roycroft to Hubbard, who became sole owner in November 1895. Hubbard's own accounts of this period describe how he established and named the press and chose the orb-and-cross logo; but, as with many of his statements, these assertions have to be taken with a grain of salt, for these were apparently Taber's creations.[11] Taber stayed on as printer of the magazine and of *The Song of Songs*, but the relationship deteriorated quickly.[12] In February, Hubbard, with the assistance of the young Cy Rosen, took over the printing of the *Philistine* and of the second book of the press, *The Journal of Koheleth*. From this point on Hubbard was free to thumb his nose at those philistine publishers who rejected his manuscripts and he would apply his mastery of the art of publicity in the service of the art of bookmaking.[13]

At first *The Song of Songs* did not sell well.[14] Hubbard was not a book designer and his answer to Morris's clarion call was well-intended but weak. Neither the Morrisian borders and initials nor Bertha Hubbard's charmingly clumsy title page saved the day.[15] But sales of the book soon picked up and the circulation of the *Philistine* was growing: the Roycroft Printing Shop was on its way.

Fig. 17: Bertha Hubbard's title page for *The Song of Songs*, by Elbert Hubbard, 1896.
(Courtesy Elbert Hubbard-Roycroft Museum)

The Roycroft Books

Hubbard realized that while the buying public was eager for his opinionated magazine, that same public, which had never been shown that a book could be an object of beauty in its own right, would need to be convinced to buy his books. Advertisements extolling them appeared regularly in the magazine, book lists and catalogues were issued and sent to subscribers, and many books were sent, "on suspicion," to previous buyers.[16] Combined with his controversial fame as a lecturer and his natural talent for self-promotion, this barrage of publicity stirred interest and generated faithful customers, but something more was needed to generate and sustain sales.

This is where Hubbard gave full rein to his remarkable aptitude for marketing.[17] Limited editions appealed to the keep-up-with-the-Joneses instinct, which was as prevalent then as it is now, so Hubbard stressed heavily the status-enhancing aspect of the Roycroft books.[18] A typical book had a press run of nine hundred copies on regular paper, with an additional edition of from twelve to one hundred copies printed on Japan vellum;[19] occasionally, a very few copies were printed on genuine animal vellum.[20] In addition to these options of printing media, each book was available in an enticing variety of bindings: soft suede, suede on boards, plain boards, three-quarter leather, and full leather. Much was made also of Hubbard's signature, which added the personal touch and guaranteed the authenticity of the limitation statement.[21] Hubbard's masterstroke of genius, however, was his decision to use color in a limited number of the books in the print run—not just a printed second color in the running or shoulder heads, but hand-decorated initials and illuminations, such as those used in the medieval manuscripts of which he and Taber were fond.[22] This use of illuminations and original ornaments had many advantages: it exhibited craftsmanship, it outdid the competition, *and* it compensated for some of the flaws evident in the incunabula of the press—the uneven inking, the inconsistent presswork, the hesitant page make-up, the poor second-color registration.

Because of the wide range of prices at which the books were offered, depending on the quantity of the run, the type of paper, the binding, and the presence or absence of illuminations, Hubbard's pool of customers was significantly broadened. Roycroft could appeal to the average person who wanted a pretty book for relatively little money ($2), as well as to the wealthy collector who could, and did, afford a luxuriously bound volume for $100.[23] And the fanatical collector could build a significant library of "variants" of a single title.[24]

Illuminations

This use of handcoloring, unique in the private press world of the day, was made possible by Bertha's talent with watercolors,[25] and she assumed the role of illuminator with the help of a young neighbor, Minnie Gardner.[26] As the number of books grew, so did the illuminators' work and the need for a more formal arrangement; Hubbard subsequently put William W. Denslow, a Chicago artist who later attained fame for his illustration of *The Wizard of Oz*,[27] in charge of the illumination department. Samuel Warner,[28] a solid journeyman artist, had been hired in 1895 and complemented Denslow, whose sense of book design did not measure up to the quality of his illustrations and cartoons for the *Philistine*.[29] The Roycroft Press now had an art department, and the quality of book design improved dramatically.

In addition to the singular attention to the book as a unit and to the various elements that contribute to a successful book—choice of paper and typeface, careful inking, consistent impression, and accurate register—the Roycroft books stand out for their glowing decorations and illustrations. Some of these, free-hand paintings, occupy a full page (such as the recto

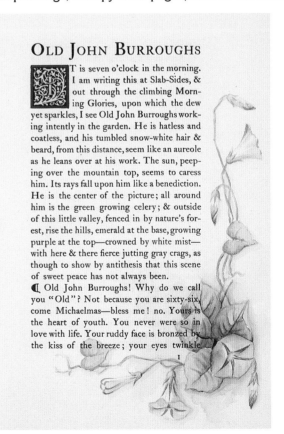

Plate 15: *Old John Burroughs*, by Elbert Hubbard, 1901 (unspecified limitation on Roycroft paper). Three-quarters leather cover with marbled boards, 8⅛ × 5⅜ in. Title page attr. to Samuel Warner. Illumined by Alta Fattey.
Private collection.

of the title page), while most adorn the margins or fill the blank bottom of a page. Most are good, a few are superb, but all contribute to the aesthetic appeal of the books. In order to meet the growing demand while maintaining the quality of the work, the standard initials and marginal decorations were printed in outline and then filled in with watercolors by Bertha and her assistants. In addition, a few special copies were adorned with original hand-painted illustrations or illuminations—on the title page, in the margins, and on the colophon page.[30]

The first book planned specifically for decoration, Vernon Lee's *Art and Life* (1896), was printed on Japan vellum and offered bound in suede as well as in gray boards with white cloth spine.[31] The Morrisian capitals, printed in black and white, and the outline drawings,[32] printed in red in the margins, were ready for hand-coloring. This established the usual procedure for the next four years.[33] *Ruskin and Turner*, published three months later, was the first Roycroft book to be printed both on Japan vellum (26 copies) and on Whatman (473 copies), a paper that lends itself well to watercolor. This compilation of two earlier *Little Journeys* was supplemented by twelve photogravures of J. M. W.

Turner's paintings ("taken especially for us in the National Gallery in London") and was the first book to be offered in three different bindings: gray boards with cloth spine, three-quarters (spine and four corners) leather, and full leather. The Kelmscott-style initials reflect Morris's influence on Warner. The twenty-six copies on Japan vellum were illuminated by Bertha Hubbard and Clara Schlegel; the other illuminators decorated an unspecified number of copies on Whatman paper.

Consistency seems to have been a problem in the early years: some copies of Adeline Knapp's *Upland Pastures* (1897) are decorated throughout and contain hand-drawn illustrations, while others have only a few hand-painted initials. Other copies have hand-drawn illustrations, but contain some outlines left unpainted. The illuminators worked on large unbound sheets as they came off the press so it is likely that the binders, under pressure to complete the books as soon as possible to satisfy expectant buyers, overlooked such minor inconsistencies and concentrated on having the pages appear sequentially, which, to their credit, they always managed.

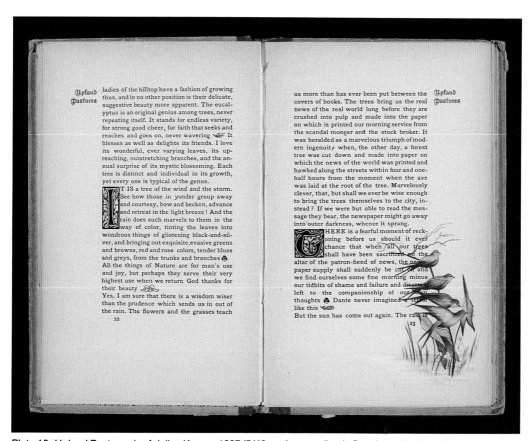

Plate 16: *Upland Pastures*, by Adeline Knapp, 1897 (5/40 on Japan vellum). Gray boards with red cloth spine, 8¼ × 5½ in. Decorated by Bertha Hubbard.
Collection of Richard Blacher.

Under the artistic leadership of Denslow and Warner, the quality of Roycroft book design improved. The presswork also improved, as did that of the printing, as Cy Rosen developed into a master printer. The experiments with type and paper resulted in a more evenly inked page with little or no show-through. The combination of illuminations and increasingly assured book designs produced some of the more beautiful books of the late 1890s, such as *The Book of Job*, illumined by Clara Schlegel, and *As It Seems To Me*, with illuminations by Denslow.

VII

WHAT does it all mean, poet? Well,
Your brains beat into rhythm, you tell
What we felt only; you expressed
You hold things beautiful the best,
And pace them in rhyme so, side by side.
'T is something, nay 't is much: but then,
Have you yourself what 's best for men?
Are you—poor, sick, old ere your time—
Nearer one whit your own sublime
Than we who have never turned a rhyme?
Sing, riding 's a joy! For me, I ride.

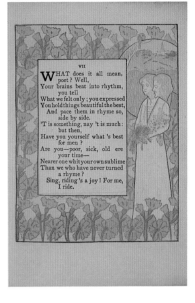

Plate 19: *The Last Ride*, by Robert Browning, 1900 (469/940 on Roycroft paper). Full vellum cover with cloth ties, 7¾ × 6 in. Page design by Samuel Warner (after Henri Caruchet). Decorated by Loretta Hubbs. *Private collection.*

THE BOOK OF JOB As Translated from the Original by Rabbi Abraham Elzas; with some Comments on the Poem by Elbert Hubbard

DONE INTO A BOOK AT THE ROYCROFT SHOP WHICH IS IN EAST AURORA, NEW YORK, U. S. A. MDCCCXCVII.

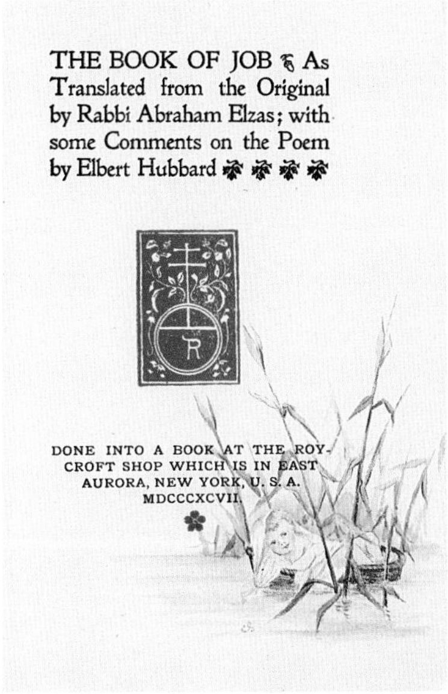

Plate 17: *The Book of Job*, by Elbert Hubbard, 1897 (16/350 on Whatman). ½ cloth cover with gray boards, 8¼ × 5⅜ in. Illumined by Clara Schlegel. *Collection of Richard Blacher.*

Roycroft's triumphal entry into the twentieth century was the edition of Browning's *The Last Ride* (1900), with its carefully printed text nestled inside delicately painted pictorial page frames. Hubbard could be rightly proud of this little gem of bookmaking, but he failed to acknowlege—or, perhaps, was not told by Warner, to whom the book has been attributed—that it was a plagiary, taken, illustration and page design, from a book published in Paris in 1896.[34] Hubbard used the complete scheme of illustrations again, in 1903, for his *Gray's Elegy*.

AS IT SEEMS TO ME

I.

BY RULE OF THREE.

SOME years ago at College I read, on compulsion, a book on Rhetoric. Reasons were to me then as plenty as blackberries, and I recollect that on examination my answers given to this, that and the other were so glib and trite, and my thesis so amusing, that I carried off a Prize. But during the struggle for prizes that have a value as collateral, the Prize and the Rhetoric were forgotten. Yet Fate decreed it so, and one day last week I met a Harvard youth, whose ambition was Literature, and he was in the grinding turmoil of a Volume. He was studying on compulsion, with intent to work off a Condition, and the book he was reading with such violence was the Rhetoric of my College days. With a flush of pride it came to me that I was a Prizeman, and I offered, out of the goodness of my heart, to tutor the youth, so that after five lessons of an hour each he could grind the Condition to powder.
To prove my fitness, the young man put me through a slight quiz, and alas! all of the beautiful truths and facts of the Rhetoric had slipped me, save this alone: "The three requisites in correct writing are Clearness, Force and Elegance."
Professor Adams Sherman Hill, who wrote the Rhetoric, begins every address with this peculiar formula. Mr. Barrett Wendell, Heir-Apparent to his ideas and Chair, does the same; and the Shock-

9

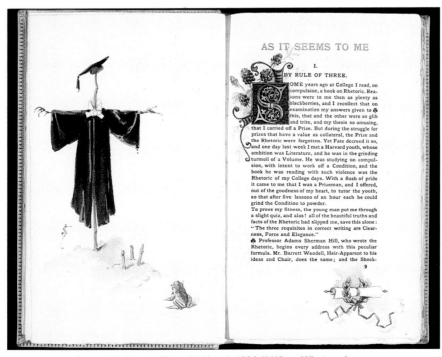

Plate 18: *As It Seems To Me*, by Elbert Hubbard, 1898 (2/40 on Whatman). Full vellum cover (ties missing), 9 × 5⅝ in. Illumined by W. W. Denslow. *Collection of Richard Blacher.*

OVE LETTERS
OF A MUSICIAN
by Myrtle Reed

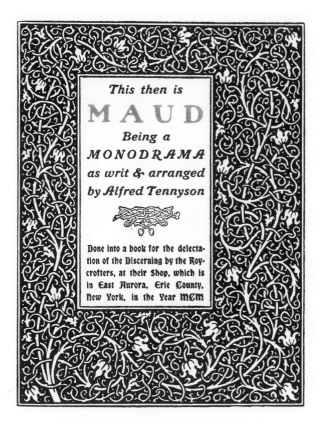

Fig. 18: W. W. Denslow's title page for *Love Letters of a Musician*, by Myrtle Reed, 1898.
(Courtesy Jean-François Vilain and Roger S. Wieck)

Fig. 19: Samuel Warner's title page for *Maud*, by Alfred Tennyson, 1900.
(Courtesy Elbert Hubbard-Roycroft Museum)

Title Pages

Walter Blaikie, the great nineteenth-century British designer, called the title page the "crowning glory of a good book,"[35] and the Roycrofters paid particular attention to that aspect of their books. The evolution of their title pages parallels the artistic maturation of the Roycroft designers and Hubbard's growing understanding of the appeal title pages held for prospective buyers. The hesitant title page of *The Song of Songs* was soon replaced by a Morrisian block of type, flushed left and right and filled out with fleurons of stylized leaves and acorns, as in G. B. Shaw's *On Going to Church* (1896), with the ruled-in Roycroft logo below, printed in red. Illumination gave special copies a vibrant and appealing look, but regular copies must have seemed austere to the less affluent buyer. Hubbard was not a designer and gave his artists free rein to invent solutions to that dilemma, and the result was an extraordinary variety of designs. These young artists were not bound to a particular tradition and, in a sponge-like manner, they had a tendency to absorb many styles—Medieval, Renaissance, Arts and Crafts, Art Nouveau. The goal of this purposeful heterogeneity was, clearly, an increased number of customers.

Myrtle Reed's *Love Letters of a Musician* (1898) breaks the block-of-type mold with a large, medievaliz-

ing *L* extending half-way down the page. The red outline gives color to the page in the regular copies and is ready for hand-coloring in the special ones. For *Aucassin et Nicolete* (1899), Warner placed the type within a heavy border of stylized flowers of vaguely Art Nouveau inspiration.[36] Warner used this scheme again, sometimes more effectively, as in his design for Tennyson's *Maud* (1900), this time with an elegant Morrisian border that is equally pleasing in both the regular and hand-colored copies.

In 1899 Hubbard published one of his many editions of *The Rubáiyát of Omar Khayyám*, translated by Edward Fitzgerald.[37] A large ornamental *T* designed by Denslow and printed in two colors anchors and enlivens the block of type, which is ruled in on three sides by rows of fleurons. The text is decorated throughout by ornamental initials printed in three colors. Printed color, an attractive and economic alternative to hand illumination, became increasingly more common in the mature years of the Shop.[38] That same year Warner designed an elaborate title page for *The Rescue of Helen* (which he used again in the 1900 edition of *The Rubáiyát*): a border of twining branches on the left, extending to the right to create two frames, one for the title and one for the imprint.

Plate 20: *The Rubaiyat of Omar Khayyam*, trans. by Edward Fitzgerald, 1904 (24/100 on Japan vellum). Modeled leather cover attr. to Frederick Kranz, 5¼ × 7 in. Title page designed by Samuel Warner. Anonymous decorator. *Collection of Richard Blacher.*

Five figural title pages, most uncommon in the history of the press, appeared between 1900 and 1902, each a striking variation on the theme of incorporating a figure and a decorated border. For *Walt Whitman* (1900), Louis Rhead created a border of classical inspiration surrounding two rectangles, the left rectangle enclosing the block of type and the right framing a stately muse.[39] In 1901 Warner drew the profile of a pensive young woman against a leafy background for the title page of Edgar Allan Poe's *Poems*.[40] Jerome Connor's scheme for Irving Bacheller's *The Story of a Passion* (1901) places the old violinist in the center of three rectangles framed within a symmetrical border of stylized leafy branches and flowers. Also in 1901, Connor composed an impressive title page spread clearly inspired by Morris and printed in brown ink, for Olive Schreiner's *Dreams*. The left page depicts a medieval pilgrim gazing at a stylized landscape, framed by a border of equally stylized birds and twining vines. On the facing page the title is superimposed over a network of interlocking lines, also framed by flowers and birds. The only flaw in the design is that the title is hard to distinguish from the background. The fifth and last figural scheme was for Hubbard's *Contemplations* (1902), one of the most impressive Roycroft books.

Fig. 21: Jerome Connor's title page for *Dreams*, by Olive Schreiner, 1901.
(Courtesy Elbert Hubbard-Roycroft Museum)

Fig. 20: Samuel Warner's title page for *Poems*, by Edgar Allen Poe, 1901.
(Courtesy Elbert Hubbard-Roycroft Museum)

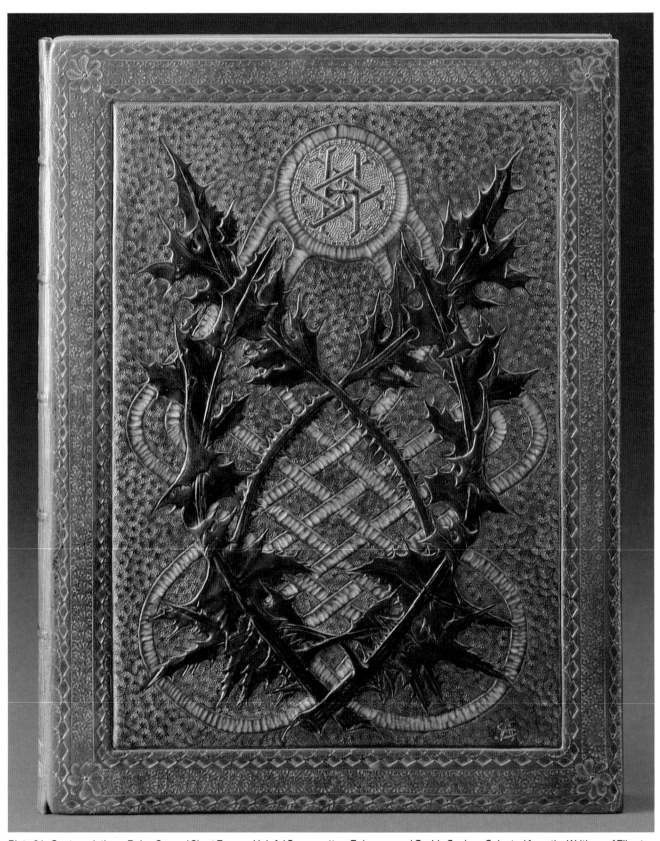

Plate 21: *Contemplations: Being Several Short Essays, Helpful Sermonettes, Epigrams and Orphic Sayings Selected from the Writings of Elbert Hubbard by Heloise Hawthorne*, by Elbert Hubbard, 1902 (88/100 on Japan vellum). Modeled leather cover designed by Frederick Kranz, executed by Axel Sahlin (signed), 11½ × 9 in.
Elbert Hubbard-Roycroft Museum.

Richard Kruger designed a complex, architectural page, inspired by the *Decretales* of Saint Gregory by Joanis Petit, published in 1529. The fairly long title of *Contemplations* is ruled in red below a large vignette, also printed and ruled in red: St. Gregory on his papal throne is shown presenting a book to a kneeling man and a group of onlookers (presumably the scribes who will copy and disseminate the saint's words). The interior design is in the manner of the early printed books, in which the text is surrounded by commentary; the book was flawlessly printed by Cy Rosen.

When Dard Hunter, who would become the best-known Roycroft designer, came to the community as a teenager, he found an established business, capably managed by Hubbard and his second wife, Alice, ready to welcome and nourish his genius.[41] The quality of Roycroft book design and presswork had been improving steadily over the years. The pressmen's skill at color printing had become impeccable, a development that contributed to the gradual abandonment of hand illumination.[42] Hunter's masterful sense of book design and his full use, in his title pages, initials, borders, and colophons, of the printers' skills with multi-color printing, enabled him to create some of the most memorable books of the turn-of-the-century era.

Plate 23: Dard Hunter, *Four Initials for Rip Van Winkle*, 1905. Pen and ink on paper, 4½ × 4½ in. (each).
Collection of Jean-François Vilain and Roger S. Wieck.

background. Each of the six chapters opens with a square woodcut, also printed on an ivory background, that suggests a medieval historiated initial, with a red capital letter in the top right corner of each woodcut aligned with the first line of text. The designs borrow something of Art Nouveau while still being clearly Arts and Crafts.

Hunter's title page for Ralph Waldo Emerson's *Nature* (1905) is a masterpiece of balance, with a stylized fruit tree supporting five large lines of text separated by orange rules. The tree motif is echoed in the three chapter-opening vignettes (each used three times) as well as in the cul-de-lampes (end-of-chapter designs) and the colophon. One of the most compelling of Hunter's title pages is that created for *Justinian and*

Plate 22: *Pig Pen Pete Or Some Chums of Mine*, by Elbert Hubbard, 1914 (unspecified number of 1000 on Japan vellum). Three-quarter stamped pigskin cover with marbled boards, 7½ × 5¼ in. Title page and initals designed by Dard Hunter. Anonymous decorator.
Collection of Don Marek.

Hunter was influenced by the English Arts and Crafts designers, as well as by the Glasgow School and the Vienna Secession Movement, but he melded all these influences into a distinctive style that has become emblematic of the American Arts and Crafts movement. For each book he created a distinctive title page, initials, and colophon—each is recognizably Hunter's but each is unique and fitted for the purpose at hand.

Hunter's first complete book design, for *Rip Van Winkle* (1905), was astonishingly mature. The elegant and playful title page balances the red and black lettering with the woodcut of a landscape printed on an ivory

Fig. 22: Dard Hunter's title page for *Justinian and Theodora*, by Elbert and Alice Hubbard, 1906.
(Courtesy Jean-François Vilain and Roger S. Wieck)

Fig. 23: The first Print Shop, ca 1898.
Photograph by Frances Benjamin Johnson.
(Courtesy Turgeon-Rust Collection)

Fig. 24: Roycroft binders at work, 1908.
(Courtesy Turgeon-Rust Collection)

Theodora, coauthored by Elbert and Alice Hubbard and published in 1906. The two-page spread is divided into three horizontal sections. The bottom consists of thin stems, white on a black background, blossoming into seven stylized orange daffodils in the top portion. The central space is occupied by the title and authors' names in hand-lettered orange capitals and the sub-title, hand-lettered in black capitals. The daffodils re-appear at the top corner of each page, framing the running heads, and again in the colophon.

The increasing success of Hubbard's commercial writing and of the community's other business ventures, such as furniture-making and metalwork, was paralleled by a decline in the quality of the Roycroft books. The designers, although talented, lacked Hunter's vigor and originality. Many title pages, initials, decorations, and colophons (especially Hunter's) were recycled. The most talented artist of that period was Raymond Nott, who designed most of the books after 1910. Henry David Thoreau's *Friendship, Love, and Marriage* (1910) and Alice Hubbard's *The Myth in Marriage* (1912) are among Nott's most distinctive designs, although they are strongly influenced by Hunter's work.

Bindings
In the early days of the Press, Hubbard had his books bound by a commercial bindery in Buffalo, in grey boards with white cloth-covered spines, or in yellow boards with red cloth spines.[43] Hubbard soon realized the marketing potential of offering a choice of bindings to match the various versions he offered of each title (regular paper, Japan vellum, limited editions, illumined, etc.), so in 1896 he hired Louis Kinder to start the Roycroft Bindery.[44]

Kinder was an accomplished binder, and during his tenure at Roycroft, he produced works considered masterpieces of the art of bookbinding. Kinder also attracted and trained talented artists—among them Lorenz C. Schwartz, Harry Avery, John Grabau, Walter Jennings, and Charles Youngers, who took over after Kinder left in 1912.[45] Kinder's first priority was to organize a trade bindery that could handle the thousands of books issued by the press and to train the young employees to become production binders. Only when this system was well established, in 1900, was he able to organize a fine-binding section.[46]

Fig. 25: A young Roycroft bookbinder, ca. 1898.
Photograph by Frances Benjamin Johnson.
(Courtesy Roycroft Arts Museum)

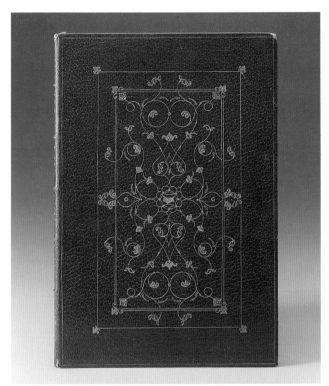

Plate 24: *Friendship*, by Henry David Thoreau, 1903 (5/50 on Japan vellum). Full leather cover designed and executed by John Grabeau (signed), 11⅝ × 8 in. Ornaments designed by Samuel Warner. Decorated by E. S. Harvey.
Collection of Richard Blacher.

Plate 26: *Friendship, Love and Marriage*, by Henry David Thoreau, 1910 (unspecified limitation on Japan vellum). Modeled leather cover designed and executed by Frederick Kranz (signed), 8¼ × 5⅜ in. Title page and initials designed by Raymond Nott.
Private collection.

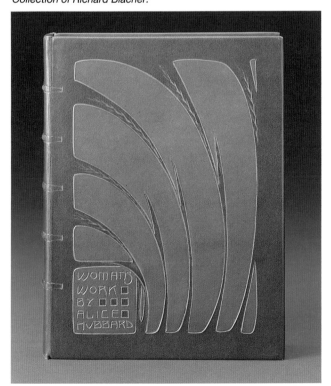

Plate 25: *Woman's Work: Being an Inquiry and an Assumption*, by Alice Hubbard, 1908 (unspecified limitation on Boxmoor). Modeled leather cover designed by Dard Hunter, 9 × 6 in. Title page, initials, and ornaments designed by Dard Hunter.
Elbert Hubbard-Roycroft Museum.

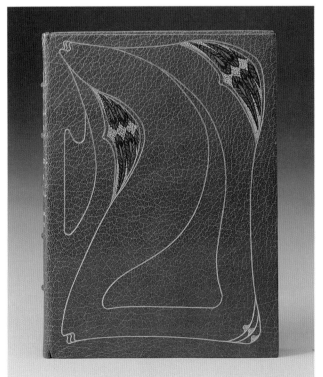

Plate 27: *The Ballad of Reading Gaol*, by Oscar Wilde, 1905 (93/100 on Japan vellum). Full leather cover designed and executed by Harry Avery (signed), 7¾ × 5⅞ in.
Roycroft Arts Museum, Boice Lydell.

The majority of the books were bound "Roycroftie" in inexpensive limp suede—usually red, green, or tan—glued over thin cardboard. The materials used were of poor quality and have tended to disintegrate with age. Most of the suede covers were plain, with the title and author's name stamped in gold within a central medallion. A few, such as *Rip Van Winkle* and *Nature*, were decorated with the title page design stamped on the front cover.

Plate 28: *Nature*, by Ralph Waldo Emerson, 1905 (unspecified limitation on Roycroft paper). Full suede cover designed by Dard Hunter, 8¾ × 5½ in. Title page, initals, and ornaments by Dard Hunter.
Elbert Hubbard-Roycroft Museum.

Larger volumes, the *Little Journeys* among others, were bound in paper-over-boards and three-quarters suede (spine and four corners in suede). The books printed on Japan vellum usually were bound in boards, often with a layer of moiré paper over the boards, and three-quarter leather. The spines were usually attractively tooled in gold.

Although Hubbard gave a variety of names to the leather bindings, there were basically three types: stamped, modeled, and tooled. The latter, especially Kinder's, rank among the most impressive achievements of the bookbinder's art.

Stamped bindings were made with a die blind-stamped on the leather. These were the least expensive and used for production bindings, especially during the years of decline. This type of binding was used most effectively on the shop's superb folio (8″ × 11.5″) edition of *The Complete Writings of Elbert Hubbard*,

designed by Dard Hunter, and published in twenty volumes between 1908 and 1915.[47]

For modeled bindings, a metal plate bearing a design in relief was placed against the back of the skin and hammered in; the resultant cavities were filled in with cement. This technique took more time than blind-stamping but allowed the binder to be more creative, and it was possible for the same design to be used more than once, as was Frederick Kranz's cruciform design for *The Man of Sorrows* (1904).[48]

Plate 29: *The Man of Sorrows*, by Elbert Hubbard, 1904 (91/102 on Japan vellum). Modeled leather cover designed by Frederick C. Kranz and executed by J. Juenker, 9 × 6 in. Anonymous decorator. *Elbert Hubbard-Roycroft Museum.*

Tooled bindings, requiring great skill, were reserved for special copies, and were the responsibility of Kinder or his most talented assistants. The designs were incised on the skin with a variety of tools and filled in with gold. Some tooled bindings, called "intarsia" by Hubbard, were also decorated with various inlays of dyed leather, ivory, or mother-of-pearl.[49]

Kinder's binding of Charles Dickens's *The Holly Tree* (1903) is a model of quiet refinement. Rows of interlocking gold circles on green leather are set off, at each intersection, by rings of jewel-like black and purple inlays enclosing lozenges of black and brown leather inlays.

For Walt Whitman's *Song of Myself* (1904), Harry Avery, one of Kinder's most inventive assistants, tooled a restful geometric meditation in gold on red leather, elegantly combining circles, ovals, and squares.

The binders often stamped their names or initials and, sometimes, the Roycroft logo at the bottom or edge of one of the inner covers, although many works are not signed.[50] One binding for *The Last Ride*, for example, reproducing from one of the text pages a

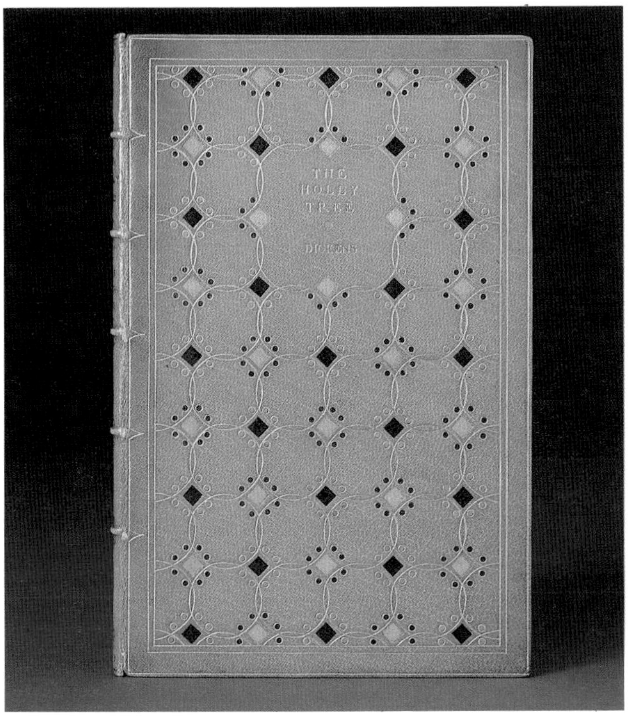

blue-robed angel playing the lute among green trees, bears only the initials *M.R.P.*[51]

On occasion the Bindery used an uncommon

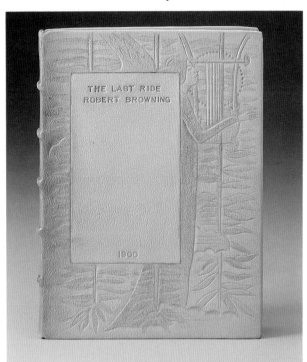

Plate 32: *The Last Ride*, by Robert Browning, 1900 (110/940 on Roycroft paper). Modeled leather cover designed by Samuel Warner (after Henri Caruchet), executed by M. R. P. (signed), 7⅞ × 5⅞ in. Illumined by Fanny Stiles.
Collection of Richard Blacher.

Plate 30: *The Holly Tree*, by Charles Dickens, 1903 (17/100 on Japan Vellum). Full leather cover designed and executed by Louis Kinder (signed), 8¼ × 5½ in. Title page and borders designed by Samuel Warner. Anonymous decorator.
Collection of Richard Blacher.

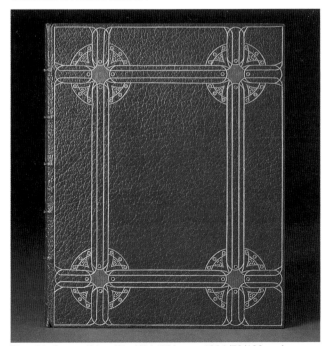

Plate 31: *Song of Myself*, by Walt Whitman, 1904 (76/100 on Japan vellum). Full leather cover designed and executed by Harry Avery (signed), 8¼ × 7 in. Title page designed by Samuel Warner. Anonymous decorator.
Collection of Richard Blacher.

Plate 33: *The Doctors: A Seizure in Four Satires*, by Elbert Hubbard, 1909 (unspecified limitation on Roycroft paper). Sheepskin cover with coarse linen ties, 8⅜ × 6¼ in. Title page and ornaments designed by Dard Hunter.
Private collection.

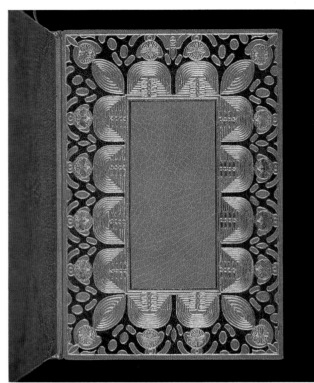

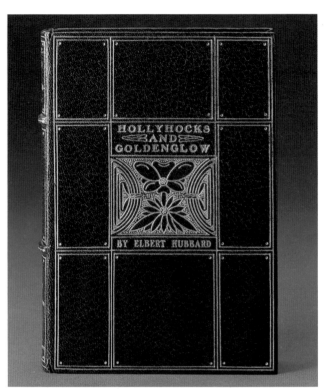

Plate 34: *Pig Pen Pete Or Some Chums of Mine*, by Elbert Hubbard, 1914 (unspecified number of 1000 on Japan vellum). Full leather cover designed and executed by Lorenz Schwartz (signed), 7½ × 5½ in. Title page and initials designed by Dard Hunter. Anonymous decorator. *Elbert Hubbard-Roycroft Museum.*

Plate 36: *Hollyhocks and Goldenglow*, by Elbert Hubbard, 1912 (unspecified limitation on Strathmore). Full leather cover designed and executed by Lorenz Schwartz (signed), 7½ × 5½ in. Anonymous decorator. *Collection of Eleanor Jackson Searl.*

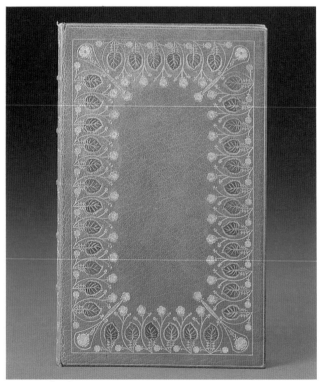

Plate 35: *The Boy from Missouri Valley*, by Elbert Hubbard, 1904 (unspecified limitation on Roycroft paper). Cover designed and executed by Frederick Kranz (signed), 8¼ × 6⅛ in. Title page designed by Samuel Warner. Anonymous decorator. *Private collection.*

Plate 37: *Self Reliance*, by Ralph Waldo Emerson, 1902 (73/100 on Japan vellum). Full leather cover, 8³⁄₁₆ × 5¼ in. Title page, initial, and ornaments attr. to Samuel Warner. Decorated by Minnie Tisdale. *Roycroft Arts Museum, Boice Lydell.*

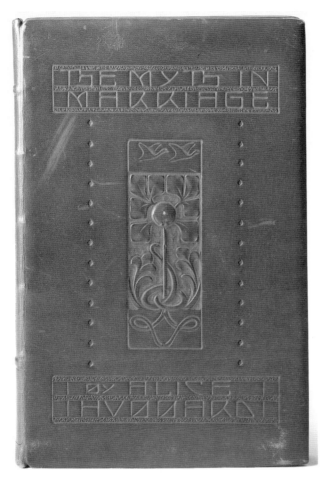

Fig. 26: Lorenz Schwartz's stamped leather cover for *The Myth in Marriage*, by Alice Hubbard, 1912.
(Courtesy Elbert Hubbard-Roycroft Museum)

Books of the Later Years

The innovative years of Roycroft bookmaking entered a gradual decline and by the time of Elbert and Alice's death, in 1915, the bookmaking had become indifferent. Hubbard's original motto, "Not how cheap, but how good," was replaced by "How quickly, and inexpensively can this be done?" Elbert Hubbard II (Bert), as son and heir, lacked his father's charisma and his step-mother's writing and managerial skills, but he was a sound manager nonetheless, keeping the press and the community alive until 1938. The work produced at the press was of decent quality overall, although Bert recycled too often—probably by necessity—the old designs, initials, and decorations. The few books with original designs lacked the vitality of their predecessors.

Fig. 27: Elbert Hubbard II, 1916. Photograph by Elliott Studios, Columbus, Ohio.
(Courtesy Roycroft Arts Museum)

medium. Some copies of *The Last Ride* (1900) and Robert Louis Stevenson's *Virginibus Puerisque* (1904) were issued in vellum with silk ties. A few sets of the *Little Journeys* were bound in boards with vellum spines and corners, with gold lettering. Hubbard's *Good Men and Great* (1908) is bound in heavy boards and features a leather strap with a metal clasp at the fore-edge. In 1909 a few copies of Hubbard's *The Doctors* were bound in full sheepskin with coarse linen ties.[52]

The majority of the bindings issued after 1910 were suede or stamped leather. The latter can be very effective, as is the elegant cover designed by Lorenz C. Schwartz in 1912 for Alice Hubbard's *The Myth in Marriage*. But many were clumsy and perfunctory: the stagnation that afflicted the design department had by then reached the Bindery.

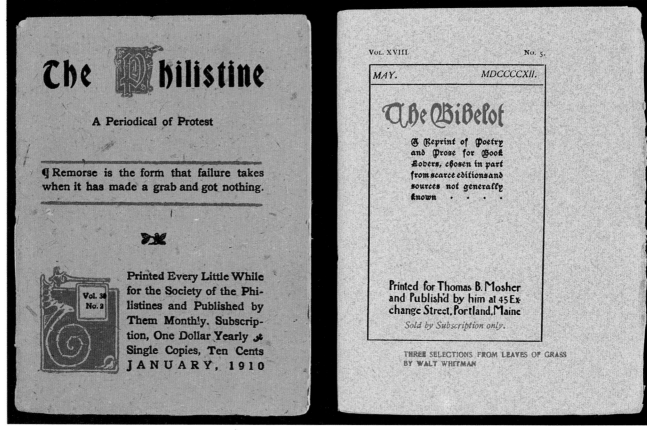

Plate 38: *The Philistine: A Periodical of Protest*, Vol. 30, No. 2
(January 1910). Cover motif designed by W. W. Denslow, 6 × 4⅝ in.
Private collection.

Another enduring "dinky" was the *Bibelot.*
(Courtesy Jean-François Vilain and Roger S. Wieck)

The Little Magazines

The Philistine

The early development of the Roycroft publishing enterprise was intimately tied to the growth and development of the *Philistine*. It was tied as well to the the success of the *Little Journeys* and of the later magazine, the *Fra*, and to Hubbard's busy schedule of lectures, each bringing more subscribers to his magazines and more buyers for his books.

The social, economic, and intellectual ferment of the last decade of the nineteenth century created a proliferation of little magazines in which their creators were free to express themselves without restraint. Most of these "dinky" magazines (so named because of their small size and lack of pretensions) lasted only a few issues, while some, like the *Philosopher*, the *Phoenix*, and the *Whim,* endured a few years. Only two, Thomas Mosher's *Bibelot* and Hubbard's *Philistine*, lasted twenty years. Of the two, Hubbard's "periodical of protest" (as he liked to call it) was by far the more successful, boasting in 1911 a subscription list of two hundred thousand.[53] The magazine was a joint venture with Taber and McIntosh, but after their break-up Hubbard assumed the editorship.[54] Although Hubbard at first

wrote most of each issue, including the advertisements,[55] he featured the works of a large number of well-known contemporaries, including Michael Monahan, Gelett Burgess, George Ade, Bliss Carman, Ouida, and William Marion Reedy.[56] In the January 1899 issue, Hubbard announced that he would write everything in the "magazinelet," including the testimonials for the books,[57] and he continued to do so, every month for the next sixteen years.[58] So emblematic was the *Philistine* of Hubbard that from time to time he reprinted favorite essays in the same format as that of the magazine. The magazine was so successful that it inspired a deliciously wicked pastiche, the *Bilioustine*, in which the Fra receives as many knocks as he was wont to give.[59]

Bound in rough yellow butcher paper, the *Philistine*, a little booklet of thirty-two pages, measuring only six by four and one-half inches, is really quite a successful design. The bold initial *P* is printed in red, and Denslow's familiar sea horse, also in red, holds in his mouth a placard containing volume and issue number. The inside is also well designed, with wide margins and good use of Warner's initials (and later those of Hunter). In addition, the back cover usually sports a cartoon by one of the Roycrofters: Denslow, Burt Barnes, and Albert Miller, among others.

Subscribers grew steadily from the original twenty-five hundred, but in 1899 a brief essay published in the March issue boosted the number to over one hundred thousand. The essay, although untitled when it first appeared, was "A Message to Garcia," a glorification of

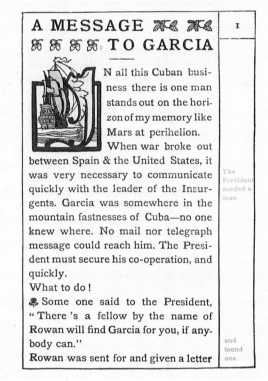

Plate 39: *A Message to Garcia*, by Elbert Hubbard, 1899 (this edition printed ca. 1900, unspecified limitation on Roycroft paper). Full suede cover, 8¼ × 6¼ in. Initial designed by W. W. Denslow. Anonymous decorator.
Elbert Hubbard-Roycroft Museum.

blind obedience to orders, based on an actual event during the Spanish-American War. A young lieutenant, Andrew S. Rowan, braved many dangers to deliver a message from his superior to insurgent General Calixto Garcia in the mountains of Cuba. Americans in general, and the business community in particular, avidly welcomed the heroic essay and orders for the March issue poured in. Not one to miss such an opportunity, Hubbard started printing the "Message" as a booklet, in various formats and, of course, bindings.[60] One of these later variants is a bilingual edition published in 1910 in Japanese with a charmingly awkward translation back into English.[61] Another notable variant is the John Wanamaker edition, complete with panegyric to the company's founder, for distribution to customers and employees alike.[62]

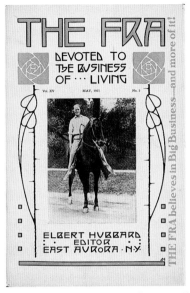

Plate 40: *The Fra*, Vol. 15, No. 2 (May 1915). Cover motif designed by Dard Hunter, 14 × 9 in.
Private collection.

The Fra

Hubbard's wizardry as copywriter was widely known, but the *Philistine* could not accommodate all the requests for ad space. In addition, the small format of the magazine meant that advertisers could not use the standard ads they prepared for other national magazines.[63] In 1908 Hubbard announced the creation of the *Fra*, a large format magazine (14″ × 9″) printed on coated stock, and designed by Dard Hunter. Hubbard likened the Roycroft community to a medieval phalanstery of which he was the leader, calling himself "the Fra." That nickname became nearly as famous as his own name and using it for the title of the new venture made eminent sense. The quality of the photographic reproduction in the *Fra* is much better than in the *Philistine* due to the use of coated stock. Physically, this is one of the handsomest magazines of the period. Hunter's emblematic lettering and rose borders create startling covers, and the page layout, decoration, and typography inside meet the expectations raised by the outside. Raymond Nott took over the design after Hunter left, but his own illustrations and initials are very reminiscent of his predecessor's.

This time around Hubbard did not write everything; instead he secured the help of a variety of contemporary luminaries, including Luther Burbank, Gutzon Borglum, Carl Sandburg, and Sadakichi Hartmann. Alice Hubbard herself contributed to the magazine and had a greater say in its editorial direction: the flippant tone of the *Philistine* was replaced by more serious discussions of social and economic matters.[64] At first, as with the *Philistine*, the advertisements were written mostly by the Fra;[65] that task soon devolved to Felix Shay, who had an uncanny ability to write like his boss.

THE SATIRES

Elbert Hubbard was nothing if not a man who enjoyed a good laugh. In the June 1912 issue of the *Fra*, he observed that "Satire is a giant Wasp playing in and out of the mouth of a sleeping clown." Not surprisingly, satirists and cartoonists pounced eagerly upon his own hyperbolic character, some, like W. W. Denslow, from within the Roycroft camp. Especially trenchant, however, were the authors of two privately-printed booklets that mimicked Hubbard's own little magazines.

A Little Spasm at the Home of Wolfgang Mozart, purportedly published by the Rakeoffers at Rising Sun, New York, as part of their series devoted to Great Organ-Grinders, was the 1901 creation of Clifford Richmond of Easthampton, Massachusetts. From the opening epigrams ("Life without terra cotta is guilt" and "Industry without sham is nit") to the closing ads for limited edition books "printed on Jimdandy Wall Paper" with "limp cover of bed-ticking," readers of the *Little Journeys* were sure to recognize Richmond's target. With ornamental initial letters and Morrisian page designs, Richmond's presentation of this "lost" Hubbard manuscript, recently recovered after accidentally being thrown from a train window, lampooned both the substance and the style of Roycroft publications. Each chapter was supposedly written at a different stop on Hubbard's lecture circuit (including such unlikely venues as Peculiar, Missouri; Gratis, Ohio; and Ego, Alabama). The Fra's long hair, his sex appeal, his ideological posturing, his penchant for publicity, his fledgling courtship with big business—none escaped Richmond's pointed jabs.

Plate 41: *A Little Spasm at the Home of Wolfgang Mozart*, 1901.
Published by The Rakeoffers, Rising Sun, New York [Clifford Richmond, Easthampton, Massachusetts].
Elbert Hubbard-Roycroft Museum.

Plate 42: *The Bilioustine*, Vol. 2 (1901). Published by The Boygrafters, West Aurora, Illinois [William S. Lord, Evanston, Illinois]. *Private collection.*

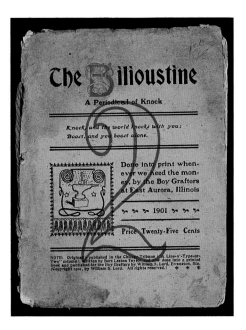

Even more wickedly comic was *The Bilioustine: A Periodical of Knock*, a 1901 parody of the *Philistine* in two volumes from the pen of William S. Lord of Evanston, Illinois. It was printed on brown butcher paper "whenever we need the money, by the Boy Grafters," under the direction of Fra McGinnis, "very long in hair, and . . . the original goo-goo eye man." The stated objective of the work being produced at the "Philandery" was to "do things into gold bricks and other articles calculated to con the community, especially that part of it which is female and literary and adores speaking eyes and conversational long hair."

Readers were invited to send for a lock of the Fra's hair, on suspicion, or a set of *Little Journeys to the Scenes of Famous Explosions*, or a bas relief of Fra McGinnis modeled in chewing gum. They were treated to the Boy Grafters' "Articles of Faith" ("I believe in Watt'ell paper and Japan vellum, in long hair and hand-painted initials") and Fra McGinniss's words of wisdom ("Next to boiling an egg there is nothing easier to do than an epigram. Just take a pertinent saying by some dead genius and turn it inside out.") Lord managed to mock the Roycroft campus, Hubbard's theatricality, and his reputation as a teetotaller, all in one brief passage from an account of a visitor's meeting with Fra McGinnis:

I found the Fra in the alley that skirts the Philandery, standing in a negligee attitude, with a far-away expression in his eyes. I waited till he had completed his pose, and then introduced myself.

"Let us go to the Philandery," said he, "and do a few thoughts into conversation."

"Is there," I inquired, "any place near by where one can do a Jamaica ginger highball into a renewed interest in life?"

And in a perfect parody of the typical Roycroft colophon, workers were given elaborate credit for their roles in assembling the *Bilioustine*:

So here endeth the Little Journey, as written by hand by Mr. Criticus Flub-Dubbe; the tail-piece being hand-painted by Saint Sally of the Philandery Alley; the paper cut by hand by Sindbad the Buzz-Saw; the ink mixed by Saint Johnny the Devil; the proof pulled by Saint Jimmy the Dope Fiend, and read by Larry the Lynx-Eyed; the page closed by Daniel the Foreman, and stereotyped by Simon the Shirtless; and the press fed by Saint Phillip the Profane.

MV

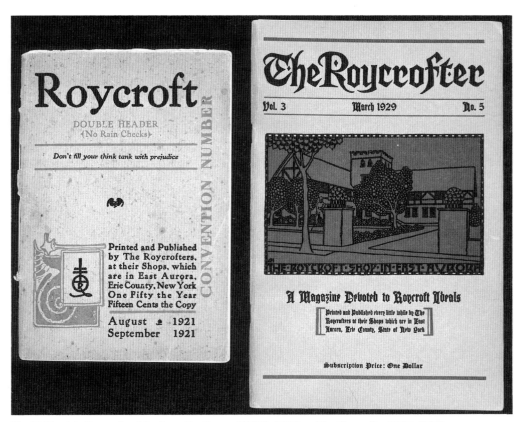

Fig. 28: Two late Roycroft publications, the *Roycroft* (1917–1926) and the *Roycrofter* (1926–1932).
(Courtesy Bruce Bland)

Roycroft and The Roycrofter

The *Philistine* did not survive the Hubbards's death on the *Lusitania* in 1915. The *Fra*, less idiosyncratic, was kept alive for a while by Elbert Hubbard II, with Shay's assistance. Absent Elbert's charisma and ability to attract business and Alice's organizational skills, the task proved insurmountable, and in September 1917 Bert published a new magazine, *Roycroft*, which he described in the first issue as the "illegitimate offspring of the *Philistine* and direct descendant of *The Fra*."[66] *Roycroft* was a hybrid of its predecessors. Slightly larger than its illegitimate parent and much smaller than its legitimate ancestor, the new magazine's cover echoed faithfully that of the *Philistine*, while the interior design, with its two-column format and Hunter's initial vignettes, was a smaller version of the *Fra*. The new magazine carried a healthy load of advertisements (forty pages, half of which were devoted to Roycroft products) and survived for a few years by combining reprints of Elbert's pieces with essays by Bert, Shay, and other contributors. Ad space became harder to sell and in 1926 *Roycroft* was replaced by the *Roycrofter*. The new magazine had a larger trim size (9″ × 6″) and is distinguished by the linoleum cuts, designed by Dard Hunter in the heyday of Roycroft, incorporated into the cover design.

Little Journeys

Among Hubbard's prodigious literary work, his *Little Journeys* stand out for many reasons: the breadth of their topics, the regularity of their publication, their physical appearance, and the insights they afford into their author. When Hubbard first decided to visit England, Harry Taber suggested to him that he write essays about the famous authors whose houses he planned to visit. Hubbard searched for a publisher willing to produce and market his booklets, and eventually convinced Putnam's, the publisher of his fourth novel, *No Enemy (But Himself)*, that the *Little Journeys* had potential.

Every month for the next twenty years Hubbard's readers could expect to read a new *Little Journey* to the home of a famous person.[67] It is hard to do justice to anybody's life in less than twenty pages, let alone to the life and work of figures such as Kant, Mozart, or Parnell, but Hubbard did not really try to be the "compleat" biographer. He chose instead events in the life of his subject that either resonated with his own, or allowed him to philosophize about a pet topic. Neither did Hubbard let facts interfere too meddlesomely with his view of what the world should be. In his *Little Journey to the Home of Austin Abbey,* for instance, he poignantly described his encounter with the painter

Plate 43: *Little Journeys to the Homes of Eminent Artists: Velasquez*, Vol. 10, No. 5 (June 1902). Cover designed by Samuel Warner.   *Little Journeys to the Homes of Great Teachers: Thomas Arnold*, Vol. 23, No. 2 (August 1908). Cover designed by Dard Hunter.   *Little Journeys to the Homes of Great Business Men: Philip Armour*, Vol. 24, No. 5 (May 1909). Cover designed by Dard Hunter. 8 × 6 in. (each). *Memorial Art Gallery of the University of Rochester.*

and his wife, surrounded by their loving children. An upset Abbey soon wrote that a great tragedy in his life was the fact that he and his wife were unable to have children and that Mrs. Abbey was distressed by Hubbard's callous disregard for the truth.[68]

Hubbard was keen on retrieving the publishing rights to this successful magazine from Putnam and Sons, and he finally succeeded in 1900.[69] Until then the *Little Journeys* had been issued in a vest-pocket format (7″ × 4¼″), much like the early American chapbooks, covered in light gray wrappers and typographically undistinguished. The first *Journey* published by the Roycroft (Vol. 6, No. 1, *William Morris*), appeared in the soon-to-be-familiar trim size (6″ × 8″) bound in army-green wrappers,[70] with the name of the subject of the essay and the Roycroft logo printed in red. The interior design is simple and elegant, with the decoration kept to a minimum. The Morrisian title page, borders, and initials were designed by Warner. In addition, a portrait of each subject, drawn by Otto Schneider or Jules Gaspard, appeared as the frontispiece. Beginning in January 1908, the *Little Journeys* took on a more modern look when Dard Hunter redesigned the booklet, using a stylized motif of grape leaves for the title page and initials. One year later Hunter created what was to be the standard design for the *Little Journeys* in a style inspired by the Glasgow School and the Vienna Secession.[71]

Hubbard, ever the diligent marketer, also issued each essay in paper wrappers and in suede, some copies of which were limited and hand-illumined. In addition, as with the *Philistine*, Hubbard offered bound volumes, each consisting of six issues, in a variety of bindings ranging from three-quarter suede to luxurious full leather, all hand-illumined, and "signed" by the author.[72]

The Roycroft Quarterly

The *Roycroft Quarterly* was the first, and remains one of the most elusive, of the Roycroft periodicals. The maiden issue, published in 1896, grew out of a dinner organized in honor of Stephen Crane by the "Society

Plate 44: *The Roycroft Quarterly*, No. 1 (May 1896). Cover designed by Sewell Collins, 7½ × 5¼ in. *Elbert Hubbard-Roycroft Museum.*

THE ROYCROFT STUDY HABIT

Beginning around 1910, readers of the *Fra* were encouraged to form study groups called "juntas," in the tradition of a similar club established by Benjamin Franklin. Each issue of the *Fra* contained a page of questions designed to stimulate discussion about that month's articles; the queries were often worded, however, to gently steer participants toward conclusions consistent with the Roycroft philosophy:

▶ Why should grammar be called "the grave of letters"?

▶ Is it a compliment to be called "provincial"? If so, why so, and if not, why not?

▶ How does a fashionable church service compare with a high-class vaudeville show?

▶ Do you approve of women ministers?

▶ What would happen if the government were put on a business basis?

▶ To what extent is Ridicule an agent of Reform?

Hubbard, proud graduate of the School of Hard Knocks, championed the junta as "an In-Absentia University" and "a convenient form of mental massage," designed to promote "Personal Betterment and the Advancement of the Race as a whole." Through a program patterned after one at the nearby Chautauqua Institution, junta members could work toward award pins and certificates of achievement by sending their answers back to the Roycroft for marking, free of charge. To the intellectual pilgrim who could not assemble a group of similarly motivated friends, Hubbard suggested organizing an evening study group for family members. The smallest junta, called "The Solitaire," consisted of just one member: a woman who lived at Watson's Ranch in a remote part of Nebraska.[1]

MV

Plate 45: *Roycroft Study Junta Pin* (manufactured by BS&B Bronze). Copper, ¾ × ⅜ in. *Collection of Richard Blacher.*

Plate 46: *Pin with Enameled Orb* (manufactured by S. D. Childs & Co., Chicago). Copper and enamel, 1⅛ × ¾ in. *Collection of Richard Blacher.*

HUBBARD AND CHAUTAUQUA

When Elbert Hubbard stated in the October 1909 *Philistine*, "The Chautauqua is here to stay," he spoke from personal experience with the phenomenon. By the time he became involved in the late 1880s, Chautauqua had transformed itself from its 1874 beginning as a Sunday School teacher's retreat on the shores of a pleasant western New York lake into a center for intellectual and spiritual questing, which it remains to this day.

The Chautauqua Literary and Scientific Circle, begun in 1878 and referred to as the "oldest continuous book club in America," established Chautauqua's commitment to adult education with its program of prescribed readings across the disciplines.[1] The CLSC program, still active today, was enthusiastically adopted by many across the country, including Mr. and Mrs. Elbert Hubbard and Miss Alice Moore in East Aurora. For many, it was their only opportunity for higher education and a life of the mind.

In a letter from Hubbard in 1890 to Miss Kimball, executive secretary of the CLSC, he reminded her that he was entitled to a garnet seal and three white seals in recognition of papers that he had submitted as requirements for graduation from the CLSC program. Ever the salesman, he concluded his letter by mentioning, "The envelope containing these papers had on one side a large advertisement of Sweet Home soap which by the way is a most excellent article."[2]

Hubbard's relationship to Chautauqua went beyond his presidency of the East Aurora circle in 1890[3] and membership in the class of 1894. From 30 June to 2 July 1896, he appeared on the Chautauqua platform, where he gave a series of talks that were likely based on information used in the *Little Journeys*: "In the Home of Victor Hugo," "In the Haunts of Goldsmith," and "In the House of John Ruskin."[4] He was also listed as a speaker for the 1897 summer program. Given the Christian orientation of this community of minds and Hubbard's published attacks on organized religion, it is no wonder that some Chautauquans found Hubbard's presence inappropriate and unwelcome. In a letter to Dr. John H. Vincent, co-founder of the Chautauqua Assembly, the pastor of the East Aurora Baptist Church warns of Hubbard's "pernicious" influence:

> In looking over the Chautauqua Program for the coming summer, I find the name of Mr. E. G. Hubbard of this place, page 6. Can it be that Mr. Hubbard's record is unknown to the gentlemen who arranged the Program? Is it unknown what the March and April numbers of the "Philistine", which he edits, contain? Mr. Hubbard is a disciple of Ingersoll, and is, I suppose, just as strongly opposed to the religion of Christ as Ingersoll.
>
> By some means he had been invited to speak, a few evenings ago, in the Delaware Ave. Baptist church, Buffalo. His recent utterances (see Apr. no. of Philistine) caused the withdrawal of the invitation. I am sure I have seen nothing more vile in print than some of his published utterances. Mr. Gifford the pastor of the above-mentioned church said when Mr. Hubbard's article came before him, "The Philistine cannot come into the camp of Israel."
>
> Mr. Hubbard's influence here is bad. Any recognition he receives from Christian institutions only enables him to advertise himself and his ware, and strengthen himself with the thought he is recognized as great even among Christians.
>
> I sincerely hope that Chautauqua is too Christian in spirit, to allow its noble name to be a bolster to such a man as Mr. Hubbard.[5]

There is no record of Vincent's response, but Chautauqua's historian, Alfreda L. Irwin, comments that Vincent was known for his openmindedness.[6] The influence of the Chautauqua program, if not its philosophy, remained visible in Hubbard's own promotion of speakers and performers, his publishing ventures, which stressed life-long learning, and, through these, his fostering of a lifestyle based on ideological convictions.

of Philistines" in December 1895. The demand for a memento of that dinner (which today would be termed a "roast") led to the publication of a little booklet containing testimonials to Crane, a brief essay by Hubbard, and a few poems by Crane. Typographically undistinguished, the booklet is mostly remarkable for the elegantly restrained, two-color cover with an illustration by Sewell Collins.[73] Only two more issues appeared, both in 1896: Shaw's *On Going to Church* and Fr. George Zurcher's *Foreign Ideas in the Catholic Church*. The public response was tepid and the periodical was abandoned for the far more profitable *Little Journeys*.

Plate 47: *Motto: We are all Children in the Kindergarten of God*. Ink and colors on paper, 10½ × 8¼ in.
Private collection.

The Roycroft Ephemera

In addition to the many books and magazines they published, the Roycrofters produced an equally prodigious amount of ephemeral material, upon which the designers and pressmen lavished the same care they brought to the production of the "legitimate" publications.[74] These ephemera include booklists, catalogues advertising the books and other products of the community, mottoes (epigrams written by the Fra) suitable for framing, little booklets advertising the Roycroft community, pamphlet reprints of some of Elbert and Alice's briefer essays, and a vast number of advertising pamphlets.

One of the better-known of these promotional pam-

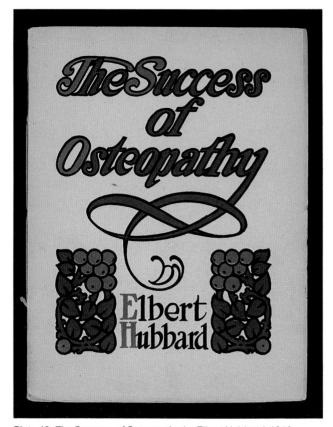

Plate 48: *The Success of Osteopathy*, by Elbert Hubbard, 1912. Cover design attr. to Raymond Nott, 8 × 6 in.
Private collection.

phlets demonstrates Hubbard's ambivalent attitude towards big business, upon which he depended for his advertising revenue: in 1910 he wrote, on commission, a *Little Journey to Standard Oil Company*. He gave it

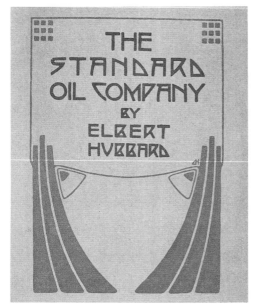

Fig. 29: Dard Hunter's "octopus" cover for *A Little Journey to Standard Oil Company*, by Elbert Hubbard, 1910.
(Courtesy Dard Hunter III)

to the young Dard Hunter to design, trusting his talent and imagination to dress the words in exciting garb. Dard submitted one of his liveliest cover designs, slyly incorporating a stylized octopus to symbolize Standard's multifarious activities. After some hesitation Hubbard gave his "nil obstat," trusting, rightly, in his client's lack of sensitivity to symbolism.[75]

Another of Hunter's arresting covers, for the *Motto Book* (1914), reflects a strong Art Nouveau influence.

Plate 49: *The Motto Book*, by Elbert Hubbard, 1914. Cover design by Dard Hunter, 7½ × 5¼ in.
Private collection.

The design consists of two black poppy stems writhing up from two large green leaves, each terminating in a pair of bright orange flowers, the whole surmounted and balanced by Hunter's emblematic lettering, printed in green.

Hubbard's attention to details is especially apparent in the catalogues issued by the press every year—supplemented by an occasional booklist. Each offers prospective buyers a preview of the quality they can expect to find in the Roycroft books themselves. The catalogues are carefully printed in two colors, the page make-up is elegant, and special attention is given to the title pages by the house artists: Warner, Nott, and Hunter each contributed some impressive works. As with other products of the press, the catalogues came in a variety of bindings. The majority were issued in paper wrappers but a few, notably the 1900 publication, were issued in suede bindings. In addition, the title pages of some copies were hand-illumined.

Conclusion

One hundred years after the Roycroft Printing Shop was founded, Hubbard's controversial personality still colors the way its products are perceived. Early unfavorable opinions of the books have been accepted uncritically by succeeding generations of bookmakers and booklovers, and praises have been ignored by modern bibliophiles as misguided. Hubbard had many faults but also many fine qualities, and so do the books that he wrote and published. Some Roycroft books can be charitably forgotten, many more are outstanding examples of bookmaking, but all contributed to the awakening of the American public to the value of a book as art object, and to the spreading of the tenets of the Arts and Crafts movement.

The author is indebted to many people who helped in the development of this essay. To David B. Ogle, who shared his extensive knowledge of the Roycroft Shop, and read the manuscript so carefully. To Bruce Bland, always there to verify an obscure point. To the "keepers of the faith," Robert Rust and Kitty Turgeon, whose encyclopedic knowledge of the Roycroft community was invaluable. To Marie Via, who cheerfully put up with British spellings and a French accent. To Ralph Zickgraf, patient colleague, for his editorial punctilio. And finally to Roger Wieck, *sine quem non*, for reading and editing many drafts, and most importantly, for being there.

Plate 50: *Desk Calendar*, 1908. Designed by Dard Hunter. Paper, wood, and metal, 7¾ × 7¾ in.
Collection of Jean-François Vilain and Roger S. Wieck.

THE FRA ON TRIAL

Advertisements for the *Philistine* acknowledged that "every issue causes sudden cancellations from the grumpy, who subscribe not knowing it is loaded." On at least one occasion, however, Elbert Hubbard's desire to nettle the complacency of his readers went too far. On 2 November 1912, he was indicted on six counts of violating the federal criminal code: various issues of the *Philistine* were said to have "contained among other things certain matters in print of an obscene, lewd, lascivious, filthy and indecent character . . ."[1] The straw that broke the rather straitlaced camel's back was a joke published in the November 1912 issue:

> The new stenog's name was Miss Mary Merryseat. But Old Man Lunkhead, Senior Member of the firm of Lunkhead Sons & Co., Ltd., never having taken a course in Dickson's Memory Method, called her Gladys.

Hubbard was convicted on all counts in January 1913. The matter was resolved with a $100 fine on the first count, suspension of the remaining five, and a warning to Hubbard from his attorney that "the *Philistine* and your other publications must henceforth be like Caesar's wife."[2]

When Hubbard made plans for his ill-fated voyage on the *Lusitania* in 1915, he learned that he could not obtain a passport while under suspended sentence. He applied to the Department of Justice for a pardon, rationalizing: "Technically . . . my offense was a felony— actually it was a matter of bad literary taste, for which unhappily the law provides no penalty."[3] On 23 March 1915, Woodrow Wilson signed a full and unconditional pardon for Elbert Hubbard, restoring his civil rights and, ironically, sealing his fate at the hands of a German U-boat captain.

Fig. 30: Elbert Hubbard's presidential pardon. *(Courtesy Elbert Hubbard-Roycroft Museum)*

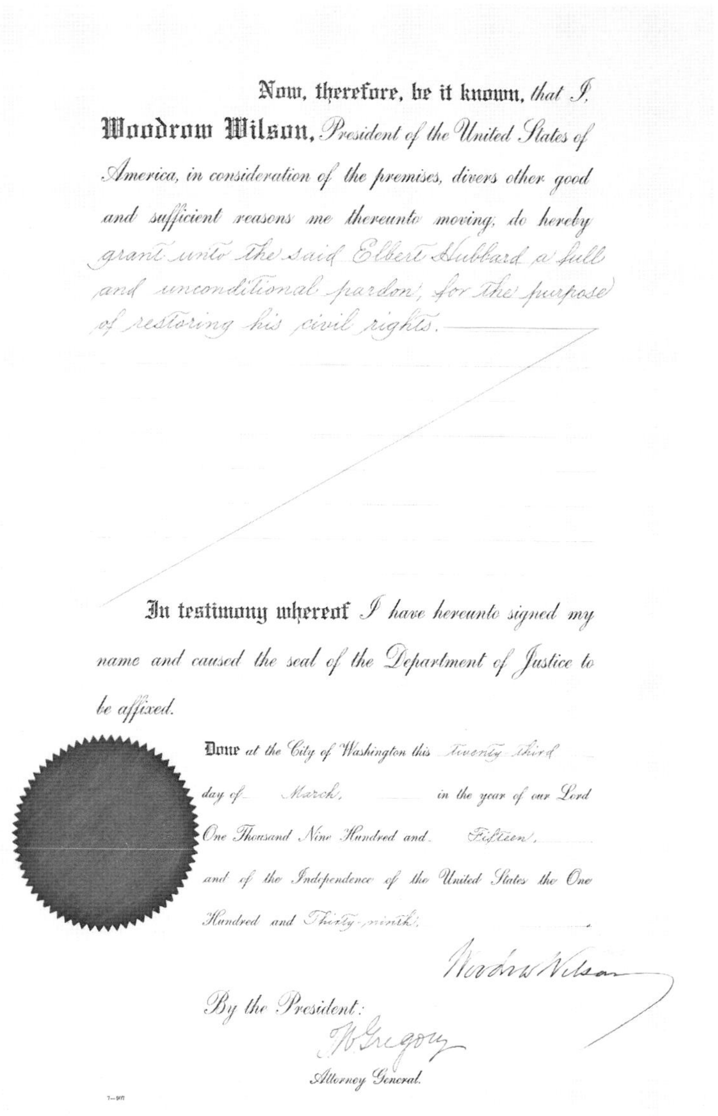

Now, therefore, be it known, that I, **Woodrow Wilson**, President of the United States of America, in consideration of the premises, divers other good and sufficient reasons me thereunto moving, do hereby grant unto the said Elbert Hubbard a full and unconditional pardon, for the purpose of restoring his civil rights.

In testimony whereof I have hereunto signed my name and caused the seal of the Department of Justice to be affixed.

Done at the City of Washington this twenty third day of March, in the year of our Lord One Thousand Nine Hundred and Fifteen, and of the Independence of the United States the One Hundred and Thirty-ninth.

Woodrow Wilson

By the President:

TW Gregory

Attorney General.

ENDNOTES

[1] This is Morris's modest assessment of his splendid undertaking.

[2] "The Ideal Book" was a lecture delivered in 1893 by Morris. It is reprinted in *The Ideal Book: Essays and Lectures on the Art of the Book* by *William Morris*, ed. William S. Peterson (Berkeley: University of California Press, 1982).

[3] The painter Edward Burne-Jones, Morris's lifelong friend and collaborator, who was also fond of the Middle Ages, coined this description of the Kelmscott books.

[4] Will Ransom, *Private Presses and Their Books* (New York: R. R. Bowker, 1929), 126. (Also quoted, but unacknowledged, in Joseph Blumenthal, *The Printed Book in America* [Boston: David R. Godine, 1977] 52.) Ransom, whose passion for printing was first aroused by Roycroft books, was the first historian of the art of the book to acknowledge Hubbard's importance. Blumenthal, whose Spiral Press printed Robert Frost's works, reluctantly acknowledges that, although "it is fashionable to scoff at Hubbard," the latter helped spread Morris's message.

[5] A. K. Dirlam and E. E. Simmons, *Sinners, This Is East Aurora* (New York: Vantage Press, 1964), 16. This is a brief, enthusiastic, and flawed, but fairly objective, memoir of Roycroft written by two longtime Roycrofters.

[6] There is an interesting parallel with the foundation of the Kelmscott Press: in 1888 the Arts and Crafts Exhibition Society in London organized a series of lectures on the Arts and Crafts. Emery Walker, a friend and neighbor of Morris's, spoke on "Letterpress Printing and Illustrations," using magic lantern slides of early and later books. This lecture, attended by Morris, was of crucial importance for the renaissance of book-making, and the birth of the Kelmscott Press can be attributed directly to it. See W. S. Peterson, *The Kelmscott Press: A History of William Morris's Typographical Adventure* (Berkeley: The University of California Press, 1991) for a fascinating and scholarly account of the Kelmscott Press.

[7] *The Man: A Story of Today* had been published by J. S. Ogilvie in 1891; Arena Publishing Co. of Boston published *One Day: A Tale of the Prairies* late in 1893.

[8] This putative meeting calls to mind the Italian expression: "Si non e vero, e bene trovato" ("Even if it is not true, it is a good idea anyway"). The "visit" establishes a direct link between the great man and the newcomer. For Hubbard's views on the Kelmscott books, see the Roycrofters' 1900 catalogue, p. 2.

[9] Paul McKenna, *A History and Bibliography of the Roycroft Printing Shop* (North Tonawanda, N.Y.: Tona Graphics, 1986), 35; also see Dirlam and Simmons, *Sinners*, 23.

[10] The year 1894 was an unusual one for Hubbard: he published his third and fourth books, he started his *Little Journeys* on their long voyage, and in September Alice Moore gave birth to their daughter Miriam. A year later his wife, Bertha, gave birth to their child, Katherine.

[11] A contract dated November '95 assigns title to the *Philistine* **and** to the Roycroft Printing Shop to Hubbard. See McKenna, *A History and Bibliography*, for a more elaborate discussion. Also see Richard J. Wolfe and Paul McKenna, *Louis Herman Kinder* (Newtown, Pa.: Bird and Bull Press, 1985), 21; also p. 22 for a photocopy of the 29 November 1895 contract between Taber and Hubbard.

[12] Dirlam and Simmons maintain that the break occurred over Hubbard's insistence on discussing sex in the magazine.

[13] Ransom, *Private Presses and Their Books*, 126.

[14] Dirlam and Simmons mention that three hundred of the six hundred copies printed were given away. Felix Shay, in his sycophantic *Elbert Hubbard of East Aurora* (New York: W. H. Wise & Co., 1926), repeats Hubbard's assertion in the *American Printer and Lithographer* 10, no. 23 (February 1900) that the book was sold out as soon as it was off the press. Susan Otis Thompson has called the book "distinctly amateurish." (*American Book Design and William Morris* [New York: R. R. Bowker, 1977], 171)

[15] Bertha Crawford Hubbard was Elbert's first wife.

[16] "The Roycrofters do not sell their books through stores or agents, but are very glad to send any of their wares to the Elect 'on suspicion'." (*Some Books for Sale at our Shop* [East Aurora: The Roycrofters, 1899])

[17] Ransom was the first to recognize Hubbard's genius for publicity: "That is really how the tradition first came to America . . . was expressed in terms of the national characteristic, publicity, by a master of that delicate art . . ." (*Private Presses and Their Books,* 126)

[18] The controversial topic of the Roycroft limited press-runs is a thorny one, addressed by McKenna and, more carefully, by David B. Ogle in his book, *On a High Shelf: Roycroft Books and Bookmakers* (Tavares, Fla.: S. P. S. Publishers, forthcoming). The most charitable attitude is to accept that some books were issued in true limited editions, while others were not.

[19] Japan vellum is a stiff, extremely smooth, long-fibered paper, made from macerated mulberry leaves, which resembles animal vellum. The impression of the carefully inked type on Japan vellum is brilliant and three-dimensional.

[20] This was common practice among private presses and literary publishers. See Jean-François Vilain and Paul Bishop, *Thomas Bird Mosher and the Art of the Book* (Philadelphia: F. A. Davis, 1992), 9.

[21] Here again, the topic of Hubbard's signature is much debated. In the beginning, Hubbard did sign all limitation statements, but it is obvious that, with the great number of books published and the various claims on Hubbard's time, this became impossible, and soon the task of signing his name was assigned to staff members. Only books with special inscriptions, such as presentation copies, can be assumed to be signed by him.

[22] Dirlam and Simmons, *Sinners*, 33. Also see Hubbard's letter to Denslow, 14 August 1896, in McKenna, *A History and Bibliography*, 28: "There is no competition in this line, for the reason there is no demand." Hubbard intended to create that demand. Denslow's influence in this regard is also discussed at length by Ogle.

[23] The 1906 list of books offered two copies of *Justinian and Theodora* at $100 each.

[24] This inclusive collecting is much in evidence today, with variants dangled tantalizingly by book dealers in front of avid collectors.

[25] Along with many genteel women of the period, Bertha practiced the art of china painting, which she also taught to the girls working as illuminators.

[26] Hubbard, an outspoken opponent of child labor in mines and factories, found himself in the uncomfortable position of employing children as illuminators and having to defend this practice. See Freeman Champney, *Art and Glory: The Story of Elbert Hubbard* (New York: Crown Publishers, 1968), 136.

[27] Denslow's trademark sea horse (hippocampus), which always adorned his signature, also appears as decoration in the margins of many books and on the cover of the *Philistine*.

[28] Hubbard claimed that Warner was from England but he was actually from Pennsylvania.

[29] Although Warner's first signed design did not appear until 1899, he designed initials and ornaments for the *Philistine* as well as for some books. See Ogle, *On a High Shelf*.

[30] The terms have been used interchangeably. Illustrations are drawn and painted by hand. Decorations are mechanically printed and hand-colored.

[31] The book was issued in two identical editions on Japan vellum (109 and 352 copies respectively) decorated by Bertha Hubbard and Clara Schlegel. Twenty-two copies were specially illustrated by Denslow and William Faville (see Ogle, *On a High Shelf*). Suede was a popular "art" binding at the turn of the century; Ogle lists ten descriptions: calf, limp chamois, flexible velvet calf, flexible chamois, rough chamois, limp leather, velvet suede, and the faintly repulsive ooze calf, ooze leather, and limp ooze calf. Vernon Lee was Violet Paget's *nom de plume*.

[32] These drawings range from simple stars to the more complex orb-and-cross logo, animal heads, bunches of flowers, and birds on boughs. The tradition of drawing outlines to be painted later goes back to the medieval scriptoria.

[33] As Ogle points out, the use of illumination peaked during the Denslow years and waned after 1900; the last book designed for hand-illumination was *Friendship* in 1903.

[34] Jean-François Vilain, "The Last Ride," *Arts and Crafts Quarterly* 1, no. 1 (October 1986). French artist Henri Caruchet created the eleven designs for Octave Uzanne's *Voyage Autour de ma Chambre*, published in Paris by H. Floury in 1896.

[35] In an interview with the *Scottish Leader*, 18 January 1894, cited in J. G. Nelson, *The Early Nineties: A View from the Bodley Head* (Cambridge, Mass.: 1971), 39.

[36] The same design appears on the title page of Philip Hamerton's *The Intellectual Life*, also published by Roycroft in 1899.

[37] *The Rubáiyát*'s length and structure made it an ideal subject for the private presses, which could count on an almost inexhaustible market for what had become one of the hoariest, and most beloved, chestnuts of the late nineteenth century.

[38] Ogle divides the output of the Shop into four periods: Experimental (1896–1898), Mature (1899–1907), Expansion (1908–1915), and Post-Hubbard (1916–1943).

[39] British-born Louis Rhead was a popular artist and book illustrator. (His brother, F. H. Rhead, was one of the leading art potters of the day.) This is one of the few times that Hubbard commissioned an artist from outside the Roycroft community.

[40] For this design Warner is very much in debt to Will Bradley.

[41] The Hubbards encouraged Hunter's talents and funded his studies of stained glass in New York, within six months of his arrival in East Aurora in 1904, as well as study travels to Europe. Hunter, who left Roycroft in 1910, became an internationally recognized authority on paper-making. He wrote many books on the subject and printed them himself on a press he had built, on paper he had made, with type he had designed and made. Testaments to Hunter's talent, and to Roycroft's influence, are the facsimile reprints by C. F. Braun Co. of *The Battle of Waterloo* in 1966, and *Rip Van Winkle* in 1972, and the miniature edition of Hubbard's *Walt Whitman* published in 1983 by The Hillside Press, Roswell, Georgia.

[42] Ogle, *On a High Shelf.*

[43] Wolfe and McKenna, *Louis Herman Kinder*, 29.

[44] For an exhaustive study of Kinder and his work, see Wolfe and McKenna, *Louis Herman Kinder.*

[45] McKenna mentions that Lorenz Schwartz had worked with Otto Zahn, the leading bookbinder of the day, in Memphis, Tennessee. (*A History and Bibliography*, 32) A. R. Andrew mentions that other students of Zahn's came to study with Kinder, but this is not substantiated. (A. R. Andrews, *American Printer and Bookmaker* 29 [February 1900]: 329)

[46] Wolfe and McKenna, *Louis Herman Kinder*, 45.

[47] The first nineteen volumes are identical, with a design of Viennese inspiration: a majestic title page ornamented by three stylized rose trees printed in brown ink, as are the initial letters throughout. For the twentieth volume the designers went back, inexplicably, to the Renaissance for the title page; the interior design, using red as a second color, is similar to the design of *Contemplations.*

[48] When William Wise published a *Memorial Edition* of Hubbard's complete writings in 1928, he offered on the covers a garish and clumsy echo, on cardboard, of these bindings.

[49] In 1901, Hubbard offered a copy of *The Last Ride*, bound by Kinder and illumined by Harriet Robarge, for $100. (*Some Books For Sale at Our Shop* [East Aurora: The Roycrofters], 10.) In the catalog for 1900, the regular edition, bound in boards, cost $5.00. (*The Roycroft Books* [East Aurora: The Roycrofters], 4)

[50] Perhaps in deference to Kinder, who rarely signed his work.

[51] The style of the design is strongly reminiscent of the work of the League of Women Binders active in England at that time. For more information on the Guild, see A. Callen, *Women Artists of the Arts and Crafts Movement, 1870–1914* (New York: Pantheon Books, 1979), 191–194.

[52] In his autobiography, Hunter tells of an unusual book: he had designed a memorial to a widow's late husband, which he inscribed by hand on heavy vellum. The one and only copy of the memorial was sent to the bindery. The leather provided by the lady for the binding was so fine that Hunter asked about its source and learned that it was the husband's skin, carefully tanned. (Dard Hunter, *My Life with Paper: An Autobiography* [New York: Knopf, 1958], 41–42)

[53] The first little magazine was the *Chap Book*, a literary monthly published in 1894 by Ingalls Stone and Herbert Kimball, two Harvard undergraduates who later moved their company to Chicago. By 1900 Frederick Faxon had identified 200 magazines. (*Modern Chapbooks and Their Imitators* [Boston: The Boston Book Company, 1900]) The *Philistine* and the *Bibelot*, published by Thomas B. Mosher in Portland, Maine, were the most successful and longest-lived. (Vilain and Bishop, *Thomas Bird Mosher*, 75) For a more complete discussion of the *Philistine*, see Bruce Allen White, "Elbert Hubbard's 'The Philistine, A Periodical Of Protest' (1895–1915): A Major American 'Little Magazine'" (Ph.D. diss., University of Maryland, 1988)

[54] Hubbard saw the *Philistine* as a take-off on other periodicals and his revenge for their consistent refusal of his manuscripts. ("A Heart to Heart Talk With the Philistines by the Pastor of His Flock," *Philistine* 35, no. 1 (June 1912): 2–3 and Champney, *Art and Glory*, 58)

[55] The first numbers carried some ads (three pages devoted to Roycroft), but ten years later the January 1906 issue contained forty pages of ads, half of which were devoted to Roycroft products. Hubbard had contracted with Frederic W. Gardner of Chicago to sell ad space for him. The magazine's success led Hubbard to rue that decision, and he tried to circumvent the terms of the agreement, which led to a series of lawsuits. Hubbard eventually bought Gardner out. (McKenna, *A History and Bibliography*, 61) In a booklet published for Gardner (undated, but obviously before the dissolution of their contract in 1901), Hubbard writes that the circulation of the *Philistine* was 110,000, and that of the *Little Journeys* was 60,000.

[56] White counted 200 contributors in 242 issues; see note 53.

[57] "If it were possible to secure any one to write so well as myself I would not do this." ("Manifesto," *Philistine* 8, no. 2 [January 1899]: 33)

[58] The Roycrofters also sold bound volumes of the *Philistine*, each containing six issues, bound in boards with suede spines.

[59] The *Bilioustine* was published (two issues only) by William Lord of Evanston, Illinois. Lord gleefully skewers the skewerer, dispensing barbs and brickbats with wanton generosity.

[60] Hubbard claimed to have printed 1,000,000 copies by January 1900. (Dirlam and Simmons, *Sinners*, 93) Whether this is true or not, it is true that the manager of the New York Central Railroad ordered 500,000 copies. (Hubbard could not fill that order and gave him the right to reprint it.) In his letter accompanying the bound manuscript of the *Message* presented to the Buffalo Public Library in 1900, Hubbard asserted that 9,000,000 copies hade been printed (see Champney, *Art and Glory*, 91). It is also true that the *Message* became required reading in businesses, government offices, and the armed forces (where it is still required reading).

[61] Possibly a hoax since the clumsiness of the translation appears contrived. Hubbard might have been inspired by Mark Twain's exquisitely literal retranslation of the French version of his *Jumping Frog of Calaveras County.*

[62] The bewildering variety of variants of the *Message* drives devoted collectors to desperation. The booklets range from small 3" × 4" pamphlets in modest self-wrappers to 5" × 7" books bound in leather, from plain typography on inexpensive paper to elaborately hand-illuminated volumes.

[63] McKenna, *A History and Bibliography*, 65.

[64] Ibid., 65; Champney, *Art and Glory*, 132.

[65] In a letter to Sadakichi Hartmann, Hubbard wrote that he "grind(s) out copy, such as it is, in about the same way that they make Little Pig Sausages." Quoted by Charles Hamilton in *Sadakichi Hartmann Newsletter* 2, no. 1 (Spring 1971).

[66] Bert, disingenuously, claimed that the Roycrofters were pamphleteers at heart and hinted that the *Fra*'s ambitious format did violence to their natural talents. (*Roycroft* 1, no. 1 [January 1917]: 1)

[67] Nothing human seems to have been foreign to Hubbard: his subjects ranged from writers, to philosophers, to musicians, to painters, to scientists, to teachers, to politicians, to businessmen, to lovers.

[68] Cited by Dirlam and Simmons, *Sinners*, 56. These authors also quote a letter from James McNeill Whistler to Hubbard, congratulating him on the fact that his *Little Journey to the Home of James McNeill Whistler* "contains several things I never knew before."

[69] The *Journeys*' success made them an ideal additional advertising medium that Hubbard exploited fully. The *Journeys* usually included ten pages of advertisements, all for Roycroft products.

[70] Hubbard boasted that these slender volumes were stitched by hand in silk.

[71] The intermediate design first appears in Vol. 22, no. 1 (January 1908). Vol. 24, no. 1 (January 1909), inaugurates the final design.

[72] Sets of three-quarter bound volumes were also offered for sale, five in a wooden box. (*The Roycroft Wares: Some Books for Sale at our Shop* [East Aurora: The Roycrofters, 1901], 11) Subscribers were also given the choice of sending their single copies to Roycroft for binding.

[73] This design, modified from the poster issued by the Philistines to announce the dinner, features plumed and caped riders, mounted on toy horses, swooping down from the sky (an obvious spoof of Crane's poem "The Black Riders").

[74] McKenna lists over three hundred ephemera, not counting the *Message* and the catalogues. (*A History and Bibliography*, 154–164)

[75] Hunter, *My Life with Paper*, 42–43.

The Roycroft Study Habit

[1] *Fra* 6, no. 4 (January 1911), xviii.

Hubbard and Chautauqua

[1] For a good discussion of the institution's history, see Alfreda L. Irwin, *Three Taps of the Gavel: Pledge to the Future* (Chautauqua: The Chautauqua Institution, 1987).

[2] Elbert Hubbard to Miss Kimball, 1 December 1890, The Chautauqua Institution archives.

[3] "Vicinity Varieties," *East Aurora Advertiser*, 4 October 1889.

[4] Alfreda L. Irwin to the author, 20 February 1994.

[5] Rev. Robert Morris Robb to Dr. John H. Vincent, 15 April 1897, The Chautauqua Institution archives.

[6] Alfreda L. Irwin to the author, 20 February 1994.

The Fra on Trial

[1] Hubbard papers, Elbert Hubbard-Roycroft Museum archives.

[2] James Mitchell to Elbert Hubbard, 17 January 1913, Elbert Hubbard-Roycroft Museum archives.

[3] Elbert Hubbard to Buffalo District Attorney's Office, 27 January 1915, Elbert Hubbard Roycroft Museum archives.

Jean-François Vilain is publisher at F. A. Davis Company, Publishers, in Philadelphia. A confirmed bibliophile, he has written extensively about the private press movement and is co-author of *Thomas Bird Mosher and the Art of the Book*.

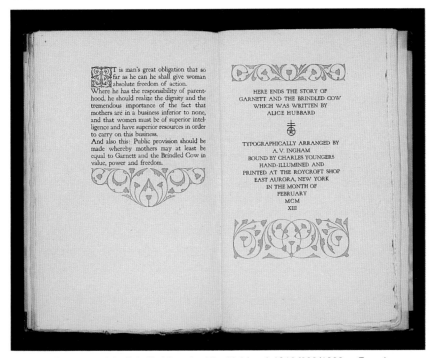

Plate 51: *Garnett and the Brindled Cow*, by Alice Hubbard, 1913 (633/1003 on French handmade paper). 3/4 leather cover with marbled boards, 9½ × 6¼ in. Anonymous decorator.
Private collection.

ALICE HUBBARD: A LIFE LESSON

As the Roycroft community mourned the deaths of Alice and Elbert Hubbard in 1915, more than one East Auroran must have reflected on this tragic, but somewhat fitting end to a remarkable marriage. From its inception, the relationship was characterized by risk, passion, and the quest for exceptional experience. Far from being overshadowed by her notorious husband, Alice Moore Hubbard perceived herself as his equal in all ways, and proved to be simultaneously his intellectual mentor, a skillful business manager, and a nationally-renowned advocate for women's rights.

Such a life for a woman, extraordinary by contemporary standards, was rare when Alice Moore graduated from Buffalo Normal School in 1883 and took her first job as a teacher.[1] This step marked the beginning of her own striving for economic independence, which she would later mandate as essential to the well-being of all women and to society in general. In 1910, after interviewing Alice in East Aurora for the sensational *New York Evening World*, journalist Sophie Irene Loeb wrote:

> Alice Hubbard is a mother. She is a successful mother. Besides being a mother, Alice Hubbard is a woman of varied occupation. She supervises the work in a manufacturing establishment employing five hundred people. She has charge of two unique hotels run as home, where visitors come from all over the globe. She is a writer on various subjects and assistant editor of two monthly magazines. She is the author of several books. She pays almost daily visits to her farm of three hundred acres, which provides all the food consumed in her extensive household.
>
> I know all this for I have seen her in the morning, noon, and night at these various tasks. So when I asked her, "Mrs. Hubbard, how do you find time to do all these things, when most mothers find it difficult to attend only to the duties of motherhood," she answered, "Because I am economically free, as I think every mother should be. The State should make it so."[2]

In ten sentences, Loeb spanned the breadth of Alice Hubbard's life as it had expanded from her neophyte teaching career to her fully-evolved, mature position as full partner with her remarkable husband. After their marriage in 1904, she quickly assumed responsibility for most aspects of the Roycroft operation. She was the general manager of the Print Shop;[3] she proofread catalogs;[4] and her byline appeared with regularity in the *Fra* as the author of advertising copy as well as articles on women's rights. In 1911 she was identified as general manager of the Roycroft shops in a notarized document,[5] while an ad in the June 1911 *Fra* named her as the principal of the Roycroft School for Boys.[6] Even interior design was not beyond her scope: Alice is credited with the decor of the Roycroft Inn's famed Salon.[7]

Alice Hubbard, like Elbert, used Roycroft publications to communicate with a national audience about her own beliefs. She regularly took a passionate, if controversial, stand on the twin needs for women's suffrage and guaranteed stipends for mothers in recognition of their critical role as caretakers of the next generation. With her own life experience to guide her, she gave voice to the anguish of many women who had no forum, even within their own homes. Her numerous articles and books, including *Woman's Work* (1908) and *The Basis of Marriage* (1910), pointed the way to a more humane society that would recognize women's unique gifts for family and community. Her poignant 1913 allegory, *Garnett and the Brindled Cow*, takes an eloquent and visionary stand on issues that continue to be debated internationally over eighty years later in the contemporary language of family leave and day care:

> It is man's great obligation that so far as he can he shall give woman absolute freedom of action.
>
> Where he has the responsibility of parenthood, he should realize the dignity and the tremendous importance of the fact that mothers are in a business inferior to none, and that women must be of superior intelligence and have superior resources in order to carry on this business.
>
> And also this: Public provision should be made whereby mothers may at least be equal to Garnett and the Brindled Cow in value, power, and freedom.[8]

Fig. 31: Alice and Elbert Hubbard in their office, ca. 1914.
(Elbert Hubbard-Roycroft Museum)

In 1911, Alice edited *An American Bible*, a compilation of writings by influential Americans whose philosophies were compatible with the Roycroft's. Never missing an opportunity to advance her husband's standing, she included Elbert Hubbard ("the most positive human force of his time"[9]) in this august group, along with Jefferson and Lincoln: "Elbert Hubbard sees, too, that just as long as one woman is denied any right that man claims for himself, there is no free man; that no man can be a superior, true American so long as one woman is denied her birthright of life, liberty and happiness."[10] Undoubtedly, it was Alice who helped him arrive at such an understanding.

As early as 1905, Alice accompanied Elbert on his Western lecture tour and gave her own talk, "Woman's Work."[11] Over time, the pace of her own lecture schedule appeared to rival her husband's, as a notice in the July 1907 *Little Journeys* revealed: eleven lectures on "Woman's Work: An Inquiry and a Suggestion" were scheduled in just over a month from coast to coast.[12] The title of a 1911 lecture in San Francisco, "The New Woman," indicates that, while her titles varied, her message did not.[13]

The lecture circuit did not free her from responsibilities at home, where her authoritative and self-assured style was not always appreciated. Cy Rosen left the Print Shop in 1912 because he did not agree with the changes she was empowered to make. Emil Sahlin, also a printer, described her as having a no-nonsense attitude, which may be have been a kind way of saying that she would not take no for an answer.[14] How significant a problem this was for the Roycroft can be surmised by analyzing dates of master metalworker Karl Kipp's departure to establish a competing shop and his subsequent return. These correspond neatly to Alice's growing influence within the organization and with her death in 1915.[15] Her micromanagement style might have been unattractive to craftsmen who had become accustomed to working with the more casual Elbert and were suddenly answerable to a more detail-oriented Alice. Roycroft scholar Paul McKenna suggests that "Alice and Elbert were a balanced pair. Where Elbert was impetuous, Alice was reserved; where he was too generous, she was too frugal. He took the part of father-patron while she watched the books."[16] It is even more likely that Alice's strength as a woman and her modern views about women's rights aroused resentment, particularly in the traditionally male bastion of printing.

Nonetheless, Alice ran a successful operation and no doubt could have done so on her own. She and Elbert had equal abilities and complementary strengths, and their symbiotic working relationship yielded much fruit. In his eulogy to Alice in the Memorial Number of the *Fra*, William Marion Reedy wrote: "Only those who knew well both Elbert and Alice knew the quality of their attachment. I so knew them, and I know that Alice's judgment upon any man or any matter of importance was the final determinant for Elbert. He would dream, but she held him to the purpose of doing."[17] Alice's own "purpose of doing" was stilled in 1915, but the urgency of her ideas endured in her writings. In 1920, only five years after Alice's death, the Nineteenth Amendment, guaranteeing both sexes the right to vote, was added to the United States Constitution. Undoubtedly, Alice's sharp and widely-circulated comments; emanating frequently from rural East Aurora, must have pricked many a man's conscience:

You Think

Then

You Think as

You Must.[18]

MBS

ENDNOTES

[1] Charles F. Hamilton, *As Bees in Honey Drown* (South Brunswick and New York: A. S. Barnes and Co., 1973), 17.

[2] Sophie Irene Loeb, *An Interview* (East Aurora: The Roycrofters, 1910), quoted in Charles F. Hamilton, *Alice Hubbard: A Feminist Recalled* (East Aurora: G. M. Hamilton and Sons, 1991), 17. The Loeb interview was first published in the Pulitzer-owned *Evening World*, known for its investigative reporting, promotion of reform, and frequent sensationalism.

[3] Paul Mc Kenna, *A History And Bibliography of the Roycroft Printing Shop* (North Tonawanda: Tona Graphics, 1986), 8.

[4] Ibid., 25.

[5] Hamilton, *As Bees in Honey Drown*, 215.

[6] H. Kenneth Dirlam and Ernest E. Simmons, *Sinners: This is East Aurora* (New York: Vantage Press, 1964), 203.

[7] Helen Sayr Gray, "A Little Journey to East Aurora," *Little Journeys to the Homes of Great Teachers: Thomas Arnold* 23, no. 2 (August 1908): i.

[8] Alice Hubbard, *Garnett and the Brindled Cow Also Other Mothers* (East Aurora: The Roycrofters, 1913).

[9] Alice Hubbard, *An American Bible* (East Aurora: The Roycrofters, 1911), 31.

[10] Ibid., 32.

[11] Dirlam and Simmons, *Sinners*, 208.

[12] Advertisement, *Little Journeys to the Homes of Reformers: John Bright* 21, no. 1 (July 1907).

[13] Hamilton, *As Bees in Honey Drown*, 210.

[14] McKenna, *A History and Bibliography*, 25–26.

[15] See accompanying essay by Robert Rust, Kitty Turgeon, Marie Via, and Marjorie Searl.

[16] McKenna, *A History and Bibliography*, 8.

[17] William Marion Reedy, "Alice Hubbard," *Fra* 15, no. 4 (July 1915): 123. McKenna describes Reedy, publisher of *Reedy's Mirror* of St. Louis, as "one of Elbert Hubbard's kindest and most constructive critics." (*A History and Bibliography*, 20) He goes on to say, "Reedy enjoyed visiting East Aurora and his comments on Hubbard and his writing are probably the most astute of all of the contemporaries of Hubbard. He also left an epitaph for Hubbard: Be kind but get the mazuma (money)."

[18] Hamilton, *Alice Hubbard: A Feminist Recalled*, inside front cover.

"Made to Last a Century"
The Work of the Roycroft Furniture Shop

FREDERICK R. BRANDT

The production of furniture at the Roycroft Shops took a secondary position to the output and promotion of objects in other media, especially printed materials. Elbert Hubbard was not a furniture designer and came into furniture production in a rather roundabout manner, unlike the Stickleys, Limbert, Rohlfs, Greene and Greene, and the other great producers of furniture whom we associate with the American Arts and Crafts movement in the early years of the twentieth century.

Fascinated by the philosophy and products of the English Arts and Crafts movement, particularly by the work of William Morris and his Kelmscott Press, Hubbard imagined himself as the American embodiment of this English social reformer and artist. Hubbard, however, had a way with words in advertising and promoting his products that was not predicated upon exactly the same philosophy as that of Morris and his fellow English reformer, John Ruskin.

Morris and Ruskin are rightly given credit for much of the early development of the movement to elevate crafts to the aesthetic level of the fine arts. Believing that art should serve and be available to all people, regardless of social background or financial status, they unintentionally laid the foundation for a frenzy of activity by individuals and companies seeking to express their own personalities in their work, rather than simply copying the styles of past civilizations.

Sociological and philosophical changes in England and America during the late nineteenth century accompanied technological developments that were meant to free workers from the burdens of poverty, disease, and early death. The early reformers realized, however, that this technology was not entirely beneficial, but tended to contribute to the substandard conditions that were forced upon the common workers. Freed from servitude to the soil, the worker was now the prisoner of the great "Satanic mills" referred to by William Blake.[1] Ruskin and Morris aimed to vanquish these social and environmental inequities and raise the standard of living, if not to the elevated social status enjoyed by Ruskin, at least to a comfortable level that would ensure health and well-being. Ruskin felt that art would have a strong curative effect on mankind; this philosophy is often reiterated in Elbert Hubbard's homilies and epigrams.

Morris emphasized hand production over machine manufacturing and tried to solve the social problems Ruskin had identified by creating his own firm, wherein he could to a large degree control the working environment. He dreamed that workers' homes would one day be filled with beautiful objects—books, furniture, fabrics, and glass—that would help to abolish the ugliness of working-class surroundings. As a result, the workers' spirits would be raised and their moral fiber strengthened. That dream was not to be realized in the larger society, however, because his demands for handcraft and quality control forced the prices of the objects produced by Morris & Co. beyond the reach of the common worker.

Hubbard, after visiting Morris's Kelmscott Press in 1894, wrote of this English artist-philosopher as a savior:

> To the influence of William Morris does the civilized world owe its salvation from the mad rage and rush from the tawdry and cheap in home decoration. It will not do to say that if William Morris had not called a halt someone else would, nor to cavil by declaring that the inanities of the Plush-Covered Age followed the Era of the Hair-Cloth-Sofa. These things are frankly admitted, but the refreshing fact remains that fully one-half the homes of England and America have been influenced by the good taste and vivid personality of one strong, earnest, courageous man.[2]

This strong praise reflects the influence Morris exerted upon Hubbard's philosophy and his resulting production, especially of books and furniture. In fact, Hubbard declared:

> I have seen several houses furnished entire by William Morris, and the first thing that impressed me was the sparsity of things . . . [The] table was not covered with a tablecloth; mats or doilies being used here and there. To cover a table entire with a cloth or spread, was pretty good proof that the piece of furniture was cheap and shabby; so in no William Morris Library or dining room would you

find a table entirely covered. The round dining table is in very general use now, but few people realize how its plainness was scout when William Morris introduced it.[3]

Hubbard then bestowed his greatest compliment upon Morris in his description of the "Morris Chair":

One piece of William Morris furniture has become decidedly popular in America, and that is the "Morris Chair." The first chair of this pattern was made entirely by the hands of the master. It was built by a man who understood anatomy, unlike most chairs and all church pews. It was also strong, durable, ornamental and by a simple device the back could be adjusted so as to fit a man's every mood.

There is a sad degeneracy among William Morris chairs; still, good ones can be obtained, nearly as excellent as the one in which I rested at Kelmscott House—broad, deep, massive, upholstered with curled hair, & covered with leather that would delight a bookbinder. Such a chair can be used a generation and then passed on to the heirs.[4]

MORRIS CHAIR

This is a close replica of the original chair made by the hands of
William Morris. Cushioned complete, $50.00.
THE ROYCROFTERS, East Aurora, N. Y.

Fig. 32: Advertisement for *Morris Chair*, ca. 1902. (As published in *Little Journeys to the Homes of Eminent Artists: Botticelli*, March 1902)

In 1902, Hubbard advertised his own version of the Morris chair, one which he undoubtedly felt did *not* fit into the category of "a sad degeneracy." The chair is described as "a close replica of the original chair made by the hands of William Morris. Cushioned complete, $50.00. The Roycrofters, East Aurora, N.Y."[5]

This brief commentary speaks volumes concerning Hubbard's own philosophy. Clearly, he recognized the advertising value of linking both his name and his style with that of the "master." The continued popularity of the chair is evident, for it appears in later catalogues with at least three different seat sizes, in oak, ash, or mahogany, with bold-grain Spanish leather or velour cushions. Some stylistic differences appear in the arms and feet, as well as variations in the ratchet back support.[6]

This early Morris chair may have been designed and/ or made by Albert Danner, as such a chair is listed in *A Catalog of Some Specimens of Art & Handicraft Done by Roycroft Workers*, dating from late 1900. Under "Miscellaneous Wood and Iron Work," item 36 is described as a "Morris chair, being a close copy of the original chair made by William Morris and now at Kelmscott House. Made by Albert Danner (with cushion complete), $35.00."[7]

It is instructive to consider the differences between Hubbard and Gustav Stickley, the leading proponent of the Arts and Crafts movement in America, with regard to philosophy and aesthetic tendencies. Hubbard, ever the salesman, made the world beat a path to his door through his popular writings in publications such as the *Philistine* and the *Fra*, as well as his national lecture tours and his importation to East Aurora of important speakers on various subjects he considered morally correct. His "mission" in life may not have been as noble and pure as Ruskin's and Morris's, but was in line with his early work as a salesman. He wanted to sell his own brand of thinking about politics, religion, morals, and the work ethic while making enough money to manage his community and produce the books, furniture, and other crafts for which his shops became famous. This manner of salesmanship can be best summed up in a quote from a 1910 catalogue that stated: "The only man who should not advertise is the one who has nothing to offer in way of service, or one who can not make good."[8]

Stickley, on the other hand, built an empire that flourished for almost two decades based on his experience as a cabinetmaker who had "arrived at many of the conclusions of William Morris, but reaching them from a direction opposite to the one taken by that great benefactor of society, who was first a thinker and afterward a craftsman."[9] He began his furniture production in 1899; by 1903, his magazine, the *Craftsman*, was offering plans for the consummate Craftsman house and everything with which it was to be filled. The interior harmony thereby created echoed the organic relationship of the house to its site.

Stickley's furniture was often referred to as "mission" style, probably from the admiration he expressed publicly for "the architecture of the Old Missions."[10] Although he admitted that his furniture fulfilled a "mission of usefulness," he preferred the term "Craftsman" furniture, referring to the name of his company. In the *Craftsman* of May 1909, he explained "How 'Mission' Furniture Was Named" by blaming it on "a manufacturer who made two very clumsy chairs," being exhibited and exploited by

> a clever Chicago dealer . . . [who] advertised them as having been found in the California Missions. Another dealer, who possesses a genius for inventing or choosing exactly the right name for a thing, saw these chairs and was inspired with the idea that it would be a good thing to make a small line of this furniture and name it "mission" furniture. The illusion was carried out by the fact that he put a Maltese cross wherever it would go . . . The mingling of novelty and romance instantly pleased the public, and the vogue of "mission" furniture was assured.[11]

Similarly, Hubbard did not like the term "mission" when applied to the output of his shops, pleading that consumers not "class our products as 'Mission,' or so-called 'Mission Furniture.' Ours is purely Roycroft—made by us according to our own ideas. We have eliminated all unnecessary elaboration, but have kept in view the principles of artistic quality, sound mechanical construction and good workmanship."[12]

Thus Hubbard and Stickley came from two different ends of the spectrum—one from that of salesman/ capitalist and the other of craftsman—to create a significant and special style of furniture that is best included under the aegis of Arts and Crafts.

Hubbard became involved in the production of furniture as an outgrowth of the expansion of his printing enterprise. In 1895 he had founded the Roycrofters in East Aurora and by the following year he had printed his first book and soon was adding wings to the original print shop. "The place got too small when we began to bind books, so we built a wing on one side; then a wing on the other side. To keep the three carpenters busy who had been building the wings, I set them to making furniture for the place. They made the furniture as good as they could—folks came along and bought it."[13]

Hubbard also claimed that although East Aurora had a population of about two thousand people, "during the year just past, over twenty-eight thousand pilgrims have visited the Roycroft Shop."[14] It was these thousands of "pilgrims" who saw and ordered the crafts, including furniture, produced in the shops.

When the Roycroft Inn was built, to lodge and feed the "pilgrims," beds, dressers, tables, and chairs were needed to furnish it. Thus the law of supply and demand took over and the Roycroft Furniture Shop was born. Hubbard insisted on calling it a "shop," stating: "Roycroft Furniture is all made in a Cabinet Shop, we do not have a furniture factory. There is a difference in furniture so made. In a factory each piece of furniture is inspected *after* it is finished. In our cabinet shop each stick of wood is inspected *before* it is put into the piece being made. After Roycroft Furniture is installed in the home, the furniture question is settled."[15]

A photograph published in the 1902 edition of *Contemplations* shows the dining room of the Phalanstery[16] furnished with round tables and some typical Roycroft chairs. The majority of the guests, however, are seated on traditional spindle-back chairs, suggesting that chairs from other manufacturers were purchased and used until the Furniture Shop could supply enough Roycroft furniture to complete the seating.[17]

By 1900, printed advertising began to replace the reliance on word-of-mouth. Ironically, one of the few advertisements Hubbard placed in a non-Roycroft periodical appears in the April 1905 issue of Stickley's *Craftsman*. A full-page advertisement quotes the result of a sale of eighteenth-century furniture at the American Art Galleries and then goes on to state:

> All the furniture here mentioned [in the quoted news article concerning the auction] was made a hundred years ago by men who had the time, talent and inclination to make it well. We think that we are making by far the best Furniture in America today. We make furniture that is an endowment investment for you—you use it and can pass it on to your heirs. It does not wear out, and like true friendship, grows better with the passing years. We have the plant, the people, the materials, and the time.
>
> If you are interested, send ten cents for cuts of our Aurora Colonial Designs / The Roycrofters at their shop which is in East Aurora, Erie County, New York State.[18]

The purchase of advertising space in the magazine of Hubbard's chief competitor was an astute solicitation of a ready audience. Despite the fact that the furniture did not have colonial revivial features, its reference to Aurora Colonial Designs made direct appeal to the middle class whose taste was turning to historical styles in interior design and building.

Fig. 33: The Phalanstery dining room, ca. 1902. (As published in *Contemplations: Being Several Short Essays, Helpful Sermonettes, Epigrams and Orphic Sayings Selected from the Writings of Elbert Hubbard* by *Heloise Hawthorne*, 1902)

Miriam Hubbard Roelofs, the daughter of Elbert and Alice Hubbard, remembers visiting the shops: "The carpenters who made all the furniture for the other workshops as well as for the Roycroft Inn were a busy crew. I remember going into their own workroom where the saws were humming and the sawdust flying. Some men were finishing pieces, others, examining and measuring lumber, and, pencil behind ear, obviously were deciding which should be used for what."[19]

Except for the graphics, some book bindings, and a few pieces of metalwork, most of the items produced by the Roycrofters were unsigned. Thus there is little indication who designed and/or built what pieces of furniture. Hubbard himself was not a craftsman or a designer. In all the shops, Hubbard hired artisans who then served as teachers and leaders of the "guilds" that produced each object. In 1904, an article pointed out that "The Roycroft Shop is a combination workshop and school, where about three hundred people are employed."[20]

A photograph from about 1900 shows seven Roycroft wood-workers but, unfortunately, their names are not recorded. The task of identifying the designers and craftsmen associated with the Furniture Shop will be a challenging aspect of future research. John Comstock, for example, has been identified recently through furniture designs in a private archive.[21] It is not yet known, however, if he created these for the Roycroft Shops or for some other manufacturer.

Roycroft cabinetmakers named in advertising copy or payroll books include Albert Danner, James (Santiago) Cadzow, Tom Standeven, William Roth, and Herbert Buffum. In all likelihood, these men were also responsible for the design of Roycroft furniture. In a wry attempt to appear humble, Hubbard commented in 1902: "In our woodworking department and the erecting of new buildings, I have deferred to James Cadzow, a small and modest man weighing two hundred & forty pounds, who can lift six hundred pounds from the floor. He was born right in the woods, and now has but one desire—to make furniture that will do us proud."[22]

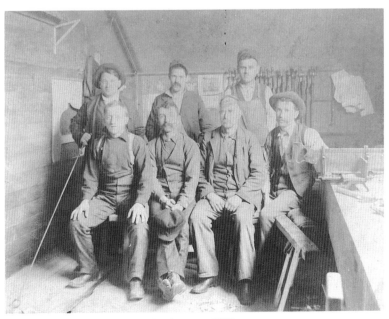

Fig. 34: A group of Roycroft woodworkers, ca. 1900.
(Courtesy Richard Jackson)

A 1900 catalog is one of the few publications in which individual makers were acknowledged. The listing includes Albert Danner, James Cadzow, Herbert Buffum, and even Ali Baba, who is credited with an "Ash pedestal, with the bark on," an "Ash pedestal," and a "Hat rack, limited edition made by Setebos and Ali Baba. Not for sale."[23] An advertisement in 1908 declares "Just for the Very Elect Few we will still make a little Roycroft furniture. We have but six men, Deacon [Herbert] Buffum and his five sons, one with a blot on his 'scutcheon, making furniture—by hand."[24]

Occasionally, Hubbard's advertisements provided colorful, if apocryphal, backgrounds for his designers. His description of Albert Danner states: "Uncle Albert served an apprenticeship of six years in Germany, left the country at nineteen—for the country's good—and came to America; joined the army, served the five years of the Civil War, and came out of it only a little worse for wear, with a bit of lead in his anatomy which the X-ray locates. He has been a cabinet maker in East Aurora ever since."[25] It is known that Danner was born in Solgau, Germany, probably in 1843, and died in 1913 in East Aurora. His skill as a woodcarver is apparent in much of the decoration on the woodwork for the Roycroft Inn.[26] Strangely, his obituary stated that he was a carpenter by trade but made no mention of his connection with the Roycrofters.[27]

The furniture produced by the Roycroft Shop is typical of that of the American Arts and Crafts movement. The wood used most frequently was quartersawn oak, although ash and African or Santo Domingo mahogany were also available. Hubbard advertised that his lumber was all "specially prepared, being air-dried from two to five years, according to thickness, then kiln-dried for three months at a temperature of One Hundred and Sixty degrees, thus retaining to a great extent the lifelike appearance and natural strength of the woods."[28] Finishes included dark, medium, and light weathered oak; Roycroft brown; Flemish, Golden, and Japanese gray; dark, medium, and light mahogany; and brown and silver gray ash.

Leather was preferred for upholstered pieces, but less expensive velour could be substituted. Hubbard described the leather as practically indestructible and fastened on with large-headed copper tacks or nails.

Although different designers apparently were in charge of the overall production of the furniture, there is a certain sense of homogeneity to its style, with emphasis on techniques common to Arts and Crafts cabinetry. Roycroft craftsmen eschewed veneers, insisting on the honesty of solid wood construction. Pegs and pins were used instead of nails and screws. Mortise and tenon joints were left exposed and became decorative as well as structural elements. The Blacksmith Shop, and later the Copper Shop, provided hinges, handles,

Plate 52: *Tall Magazine Pedestal*, ca. 1902. Oak, 63 × 18 × 18 in. Virginia Museum of Fine Arts, The Parsons Fund for American Decorative Arts.

and other fittings of copper or wrought iron, finished to harmonize with the wood.

There was one consistent exception to the straightforward design and lack of extraneous ornamentation that characterized Roycroft furniture. An incised Roycroft mark or, on early pieces, the name *Roycroft* was prominently placed on almost every piece, taking advantage of yet another advertising opportunity.

Other decorations were added to a few pieces, such as the tall magazine pedestal, where a leaf design with curling stem is deeply incised directly below the large Roycroft symbol.[29] On special orders, names

Fig. 35: Detail from *Tall Magazine Pedestal*. *(Courtesy Virginia Museum of Fine Arts)*

THE CHIROPRACTIC CONNECTION

Elbert Hubbard found a willing disciple in B. J. Palmer, the engagingly eccentric president of the Palmer School of Chiropractic in Davenport, Iowa. Palmer wore a flowing Roycroft tie, occasionally styled his long hair with a band around his forehead, and ordered Roycroft furniture for his school and clinic, some of which remains at the Palmer College today.[1] Among the most unusual pieces is a tallcase clock with the twelve letters C–H–I–R–O–P–R–A–C–T–I–C circling the face next to the hours of the day.

Fig. 36: Elbert Hubbard and B. J. Palmer, ca. 1914. *(Courtesy Palmer College of Chiropractic)*

Fig. 37: Roycroft tallcase clock, ca. 1915, commissioned by B. J. Palmer. *(Courtesy Palmer College of Chiropractic)*

Palmer also commissioned the Roycrofters to produce 13,000 special motto cards on Italian handmade paper. These bore thirteen messages in the parlance of the new science of chiropractic, which had been developed by Palmer's father in 1895. Dard Hunter's famous borders circumscribed some decidedly offbeat epigrams, all signed "B. J."

Don't Subluxate on Another's Current.

"Your Trolley's off."

What 2 do?

I want to know!

Adjust it!

Coordinate ur Carburettor.

Within two years of Hubbard's death, at least two Palmer graduates had migrated to East Aurora. Dr. A. J. Wolff arrived in October 1916 to direct the Roycroft Health Home (which had been established the previous year at Emerson Hall, the former Roycroft dormitory); unfortunately, he succumbed to diabetes within a month of his arrival.[2] And by the following spring, M. P. Sampson had established a chiropractic office on Main Street.[3]

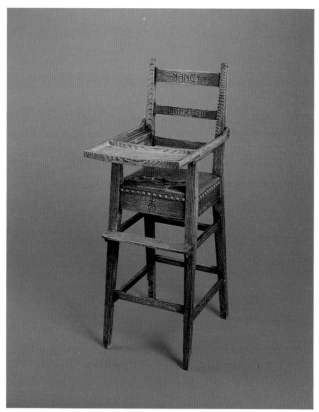

Plate 53: *Hubbard Family High Chair*, ca. 1914. Oak, leather, and brass tacks, 42 × 16½ × 24 in.
Private collection.

Plate 55: *Bookcase*, ca. 1901. Oak, glass, and iron, 61¾ × 31¾ × 15 in.
Roycroft Arts Museum, Boice Lydell.

Plate 54: *Round Table*, ca. 1906. Stamped with "R 074" inventory code. Curly maple, 30 × 36 in.
Collection of Fritz and Jane Gram.

Plate 56: *Marshall Wilder Chair*, ca. 1906. Oak, leather, and brass tacks, 35 × 17 × 16 in.
Private collection.

or initials of the owners could be added. In at least one instance, a quote was incorporated, that example being a chair designed by Dard Hunter, probably when he attended the Roycroft summer school in 1904.[30]

Roycroft designers seem to have been influenced by British styles, both contemporary and historical. The distinctive bulbous foot that one associates with the English designers Arthur Mackmurdo and C. F. Annesley Voysey appears on many Roycroft pieces and the glass inserts in the doors of some sideboards and china cabinets derive from the earlier English Gothic. The presence of both contemporary and historical references suggests the lack of a singular vision in the overall design and production of Roycroft furniture.[31]

Evidence of the strong British influence is further seen in a Roycroft wall cabinet based on the *Kelmscott Chaucer* cabinet that was designed by Voysey in 1899 and illustrated in the *Studio* in October of that year. Both are made of oak and display incised inscriptions

CHINA CABINET, No. 7
Coppered Glass Doors. 48 inches Wide, 60 inches High,
20 inches Deep. Price, $54.00

Fig. 38: Advertisement for *China Cabinet*, ca. 1905. (As published in *A Catalog of Roycroft Books and Things Year Ten from the Founding of the Roycroft Shop*, 1905–06)

on the twin doors: *Kelmscott Chaucer* on the Voysey cabinet and *Roy Croft* on the East Aurora piece. The Voysey cabinet was designed expressly to contain a richly-bound copy of the famous Kelmscott edition of *Chaucer*.[32] Similarly, the Roycroft cabinet was probably used to house a collection of Roycroft books.[33] An early Roycroft bookcase bears the same kind of graceful lettering.

Even in some of the most distinctive Roycroft pieces there is a tendency to break from the strict right angle of the typical American Arts and Crafts design in the faceted beveling of the window mullions. Stickley and his brothers would have used absolutely straight-sided mullions to divide the glass doors.

Plate 57: *Hall Chair*, ca. 1904. Designed and executed by Dard Hunter. Oak, paint, leather, and iron tacks,
51¼ x 20 x 18½ in.
Collection of Mr. and Mrs. Christopher Forbes.

Roycroft furniture design is perhaps at its best when least derivative and in unique pieces that do not appear in any other manufacturers' output. These include the Ali Baba bench, with its polished oak or ash seat and natural bark underside; the small tabouret with slatted sides; the straddle chair, which, according to an

Plate 58: *Ali Baba Bench*, ca. 1900. Oak and ash, 19½ × 42⅛ x 15¾ in.
Elbert Hubbard-Roycroft Museum.

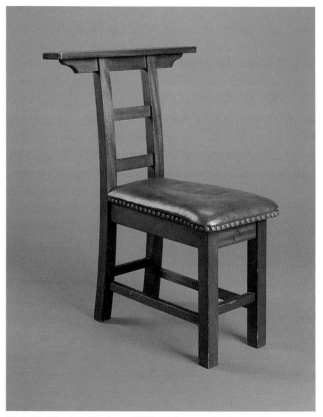

Plate 60: *Straddle Chair*, ca. 1906. Mahogany, leather, and brass tacks, 34¼ × 23¾ × 24½ in.
Collection of Charles and Honna Whelley-Bowen.

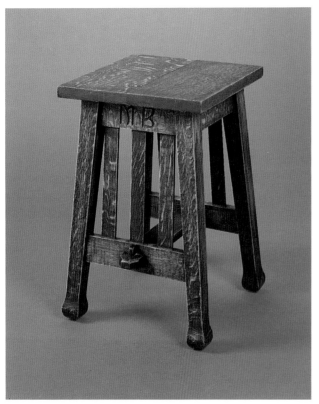

Plate 59: *Tabouret*, ca. 1906. Oak, 20 × 14 × 14 in.
Collection of Bruce A. Austin.

advertisement, "Induces Sound Sleep, an Easy Conscience and a Good Appetite;"[34] the tall magazine pedestal; the Dard Hunter designs; and pieces of furniture especially designed for the Inn.

Hubbard consistently stated in his advertising that his furniture was "hand-made from start to finish,"[35] although this was not completely accurate. He wrote, "We don't make a great deal of furniture, but what we do make is made honestly by hand," and "Beautiful hand-made furniture (Roycroft) gives a joy to both the giver and receiver,"[36] but there is little question that machinery played an important role in its production.

As a writer pointed out after a visit to the Roycroft campus in 1905, however, the machinery was used to reduce labor intensity, not for the machine duplication so prevalent at Grand Rapids, the leading center of commercial furniture production at that time:

The Roycrofter prides himself on the production of work made by hand and brain in partnership. He declares that to things made by hand there is a quality of sentiment attached that never clings to those produced in vast quantities by steam . . . The furniture building . . . is unlike the other structures of the plant. It is a wooden building of three stories and a basement. A steam engine and dynamo in the basement furnish power and light . . . The

Fig. 39: Exterior of the Furniture Shop. (As published in *The Book of the Roycrofters*, 1907)

ground floor . . . has woodworking machinery for the preliminary operation . . . Here is a disk sander, a band-saw, tenoners, shaper, a rip-saw, a mortiser . . . and a jointer . . . The cut-off saw and two planers are at the opposite side of the room.[37]

The writer also reported that the second floor housed work benches and the glue room. The third floor contained a small room for finishing the furniture after it was stained and has "the expert leather worker in charge of the upholstery, the carver and the painters engaged in staining, etc. . . . Much of this space is used for the storage of a few pieces carried in stock."[38] A photograph from about 1905 shows a stockpile of furniture, perhaps destined for a large order.

Fig. 40: Interior of the Inn showing stockpile of furniture, ca. 1905. *(Courtesy Turgeon-Rust Collection)*

This comment about the few pieces carried in stock seems to substantiate Hubbard's advice to order ahead as it would take two months to fill an order. "No stock of furniture is carried—the pieces are made as ordered . . . Every piece is signed by the man who made it."[39] The latter deliberate deception is a puzzle; there are no makers' signatures on the pieces other than the usual Roycroft symbol or name.

The Roycrofters' largest commission was for the famous Grove Park Inn in Asheville, North Carolina, in 1913. E. W. Grove put his son-in-law, Fred Seely, in charge of building what was to become one of the finest resort hotels in this country. Seely was familiar with Hubbard and the Roycroft aesthetic and intended the Roycrofters to supply all of the copper and furniture for his 150-room hotel. The original Grove Park Inn promotional booklet stated: "Seven hundred pieces of furniture and over 600 lighting fixtures of solid copper were made by hand by the Roycrofters, at East Aurora."[40] Limited manpower in the Furniture Shop dictated that the contract for the bedroom furniture be awarded to the White Furniture Company in Mebane, North Carolina.[41]

RARE FINDS

Furniture made by the Roycrofters for their own use on campus was stamped with a letter indicating the building in which the piece was located, followed by its standard catalog model number (or, if it was a custom piece, with the number of a similar model). For example, a double-door bookcase made for the office would be marked "OF 0103." Known letter codes are:

B — Bindery   OF — Office

C — Chapel   PB — Pamphlet Bindery

E — Emerson Hall   PH — Power House

R — Roycroft Inn

The furniture offered through Roycroft catalogues was made of oak, ash, and mahogany, as was much of the furniture used on campus. More rare are the walnut, cherry, bird's-eye maple, and curly maple pieces made specifically for the Roycroft Inn.

MV

Plate 61: *Bed-Room Chair*, ca. 1906. Ash, 43½ × 17 × 18¼ in. *Elbert Hubbard-Roycroft Museum.*

Plate 62: *Desk Chair*, ca. 1910. Oak, leather, and metal tacks, 48 × 18 × 18 in. *Everson Museum of Art.*

Plate 63: *Morris Settee*,
ca. 1905.
Oak and leather,
45 × 48½ x 40 in.
*Newark Museum,
Gift of Mr. and Mrs.
Christopher Forbes.*

Plate 64: *Bride's Chest*,
ca. 1912.
Oak and copper,
19⅞ × 39⅛ × 21⅛ in.
*Collection of
Thomas Portzline and
Phyllis Bieri.*

Plate 65: *Dressing Table*, ca. 1906. Mahogany, glass, and copper,
60 × 39 × 18 in.
The Strong Museum.

Plate 67: *Chest of Drawers*, ca. 1906. Mahogany, glass and copper,
60 × 43½ × 24 in.
The Strong Museum.

Plate 66: *Bedstead*, ca. 1906. Mahogany, 58 × 56 in. (headboard);
34 × 56 in. (footboard); 75 × 8 in. (side rails).
The Strong Museum.

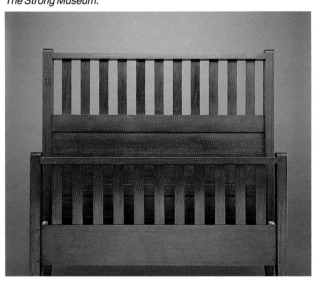

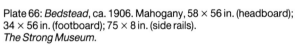

Plate 68: *Table Lamp*, ca. 1907. Wood, copper and leaded glass,
25½ × 18⅝ × 18⅝ in.
Aurora Historical Society.

With the untimely death of Hubbard aboard the *Lusitania* in May of 1915, many worried that this would mean the end of the Roycroft Shops and their production. In the July 1916 memorial edition of the *Fra*, Bert Hubbard pointed out:

> Just a year ago Elbert Hubbard sailed away on the *Lusitania*. When the unbelievable news came and the world had caught its breath, the people who knew of the Roycroft Shops looked toward East Aurora with a speculative wonder as to what was to happen. Much was said as to the probability of the Chapel becoming a home for bats; the Printshop a dungeon of darkness; the Inn a parlor of solitude; the Furniture Shop, the Copper and Leather Shops, empty chambers where rust, ruin and cobwebs would greet the chance visitor . . . Without its master, Roycroft would become a thing in history . . . But these were visions of gossips whose blood ran thin. Their prophecies were from their own empty minds. For one month only was there any slacking of Roycroft industries . . . The Roycroft Shops shall live.[42]

Bert then went on to describe the Print, Copper and Leather Shops as "working to capacity," but no other mention is made of the Furniture Shop. It was in that same year, 1915, that the Roycrofters first began to sell their products through retailers rather than relying strictly on mail order. It is unlikely that the 320 nationwide outlets sold furniture; they carried leather and copper items, but the less portable furniture probably continued to be purchased on demand from the East Aurora shop.

The Roycrofters did continue to produce furniture into the 1920s, albeit erratically. In 1923, *The Book of the Roycrofters* featured only printing, bookbinding, copper craft, and modeled leather, with no reference to furniture. In fact, the building that had housed the furniture shop was pictured as the bindery,[43] although in 1925 the *East Aurora Advertiser* noted that the Furniture Shop was producing 1,200 oak end-tables specially designed to hold the *Little Journeys* and the *Selected Writings of Elbert Hubbard*.[44]

The Depression took its toll at the Roycroft, as it did elsewhere. Attempts were made to accommodate changing public taste, which reflected, in part, a desire to escape the tedium of harsh economic times. The July 1930 issue of the *Roycrofter* offered a four-panel Roycroft screen painted by Richard Krueger and set into an oak frame carved by Charles S. Hall, who had come to the Roycroft in 1928.[45] The screen depicted white swans and silver birches reflected in the water and set off by autumn leaves. It is reminiscent of the type of decoration that had become so popular in the exotic movie palaces of the period; although it appealed to the popular taste, only the wealthy could have afforded its price of eight hundred dollars.

Both upper and middle classes were the objects of a new advertising campaign. The October 1930 issue of the *Roycrofter* offered two chests for sale. The advertising copy stated that "this old chest was brought in, in rather dilapidated condition. It was painted red, and it was much the worse for wear, but we repaired it and carved it until now it's a perfect gem of the cabinetmaker's and carver's art. It is priced at $85.00 and there is but one! . . . [The design of the other chest] is strictly original but it is a rendering of the Byzantine Style—an ecclesiastical pattern. The wood is old Pine, with hand-wrought nails, made before machine-made nails became the vogue!"[46]

This departure from the spare style that had characterized Roycroft furniture, along with the concept of reworking old pieces, was a far cry from Hubbard's original Arts and Crafts philosophy. Realistically speaking, the Furniture Shop and the mission aesthetic had run their course. People longed for the "good old days" and looked for direction to Wallace Nutting, who stressed the designs of the colonial past. The result, in the case of the carved chests, was a compromise, using "country" antiques that had been refinished by the Roycrofters, thus combining early American design with the esteem of the well-known craftsmen.

The Roycroft Shops closed in 1938 after several difficult years and eventual bankruptcy. Recently, with the renewed interest in the Arts and Crafts movement, collectors have rediscovered the beauties of Roycroft furniture, which has lived up to Hubbard's claim of being "used a generation and then passed on to the heirs." Perhaps the spirit of Roycroft furniture and its renaissance is best described in the words of Hubbard's last speech to his Roycrofters in the Salon on April 28, 1915:

> Ideas are born. They have their infancy, their youth—their time of stress and struggle—they succeed, they grow senile, they nod, they sleep, they die; they are buried and remain in their graves for ages. And then they come again . . . And this death and resurrection goes on forever. In Time, there is nothing either new or old; there is only the rising and falling of the Infinite Tide.[47]

ROYCROFT SCREEN

A Lake Scene of Swans and Silver Birches

PLAIN print can not do justice to the beauty of this Screen—a black and white description can never picture it to you. But it is highly decorative. Brilliant blues and purples predominate!— Blue skies and white swans and silver birches reflected in the water, accenuated and emphasized by the golden coloring of autumn leaves— all makes a remarkable contrast and secures a gorgeous effect! The frame is of oak, carved especially for this screen and blends with it in perfect harmony; fitted to most any style of architecture.

Painted by Richard Krueger
Frame carved by Charles S. Hall

Price $800.00

THE ROYCROFTERS, East Aurora, New York

xiii

Fig. 41: Advertisement for *Roycroft Screen*, ca. 1930. (As published in the *Roycrofter*, July 1930)

CARVED-WOOD CHESTS

We have
Old and
New chests
on sale at
Roycroft

**A Sunburst
Design**

This old chest was brought in, in rather dilapidated condition. It was painted red, and it was much the worse for wear, but we repaired it and carved it until now it's a perfect gem of the cabinet-maker's and carver's art. It is priced at $85.00, and there is but one!

We offer
other chests
priced
between
$150 and
$300

**A Byzantine
Design**

This design is strictly original but it is a rendering of the Byzantine Style—an ecclesiastical pattern. The wood is old Pine, with handwrought nails, made before machine-made nails became the vogue!

iv

Fig. 42: Advertisement for a *Sunburst Design Chest* and a *Byzantine Design Chest*, ca. 1930.
(As published in the *Roycrofter*, October 1930)

THE FINAL MOMENTS

Fig. 43: The *Lusitania*, as depicted on a promotional postcard for the Cunard Line, 1907. *(Courtesy Turgeon-Rust Collection)*

A romantic version of Elbert and Alice Hubbard's demise aboard the doomed *Lusitania* depicts them retreating to their stateroom, arm in arm, perfectly composed despite the chaos around them.[1] A letter to Elbert Hubbard II from one of the *Lusitania* survivors, Charles T. Hill of London, provides a different, and somehow even more tragic, story of their fate:

> When I reached the lifeboat on the port side of the ship, Mr. and Mrs. Hubbard were already in the boat. A good many other boats had got away. Our boat was in charge of the ship's barber (Gadd, I believe his name was), who, owing to the heavy list, and I daresay excitement, fouled the ropes in lowering it, the result being the boat struck the water with such force as to spring a leak and became water-logged. After we got clear of the *Lusitania* and as she went down, someone cried out, "Look, she's going." The movement on the part of some to see the last of the ship caused the lifeboat to capsize. When we succeeded in righting the lifeboat, unfortunately, Mr. and Mrs. Hubbard were not among those who got back in.[2]

Colin Simpson, in his book about the *Lusitania* disaster, confirms the assignment of the ship's barber as guardian of No. 14 lifeboat, but attributes its loss to structural damage:

> Boat No. 14 was also eased over the side. As lowering commenced, *Lusitania*'s bow struck the bottom. For a moment the ship flexed and the men at the davits simultaneously lost control. No. 14 fell straight down onto the wreckage of No. 12, but miraculously landed on an even keel. Some twenty survivors climbed aboard and the ship's barber managed to paddle No. 14 clear of the ship before the lifeboat slowly sank under them as water poured in through the strained and rivet-holed planks.[3]

Conflicting accounts of those last moments do not obscure the dramatic response to the Hubbards's passing on 7 May 1915. About three thousand people attended a memorial ceremony in East Aurora two weeks later,[4] and even greater numbers descended upon the small village to pay tribute at the annual Convention of the Philistines in July.[5]

MV

ENDNOTES

[1] William Blake in the prefatory poem to Milton, ca. 1809.

[2] Elbert Hubbard, *This Then is a William Morris Book Being a Little Journey by Elbert Hubbard, & Some Letters, Heretofore Unpublished, Written to His Friend & Fellow Worker, Robert Thomson, All Throwing a Side-Light or Less, on the Man and His Times* (East Aurora: The Roycrofters, 1907), 34.

[3] Ibid., 10. Photographs of the period show that Roycroft tables, too, remained uncovered.

[4] Ibid., 11.

[5] Elbert Hubbard, *Little Journeys to the Homes of Eminent Artists: Botticelli* 10, no. 3 (March 1902).

[6] For illustrations of the chair and its variations, see Brady, *Roycroft Hand Made Furniture*, 3, 43; and *A Catalogue of Roycroft Furniture and Other Things* [reprint of 1906 catalogue] (New York: Turn of the Century Editions, 1981), 23–24.

[7] I am grateful to Robert Rust for calling this catalogue to my attention.

[8] Hugh Chalmers, *Salesmanship* (East Aurora: The Roycrofters, 1910).

[9] Gustav Stickley, "Thoughts Occasioned by an Anniversary: A Plea for a Democratic Art," *Craftsman* 7, no. 7 (October 1904): 42.

[10] Richard Guy Wilson, "American Arts and Crafts Architecture: Radical though Dedicated to the Cause Conservative" in Wendy Kaplan, *"The Art that is Life": The Arts & Crafts Movement in America, 1875–1920* (Boston: Museum of Fine Arts, Boston, 1987), 125.

[11] Gustav Stickley, "How 'Mission' Furniture was Named," *Craftsman* 16, no. 2 (May 1909): 225. Stickley may be referring to Hubbard in this rather barbed commentary by referring to the familiar Roycroft orb and cross as a Maltese cross, perhaps misidentifying it on purpose. However, he might also be commenting on the work of Joseph McHugh, as has been pointed out in the recent catalogue by Anna d'Ambrosio for the Munson-Williams-Proctor Institute Museum of Art's (Utica) exhibition "The Distinction of Being Different: Joseph P. McHugh and the American Arts and Crafts Movement."

[12] *A Catalogue of Roycroft Furniture and Other Things*, 3.

[13] Elbert Hubbard, *The Roycroft Shop: A History* (East Aurora: The Roycrofters, 1908), 8.

[14] Ibid., 11.

[15] *A Catalog of Roycroft Books and Things Year Ten from the Founding of the Roycroft Shop East Aurora NY* (East Aurora: The Roycrofters, 1905–06), 23.

[16] There seems to be some difference in the spelling of this term used by Hubbard for the Inn. It appears in his publications as both Phalanstery and Phalansterie.

[17] *Contemplations: Being Several Short Essays, Helpful Sermonettes, Epigrams and Orphic Sayings Selected from the Writings of Elbert Hubbard by Heloise Hawthorne* (East Aurora: The Roycrofters, 1902).

[18] *Craftsman* 8, no. 1 (April 1905): xxxiii.

[19] Miriam Hubbard Roelofs, "The Roycrofters: A Memoir," in *The Roycroft Movement: A Spirit for Today?* (Buffalo: Buffalo State College Foundation, Inc., 1977), 6.

[20] F. F. D. Albery, "The Roycroft Shop," *Columbus Dispatch*, 28 August 1904, as quoted in *A Catalog of Roycroft Books and Things Year Nine* (East Aurora: The Roycrofters, 1904–05).

[21] David B. Ogle, "The Unknown Roycrofter," *Arts & Crafts Quarterly* 2, no. 3 (April 1989): 22–27.

[22] Elbert Hubbard, "A Social and Industrial Experiment," *The Roycroft Books: A Catalog and Some Remarks* (East Aurora: The Roycrofters, 1902), 20.

[23] *A Catalog of Some Specimens of Art & Handicraft Done by Roycroft Workers.* (East Aurora: The Roycrofters, [1900]) Hubbard does not explain who Setebos was but it might be another of his prankster nicknames.

[24] 1908 advertisement reproduced in *Furniture of the Arts & Crafts Period* (Gas City, Ind.: L-W Book Sales, 1992), K.

[25] *The Roycroft Books* (East Aurora: The Roycrofters, 1903), 27.

[26] I am grateful to Sally Sawyer, Albert Danner's granddaughter, for this information.

[27] "Albert Danner," *East Aurora Advertiser*, 20 February 1913.

[28] *A Catalog of Roycroft Furniture and Other Things* (East Aurora: The Roycrofters, 1906).

[29] The pedestal is illustrated in an advertisement in *Little Journeys to the Homes of Eminent Artists: Leonardo da Vinci* 10, no. 2 (February 1902), with the notation that it is "hand made by Uncle Albert Roycroft—seventy years young." The person referred to is in all likelihood Albert Danner, identified as the maker of this very significant piece of furniture in a 1900 catalog (see footnote 24). I am indebted to Bruce Bland, Co-curator of the Elbert Hubbard-Roycroft Museum, for this piece of information.

[30] See Cathleen Baker, "Dard Hunter—Roycroft Artist," *Arts & Crafts Quarterly* 6, no. 1 (1993): 7.

[31] Janet Ashbee, wife of C. R. A. Ashbee, founder of the Guild and School of Handicraft in England, visited the "Sage of East Aurora" and wrote both critically and yet admiringly of the shops in her *Memoirs*: "In the little forge, which smelt of home, they were making some hideous gas brackets, great unconstructional things, just for the want of knowing the first principles of design. And those tables and chairs of theirs were good." As quoted in Robert W. Winter, "American Sheaves from 'C. R. A.' and Janet Ashbee," *Journal of The Society of Architectural Historians* 30, no. 4 (December 1971): 320.

[32] Aymer Vallance, "British decorative art in 1899 and the Arts and Crafts Exhibition," *Studio* 18, no. 19 (October 15, 1899): 46. A photograph of the cabinet appears on page 42; copies of the magazine were available in the Roycroft Library.

[33] Coy Ludwig, *The Arts & Crafts Movement in New York State 1890s-1920s* (Hamilton, N.Y.: Gallery Association of New York State, Inc., 1983), 39. The Roycroft wall cabinet is pictured in the same publication on the same page.

[34] *A Catalog of Roycroft Furniture and Other Things*, 47.

[35] *A Catalog of Roycroft Books and Things* (East Aurora: The Roycrofters, 1904), 23.

[36] As quoted in Roycroft advertisements reprinted in Charles F. Hamilton, *Roycroft Collectibles* (Tavares, Fla.: SPS Publications, 1980), 44.

[37] "Roycroft Ideals and Cabinetmaking," *Wood Craft* 4, no. 1 (October 1905): 12–13.

[38] Ibid., 13.

[39] As quoted in Brady, *Roycroft Hand Made Furniture*, 57.

[40] Reprint of *Grove Park Inn: Finest Resort Hotel in the World* (Asheville: Grove Park Inn, n.d.).

[41] For more detailed information concerning this commission, see Bruce Johnson's highly informative article "The Grove Park Inn and the Arts & Crafts Movement," *Arts and Crafts Conference Catalogue* (Durham: Knock on Wood Publications, 1989). Johnson points out the addition of arms to the Plantation Dining Room chairs about 1920 to make them more comfortable to the Inn's patrons, although not as pleasing to the eye. See also Brady, *Roycroft Hand Made Furniture*, 50–53.

[42] Bert Hubbard, "Roycroft – July, 1916," *Fra* 17, no. 4 (July 1916): 110.

[43] Nancy Hubbard Brady noted that in early 1907 the Furniture Shop was closed and the Bindery was moved into what had been the furniture building. Approximately three years later, furniture production was resumed on the first floor of that same building. Letter to the author from Marie Via, 18 October 1993, quoting materials from the Roycroft Arts Museum archive.

[44] "Roycroft Activities," *East Aurora Advertiser*, 22 October 1925.

[45] Hamilton, *Roycroft Collectibles*, 118.

[46] *Roycrofter* 5, no. 2 (October 1930): iv.

[47] Fred Bann, "Elbert Hubbard's Last Talk to His Helpers," *The Book of the Roycrofters Being a History and Some Comments by Elbert Hubbard and Elbert Hubbard II* (East Aurora: The Roycrofters, 1923), 19.

The Chiropractic Connection

[1] Glenda Wiese, "A Brief History of Palmer College of Chiropractic (Palmer College of Chiropractic, Davenport, photocopy), 1.

[2] "Dr. Wolff Dies Suddenly; Was Re-establishing the Roycroft Health Home," *East Aurora Advertiser*, 23 November 1916.

[3] Advertisement, *East Aurora Advertiser*, 10 May 1917.

The Final Moments

[1] Felix Shay, *Elbert Hubbard of East Aurora* (New York: Wm. H. Wise & Co., 1926), 551. Shay's notion may have been influenced by Hubbard's own essay titled "The Titanic," in which the Fra applauds the similarly glorious passing of Mr. and Mrs. Isador Straus, victims of that earlier tragedy at sea.

[2] C. T. Hill to Elbert Hubbard II, 19 October 1923, Roycroft archives, Department of Rare Books & Special Collections, Rush Rhees Library, University of Rochester.

[3] Colin Simpson, *The Lusitania* (Boston, Toronto: Little, Brown and Company, 1972), 169.

[4] "A Fitting Memorial: About Three Thousand People Attended Services Sunday," *East Aurora Advertiser*, 27 May 1915.

[5] "Memorial Convention: Huge Crowds Make Their Little Journey to the Home of Fra," *East Aurora Advertiser*, 8 July 1915.

Frederick R. Brandt is Curator of 20th-Century Art at the Virginia Museum of Fine Arts in Richmond, where he is is entrusted with the care of the renowned Sydney and Frances Lewis Collection of decorative arts.

Plate 69: *Hanging Motto: Remember to Live*, ca. 1914. Ash and iron, 10 × 42 × 8 in. *Collection of Mark and Sarah Roelofs.*

Alchemy in East Aurora:
Roycroft Metal Arts

ROBERT RUST, KITTY TURGEON-RUST,
MARIE VIA, AND MARJORIE B. SEARL

In his *Creed of the Future*, Elbert Hubbard wrote:

> I KNOW:
> That I am here
> In a world where nothing is permanent but change,
> And that in degree I, myself, can change the form of things
> And influence a few people . . .
> And that the work I now do will in degree influence people who may live after my life has changed into other forms.[1]

Roycroft metalwork, the artisans who produced it, and the Roycroft site itself changed form as well. Base metals such as iron and copper were transformed into utilitarian and decorative objects. Craftsmen grew more proficient in their art; students learned new skills. And the Roycroft Copper Shop experienced a remarkable transmutation as it evolved from a humble blacksmith shop into an energetic and creative art metal enterprise.

The Blacksmith Period (1899–1901)

> When andirons were wanted for the big fireplaces in the shop, St. Gerome went to the village blacksmith's shop and hammered them out, with the aid of the blacksmith.[2]

Early Roycroft metal production was fired by necessity rather than by any particular creative impulse. As new buildings were constructed on campus and the Phalanstery was enlarged, lighting fixtures were needed to illuminate the sometimes cavernous spaces, as were andirons for the fireplaces by which the shops were heated. The Roycrofters also needed to produce hardware that was both sturdy and aesthetically appropriate for the furniture they were building to equip the shops.

Among the small band of early Roycrofters, Jerome Connor and Peter Robarge were experienced metal craftsmen. The muscular Connor had been a foundry worker before his arrival in East Aurora in 1896[3] and Robarge operated a blacksmith shop on Cazenovia

Street in East Aurora.[4] They were assisted by a local plumber named Ernest Standeven.[5]

Around 1899, a rude wooden building was constructed on Grove Street across from the original Print Shop.[6] For about three years, this served as the Roycroft Blacksmith Shop, where the forges shared space with the kilns of the short-lived Roycroft Pottery. The metalwork produced during this period was of wrought iron, technically not far removed from the horseshoes, barrel straps, and machine parts that constituted a blacksmith's stock-in-trade. Elaborately turned chandeliers and gas lamps were produced for the

Plate 70: *Wrought-Iron Lamp*, ca. 1901. Iron and wood, 15½ × 7 × 6¼ in.
Private collection.

75

Chapel, Print Shop, and Phalanstery dining room, as were simple knobs, handles, escutcheons, and butterfly hinges for bookcases and cabinets. At least three basic types of andirons were forged: a series that incorporated wrought curlicues, rings, hearts, and the cross-and-orb emblem, much in the style of the British designer C. R. Ashbee; an extremely simple set that consisted of a straight vertical member surmounted by a square cap; and, perhaps best known, those based on W. W. Denslow's signature sea horse design.

Plate 71: *Sea Horse Andirons*, ca. 1899. Designed by W. W. Denslow. Iron, 19¾ × 10 × 29 in. (each).
Collection of David and Susan Cathers.

Roycroft wrought iron was not signed or marked, and so must be identified through period photographs and the vague descriptions in early sales catalogues. *A Catalog of Some Specimens of Art & Handicraft Done by Roycroft Workers* (1900), for example, offered "four-light chandeliers, 36 inch spread, in Assembly room" and "andirons in Mr. Warner's studio," assuming, it seems, that many potential customers had visited the Roycroft campus, had seen the objects in use, and would remember them without further explication.

The Formative Copper Period (1902–1908)

The picturesque stone cottage (extant) that saw the birth of the Roycroft's copperworking enterprise was built in 1902. It was still called the Blacksmith Shop for many years,[7] although more from habit than as a real description of the activities taking place there, since the use of wrought iron was curtailed once work in copper began.[8]

A malleable material that was relatively easy to control, copper was the perfect choice for Roycroft artisans, who were largely self-taught or had migrated from other metalworking professions. Because it was more affordable than the traditional art metals of silver

Fig. 44: Two Roycrofters at work in the wooden Blacksmith Shop. An early wrought-iron chandelier and andirons appear at right. (As reproduced in *The Book of the Roycrofters*, 1900)

and gold, copper was also the medium of choice for many craftsmen who subscribed to the democratic principles of the Arts and Crafts movement, which maintained that beautiful hand-made objects should be available to everyone. In addition, copper conjured up romanticized visions of America's colonial past, a feature that was especially appealing in the wake of the patriotic fervor fostered by the Philadelphia Centennial Exposition of 1876.

The prototypical Roycroft copper objects demonstrated the craftsman's experimental approach to a new medium. Skills and techniques learned at the blacksmith's forge were naively transferred to the copperworking benches, sometimes with limited success. For example, the Roycrofters did not immediately grasp the importance of hammering as a means of strengthening the material rather than simply a technique for producing the desired shape. This procedure would have been foreign to producers of wrought iron, but was absolutely critical to the process of fortifying a tensile metal like copper to withstand heavy use. Consequently, the long, unhammered strap-hinges on the Roycroft ladies' writing desk have tended to stretch over the years

Fig. 45: The ivy-covered Copper Shop (built ca. 1902) as it looked in the mid-1920s. Elbert Hubbard III sits in the doorway as Karl Kipp feeds breadcrumbs to the birds.
(Courtesy Elbert Hubbard-Roycroft Museum)

and sometimes fail to provide the sturdy support needed when the drop front is lowered.

In addition to being unhammered, the early copper work was also unpatinated, leaving objects with a reddish-caramel color. Raw surfaces that would be exposed to the elements, as were the hinges and hardware on the massive doors of the Roycroft Inn, were waxed or lacquered for protection. The designs them-

Plate 72: *Ladies' Writing Desk*, ca. 1905. Oak and copper, 44¼ × 33½ × 19¼ in.
Elbert Hubbard-Roycroft Museum.

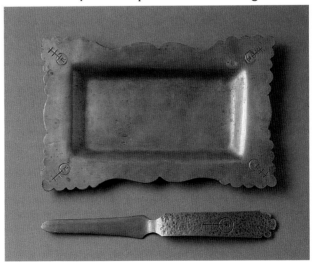

Plate 73: *Pin Tray*, ca. 1906. Copper, 4 × 6½ in.
Roycroft Arts Museum, Boice Lydell.

Letter Opener, ca. 1906. Copper, 6⅝ × ¾ in.
Roycroft Arts Museum, Boice Lydell.

selves were often uninspired, even amateurish, seemingly the product of hobbyists rather than professionally-trained artists. That began to change with the arrival, in 1904, of the gifted Dard Hunter, who was to become the Roycroft's most well-known designer in a number of media.[9] Although he was not technically an employee of the Copper Shop, Hunter's 1905 design for a set of triangular chandeliers with heart-shaped cut-outs for the Roycroft Inn marked a turning point for that department.[10] The relative sophistication of Hunter's designs led Elbert Hubbard to recognize that excellence in artistic conception must play a role equal to that of competent craftsmanship if Roycroft metalwork was to achieve commercial success as an independent product line.

Transition Period (1909–1911)

Although the cottage site appeared largely unchanged as the decade came to an end, little else remained static at the Copper Shop during the period 1909–1911. The first advertisement for copper objects (including a nut set, copper-bound lamp shades, serving-trays, belt buckles, paper-cutters, ash-receivers, and pin-trays) appeared in the *Little Journeys* of August 1909. Shortly thereafter, payroll records reveal the resolution of an ongoing identity crisis: in 1910, the more generic Arts & Crafts Department formally became the Art Copper Department.[11] About that time, four Roycroft designer-

Fig. 46: Karl Kipp, head of the Roycroft Copper Shop.
(Courtesy Elbert Hubbard-Roycroft Museum)

crafts-men tapped into the artistic ferment in Europe and were given the freedom to exploit these new ideas at the Roycroft.

Karl Kipp began his Roycroft career in the Bindery. His journey to the Copper Shop can be traced through two advertisements, in which he is unnamed but identifiable by clear references to his prominent baldness. In the *Fra* of September 1909, speaking of historic printers and binders who resented the machine, Hubbard mentioned the Roycroft's own "Fra Baldy" as a man of similar impulses. Then, in the *Roycroft Catalog* of 1910, copy describing the "anvil chorus" directed

Plate 74: *Jade Pendant*, ca. 1909. Designed by Dard Hunter. Silver, jade, and ribbon, 1¼ × 1³⁄₁₆ in. (without ribbon).
Roycroft Arts Museum, Boice Lydell.

Jade Stickpin, ca. 1909. Designed by Dard Hunter. Silver and jade, 2¾ × ⅝ in.
Roycroft Arts Museum, Boice Lydell.

Jade Pin, ca. 1909. Designed and executed by Dard Hunter (signed). Silver and jade, 1¾ × 1½ in.
Collection of Richard Blacher.

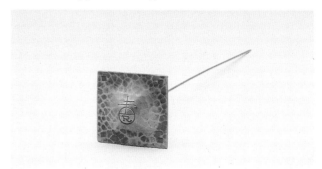

Plate 75: *Hat Pin*, ca. 1911. Copper, 9 × 1⁷⁄₁₆ × 1⁷⁄₁₆ in.
Collection of Richard Blacher.

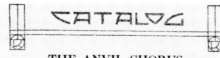

STEIN

C-2

Stein made of copper, with German silver bands set with jade. The cover is of German silver and copper. German silver handle and silver-plated lining, 4½ x 6 in. $25.00

THE ANVIL CHORUS

As done by hand in Fra Baldini's Shop.

¶ We make neither horseshoes nor coffin-nails, nor characters in Baldini's Shop—but we can give you something just as good.

¶ Oh no, that's not the chorus you were thinking about, for where the hand and hammer are so much in evidence the modern speaking-trumpet is of little use

¶ If you want Baldini to work for you, just chalk up a request on his green door and the hired man will take it in, or perhaps it will be the hired girl.

¶ You see, it's this way. So many people have been along here this Summer and have liked the Fra's bowls and lights and trays and desk-sets so well that we had to say, "Now, don't sell that until we take its picture." So, on the following pages are the pictures of Fra Baldini, His family jewels.

¶ He told us in secret that he could make anything that would come out of copper sheets by dint of careful thought and good muscle, and that he'd rather make special designs than anything he knew, but that we would have to give him a little extra time for them.

¶ Also, he wants you to bear in mind that no two pieces of copper look exactly alike. Therein lies the charm of the work and the beauty of the article

¶ We pay the freight.

Address, THE ANVIL CHORUS, care of
THE ROYCROFTERS, East Aurora, New York

Fig. 47: Advertisement for the *Roycroft Stein* in the first catalog to feature designs inspired by the artists of Glasgow and Vienna. (As published in the *Roycroft Catalog: Books, Leather, Copper, Mottos*, 1910)

by "Fra Baldini," suggested that Kipp had begun working in copper during the summer of that year. The objects presented in the 1910 catalogue, including a stein, smoking set, candlestick, book-ends, and nut spoon, were styled in the geometric manner made popular by the artists of the Viennese Sezession and the Glasgow School. Square cut-outs, applied jade cabochons, and silver overlay appeared on distinctly modern forms, and the "loving" marks of the hammer were allowed to remain on the surfaces of the objects, "like lines of experience on a thoughtful face."[12] In the vocabulary of Arts and Crafts metalwork, the hammer marks served as a decorative element as well as proof that the object in hand was the work of a craftsman, not a machine operator. These pieces signified a radical

Plate 76: *Roycroft Stein*, ca. 1910. Designed and executed by Karl Kipp (signed). Copper, silver, and jade, 6½ × 5⅝ in.
Roycroft Arts Museum, Boice Lydell.

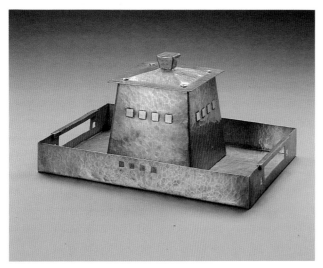

Plate 77: *Humidor*, ca. 1910. Designed by Karl Kipp. Copper and German silver, 5¾ × 5 × 5 in.

Tray, ca. 1910. Designed by Karl Kipp, executed by E.R. (signed). Copper, 1½ × 12¼ × 8¼ in.
Collection of Richard Blacher.

Plate 78: *Candelabrum*, ca. 1911. Designed by Karl Kipp. Copper, 10¾ × 8⅛ × 2¾ in.
Roycroft Arts Museum, Boice Lydell.

Plate 79: *Candlestick*, ca. 1910. Copper and German silver, 7¾ x 4⅜ in.
The Charles Rand Penney Collection of Works by Roycroft Artists at the Burchield-Penney Art Center, Buffalo State College.

Plate 80: *Jewel Box*, ca. 1910. Copper and German silver, 6⅞ × 3½ × 2¼ in.
Roycroft Arts Museum, Boice Lydell.

shift in both the quality of copper craftsmanship and the creativity of design work at the Roycroft.

A good deal of credit for the elevation of design standards belongs to Dard Hunter. His youth, his interest in modern decorative arts, his travels abroad, and his versatility in media as diverse as clay, glass, wood,

Plate 81: *Chapel Lantern*, ca. 1909. Designed by Dard Hunter. Copper and leaded glass, 9 × 15 × 9 in. *Roycroft Revitalization Corporation and The Landmark Society of Western New York.*

and printmaking helped propel the Roycroft Copper Shop beyond nineteenth-century provincialism. The lanterns he designed for the Roycroft Chapel sounded a contemporary note in the retrogressive scheme that marked the typical Roycroft interior. Under Hunter's influence, Kipp designed and executed some of the most distinctive of all Roycroft metalware, including a trapezoidal vase with German silver overlay patterned after one of Hunter's graphic designs. The two craftsmen collaborated directly on a complex figural chandelier for the Roycroft Inn (Plate 163),[13] and probably on the distinctive lamp that at various times occupied the speaker's dais in the Salon and Hubbard's own office (Plate 83).

Another addition to the "anvil chorus" at about the same time was Walter U. Jennings. Like Kipp, he had started out in the Bindery, but was sent over to the Copper Shop in 1909.[14] Equally talented as a leathercrafter and a metalworker, Jennings was later a member of the Boston Society of Arts and Crafts,[15] and contributed a distinct fine art sensibility to the work being produced in East Aurora.

Information about a fourth craftsman of the transition period is sketchy. Ernest A. Fuchs is known to have signed a bud vase and a nut spoon during these pivotal years and has left behind a sizeable collection of sketches for metal objects, including a vase,

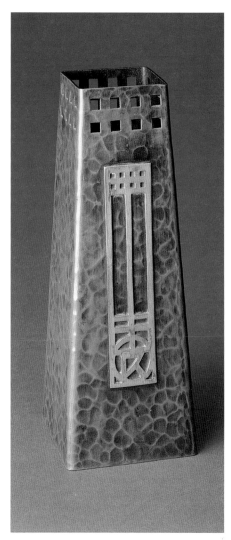

Plate 82: *Trapezoidal Vase*, ca. 1910. Designed by Karl Kipp. Copper and German silver, 6⅞ × 2⅝ × 2⅝ in. *Memorial Art Gallery of the University of Rochester, Gift of James Sibley Watson, Walter Remington, Arthur Stern III, and Bertha Buswell Bequest (by exchange).*

Fig. 48: Elbert Hubbard in his office, with the *Salon Lamp* at right, ca. 1912.
(Courtesy Elbert Hubbard-Roycroft Museum)

Plate 84: *Pierced Nut Spoon*, ca. 1910. Executed by Ernest A. Fuchs (signed). Copper, 7½ × 3¾ in.
Collection of Kitty Turgeon-Rust and Robert Rust, Roycroft Shops.

wall sconces, jewelry, and variations on a set of Roycroft candlesticks.[16]

The greatest puzzle of all, however, is how the Roycroft metal workers acquired their hammering skills. It is difficult to imagine that they could progress, without some sort of expert guidance, from the complete lack of understanding of copper manifest in the hinges of

the writing desk to the exquisite craftsmanship of the Viennese-style fern dish executed just one year later. Examination of membership rosters of the Buffalo Art Students' League and class rolls at the Buffalo Fine Arts Academy reveals Roycroft connections;[17] likewise, graduates of the Mechanics Institute (Rochester) or manual arts training classes at the East Aurora High School directly across the street from the Copper Shop may have been the "missing links." In the meantime, we are left to ponder the Roycroft Copper Shop's transition from the home-made to the hand-crafted.

The Mature Period (1912–1918)

The years from 1912 to 1918 were a time of exuberance and confusion, of triumph and tragedy, both in East Aurora and around the globe. Increased activity at the little ivy-covered Copper Shop necessitated the addition of its west wing around 1913.[18] In the previous

Plate 83: *Roycroft Inn Salon Lamp*, ca. 1910. Designed and executed by Dard Hunter (shade) and Karl Kipp (base). Copper with leaded glass shade, 23 × 17¼ in. diam.
Private collection.

Plate 85: *Fern Dish*, ca. 1910. Designed and executed by Karl Kipp (signed). Copper and German silver, 4¼ × 7 in. diam.
Aurora Historical Society.

Fig. 49: The stone Copper Shop with its cinder-block west wing (added ca. 1913). (As published in *The Book of the Roycrofters*, 1919).

year, the Roycrofters had received their largest commercial commission ever, an order for 700 lighting fixtures for the Grove Park Inn, a mammoth resort hotel being built by Edwin Grove and Fred Seely in Asheville, North Carolina. The metalworkers also produced an unknown quantity of 22½-inch American Beauty vases especially for the Grove Park Inn, as well as 2,900 pieces of hardware for the bedroom furniture.[19]

Remarkably, this enormous assignment was accomplished without Hunter, Kipp, or Jennings on campus. Hunter had left the Roycroft by mid-1910, embarking upon the path that would eventually make him the

Plate 87: *Chandelier*, ca. 1912. Designed by Victor Toothaker. Silver over copper with glass shade, 10½ × 16¾ in. (without chains). *Collection of Eleanor Jackson Searl.*

Plate 86: *Sconce*, ca. 1912. Designed by Victor Toothaker. Silver over copper with glass insert, 12 × 7½ in. *Collection of Eleanor Jackson Searl.*

Plate 88: *American Beauty Vase for the Grove Park Inn*, ca. 1912. Designed by Victor Toothaker. Copper, 22½ × 7 in. *Cooper-Hewitt, National Museum of Design, Smithsonian Institution, Museum Purchase.*

Plate 89: *Table Lamp*, ca. 1916. Copper and mica,
14¼ × 7⅜ in. diam. *Collection of Fritz and Jane Gram.*

country's foremost authority on paper-making. By 1911, although he was still employed by Hubbard, Kipp had begun to develop a private metalworking business;[20] by May of 1912 he had departed the Roycroft to devote his energies to his own studio, the Tookay Shop.[21] Shortly thereafter, Walter Jennings left Hubbard's employ to join the Tookay enterprise.[22]

The loss of three stellar craftsmen was partially offset by the contributions of Victor Toothaker, who may have received his training from his father, an Arizona blacksmith.[23] The exact date of Toothaker's arrival in East Aurora remains unknown; his name does not appear in the 1910 East Aurora census, and his future wife, Anna Knights, was still listed in that survey under her maiden name.[24] By 1912, he was working for Hubbard, in the

Plate 90: *Card Tray*, ca. 1912–18. Copper, 5¾ in. diam.
Collection of Bruce A. Austin.

Roycroft Bank as well as in the Copper Shop.[25] His illustration for the cover of the Roycroft catalog issued in that year featured a version of the American Beauty vase. This, coupled with the fact that he designed the lighting fixtures for the Grove Park Inn,[26] supports the suggestion that he designed the vase as well.

The massive Grove Park Commission placed a new emphasis on production rather than creativity and

Fig. 50: Victor Toothaker and an unidentified assistant in the front room of the Copper Shop, which housed the offices of Elbert Hubbard, Banker beginning in May 1912.
(Courtesy Town of Aurora Historian's Office)

Plate 91: *Egyptian Flower Holder*, ca. 1912. Designed by Karl Kipp. Copper and German silver, 7¾ × 4¼ in.
Collection of Rocco J. and Mary Graziano.

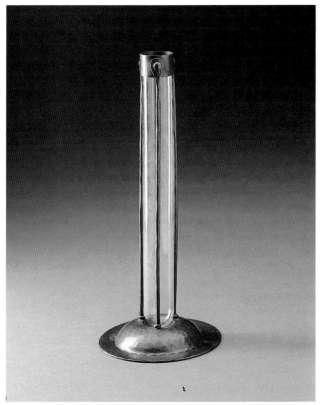

Plate 92: *Bud Vase*, ca. 1912. Copper with glass insert, 8½ × 3¾ in. *Collection of Kitty Turgeon-Rust and Robert Rust, Roycroft Shops.*

Plate 94: *Firestarter*, ca. 1912–18. Copper and brass, 11 × 10½ in. diam. (wand 20⅛ in. long). *Collection of Richard Blacher.*

handwork. Most of the Viennese-style designs were discontinued; not only were they were labor-intensive and therefore expensive to produce, but growing anti-German sentiment in the pre-war years probably reduced their public appeal. The Sezessionist motifs were replaced with decorative rivets (a Toothaker trademark) and the addition of brass elements. New forms continued to develop, some assuming shapes

Plate 93: *Smoking Set*, ca. 1912. Copper, 4⅜ × 14¼ × 6⅛ in. *Elbert Hubbard-Roycroft Museum.*

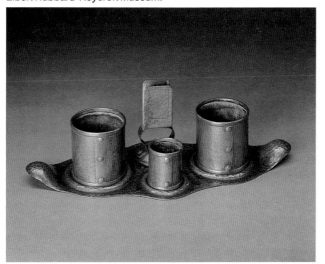

more commonly associated with pottery of the period.

The catastrophic sinking of the *Lusitania* in May 1915 triggered many changes at the Roycroft, with special consequences for the Copper Shop. Some of the craftsmen who had resigned their positions were convinced to return, including Kipp and Jennings.[27] Bert Hubbard, who assumed control of the community upon his father's death, also began to establish "Roycroft

Plate 95: *Poppy Stationery Rack*, ca. 1912. Designed by Victor Toothaker. Copper, 6⅛ × 7 × 2 in. *Private collection.*

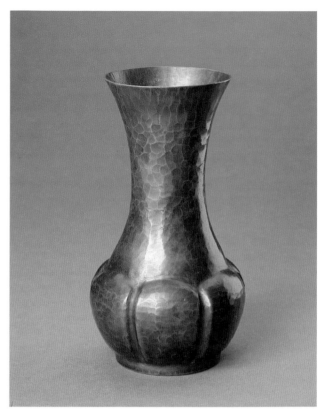

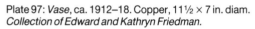

Plate 96: *Ice Bucket*, ca. 1912. Copper and brass, 11 × 10 in. diam. *Collection of Mr. and Mrs. Christopher Forbes.*

Plate 97: *Vase*, ca. 1912–18. Copper, 11½ × 7 in. diam. *Collection of Edward and Kathryn Friedman.*

Plate 98: *Vase*, ca. 1912–18. Copper, 6½ × 3⅝ in. *Private collection.*

Plate 99: *Vase*, ca. 1914. Copper and German silver, 6½ × 3 in. diam. *Collection of Bruce A. Austin.*

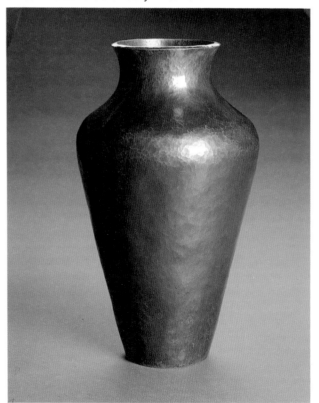

departments" at stores in larger cities; the first three were Lord & Taylor in New York, Abraham & Straus in Brooklyn, and the William Hengerer Company in Buffalo.[28] Within a few years, scores of these outlets, from Providence to Nashville to Los Angeles, were selling Roycroft metalwork, leather goods, books, and memorabilia.[29] This expansion continued the momentum toward quantity production initiated by the Grove Park commission. The little stone cottage was forced to expand again around 1916, when the north wing was added to house a separate plating room for production of objects with Aurora brown, brass and silver finishes.

Mass Market Period (1919–1929)

In the years between World War I and the Great Depression, Kipp and Jennings were joined at the Roycroft by Arthur H. Cole, who briefly attended the Pratt Institute,[30] and Leon Varley, who also sold real estate in East Aurora.[31] Jennings, who had received additional instruction at the Sloyd Training School in Boston in 1918 and 1919,[32] gave full rein to his artistic abilities and introduced a new refinement to Roycroft metalwork.

By the end of the war, evidence of Hunter's Sezessionist vision was limited to a lone vase with silver overlay offered in the Roycroft catalog, and while Victor Toothaker's signature rivets had not been altogether abandoned, definite design changes were taking place. With the addition of chasing (engraving or embossing metal) as a decorative element, Jennings began to work copper in ways traditionally reserved for silver and gold. Thus was brought full circle the Roycroft's treatment of copper, from the blacksmith's inclination to handle it like iron to the artisan's decision to treat it as precious metal. No longer was Roycroft copper characterized by deliberate and sometimes flamboyant crudeness to communicate the joy of handwork. Perhaps the Roycrofters reputation for work in the Arts and Crafts tradition had become firmly enough established to permit a more oblique expression of its tenets. But the changes in prevailing taste that occurred as people

Plate 101: *Bookends*, ca. 1920. Copper and brass, 4⅝ × 4⅛ × 3½ in. (each). *Collection of Richard Blacher.*

Plate 102: *Candlesticks*, ca. 1921. Copper, 11¹³⁄₁₆ × 3⅞ × 3⅞ in. *Elbert Hubbard-Roycroft Museum.*

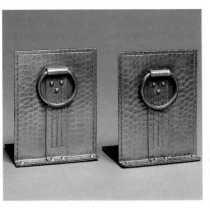

Plate 100: *Bookends*, ca. 1919. Copper, 5⅛ × 4 × 3⅛ in. *Collection of Bruce A. Austin.*

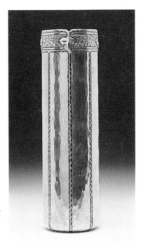

Plate 103: *Vase*, ca. 1919. Designed by Walter Jennings. Silver over copper, 10¼ × 3 in. diam. *Collection of Debbie and David Dalton Rudd.*

Plate 104: *Dresser Set: Hair Receiver and Powder Box*, ca. 1928–32. Designed and executed by Walter Jennings. Copper and brass, 2¼ × 4 in. diam. (hair receiver) and 3⅛ × 4¹/₁₆ in. (powder box). *Collection of Charles F. Hamilton.*

began to accept and even to glorify the machine as a symbol of American superiority in the marketplace may have been an equally potent factor in the Copper Shop's continued evolution. Machine-spun copper forms began to appear along with those raised by hand in the traditional manner, their quasi-industrial origin absolved to a certain degree by hammering that was frequently more complex and beautiful than ever.

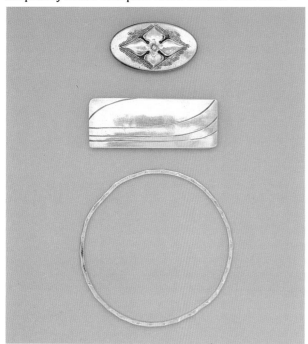

Plate 105: *Oval Pin with Floral Design*, ca. 1928–32. Designed by Walter Jennings. Silver, ¾ × 1⅜ in. diam.
Rectangular Pin with Linear Design, ca. 1928–32. Designed by Walter Jennings. Silver, ¾ × 2 in.
Bangle Bracelet, ca. 1928–32. Designed by Walter Jennings. 2⅜ in. diam.
Collection of Richard Blacher.

Roycroft craftsmen also began to experiment with several new finishes. The 1919 catalog introduced "Roycroft Bronze, a beautiful blue, under which the copper looks almost like burnished gold." The "Sheffield" finish was a silver plate, often applied over very restrained hammering, which appealed to the burgeoning interest in antiques among the middle class, as did the pea-green "Italian polychrome" finish and its more subdued cousin, "Antique Verde." Those whose taste ran to the modern, on the other hand, could choose objects with the new acid-etched surface, with or without silver-plating.

Plate 106: *Vase*, ca. 1919. Copper, 8¼ × 4 in. diam. *Collection of Fritz and Jane Gram.*

Plate 107: *Humidor*, ca. 1925. Copper and wood, 2½ × 9½ × 6¼ in. *Collection of Kitty Turgeon-Rust and Robert Rust, Roycroft Shops.*

Around 1920, the Roycrofters began an artistically significant collaboration with the Corning Glass Company. Lamp shades of iridescent Steuben glass and bubbly glass vase inserts were paired with Roycroft

Plate 108: *Bowl*, ca. 1919. Copper, 2¼ × 4¼ in. diam. *The Strong Museum.*

Plate 109: *Punch Bowl*, ca. 1919. Silver over copper, 6¹³⁄₁₆ × 12 in. diam. *Private collection.*

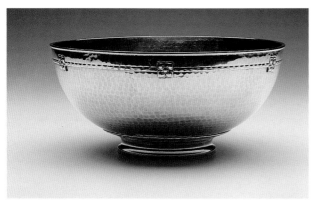

Plate 110: *Fruit Bowl*, ca. 1925. Silver over copper, 4 × 9⅛ in. diam. *Collection of Richard Blacher.*

Plate 111: *Reading Lamp*, ca. 1920. Copper with Steuben Aurene glass shade, 16⅜ × 10 in. diam. *Collection of Bruce A. Austin.*

Plate 112: *Table Lamp*, ca. 1920–25. Executed by Henry Unverdorf (base). Copper with leaded glass shade, 23 × 18¾ in. *Collection of Rocco J. and Mary Graziano.*

Plate 113: *Vase*, ca. 1925. Copper, 16¼ × 9¼ in. diam.
Collection of Richard Blacher.

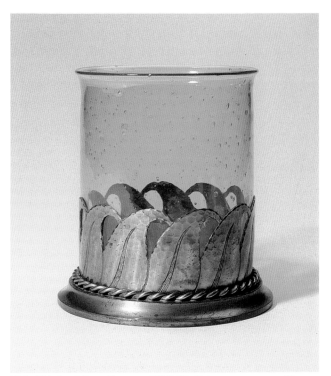

Plate 114: *Leaf-Form Vase*, ca. 1920–26. Brass over copper with
Steuben bubbly glass insert, 7⅛ × 6⅞ in. diam.
Collection of Richard Blacher.

hammered bases and surrounds. A number of stained glass lamp shades were also offered, although these were made on the Roycroft campus.

The Roycroft's product line had never been more extensive. Its metal craftsmen had forged a successful marriage of art and industry that had become the economic backbone of the community, enabling the Roycroft to outlive its creator. But signs of impending economic problems appeared in April of 1928, when Kipp was forced to begin laying off employees at the Copper Shop.[33] By the following year, the situation had not improved. On 12 April 1929, Bert Hubbard delivered a velvet-clad ultimatum to his master craftsman: Kipp would have to purchase the copper production operation and run it on his own, or he would be let go.[34] A domino effect was set in motion: the next day, seven layoffs reduced the Copper Shop staff by half.[35] One month later, Kipp resigned his position at the Roycroft, and Arthur Cole was placed in charge.[36] Three weeks after that, Cole delivered a letter of resignation as well.[37]

The Stock Market Crash in October 1929 virtually ensured that there would be no recovery.

Decline (1930–1938)
With the nation in the grip of the Great Depression, the Roycroft Copper Shop was forced to make some major adjustments in order to survive. The north wing was still

used for copper production, but the west wing was converted to a sales room and the large front room became Charles Hall's woodcarving studio.[38] Jennings, who had lost his hearing in the din of Roycroft's "anvil chorus,"[39] left the Roycroft around 1933 to establish, with Cole, the Avon Copper Shop, about 50 miles to the east. Kipp had become head designer at the Daystrom Company, manufacturers of office equipment with centers in nearby Jamestown and Olean. George Willson, one of those who had survived the layoffs of 1929, and Leon Varley were left to carry on as best they could.

Plate 115: *Vase*,
ca. 1920–28.
Silver over copper,
5 × 4½ in. diam.
*Collection of
Fritz and Jane Gram.*

UNUSUAL GIFTS IN HAND-HAMMERED COPPER AND SILVER

OWL ASH TRAY
No. 673
An Ash Tray of generous size equipped with cigar rest and ornamented with a wise little owl. Size—4½" in diameter.
Aurora Brown or Brass finish........ $3.75

HAND-HAMMERED COPPER TRAY
No. 832
8¼" long
Aurora Brown or Brass finish $2.50
Silver finish 3.00

BOTTLE STOPPLES
Chanticleer Bottle Stopple—3" high, Silver finish $1.00
Sea Horse Bottle Stopple—3¼" high, Silver finish $1.00
Bottle Stopples of Handwrought Copper with Silver finish that can be used on a great variety of different sized corks. These Stopples are equipped with a top and screw which easily adjusts itself to any cork.

VASE
No. 222—4¾" high
Etched Bronze or Etched Copper and Brass finish $4.75
Etched Silver finish 7.00

SALAD DRESSING OR BITTERS SET
A charming combination of Crackled Glass and Silver.
Tray, No. 833—11½" long.
Handwrought Copper with Silver finish $3.75
Two Crackled Glass Bitters or Salad Dressing Bottles equipped with Chanticleer and Sea Horse Stopples made of Copper with Silver finish .... Each, $1.35
Height from base to top of Stopple, 9½".
Complete set consisting of Tray, two Crackled Glass Bottles with Stopples . $6.25

INCENSE BURNER
No. 1113—3½" high
Aurora Brown or Brass finish $3.50
Silver finish 5.25

Fig. 51: A few of the gift items offered in the latter days of the Roycroft Copper Shop, including a sea horse bottle stopple. (As published in *A Catalog of Books & Things Hand-Made at the Roycroft Shops*, ca. 1932)

In speaking of the demise of the metal arts in East Aurora, *Time* magazine noted that "the Turkish corner passed on with Queen Victoria; modern decorations do not include many brass or bronze ornaments."[40] The Roycrofters attempted to keep pace with changing times by adding a few new designs in the popular Art Deco Style. Ashtrays and tumblers were small and relatively inexpensive to produce; despite Elbert Hubbard's negative views on smoking and drinking, their numbers increased, as did the offerings of purely utilitarian buckets and firewood baskets. Only the simpler examples of vases, bookends, and trays were continued, and much of the copper was spun by machine rather than raised by hand as it had been in the early days. W. W. Denslow's famous sea horse, so magnificently rendered as andirons at the turn of the century, was reduced to a caricature of its former self balancing atop a bottle stopple by 1932. Likewise, the copper-plated lantern made from a cheese grater, offered the same year, was firmly and forlornly rooted in the territory of kitsch.

a strong presence in western New York and throughout the United States that regional exhibitions, classes, and allied activities clearly had an even more direct impact.[42]

Ironically, the growth of the industrialized print industry, particularly magazine printing, facilitated unprecedented communication for promoters of the anti-industrial Arts and Crafts philosophy. Roycrofters received specialized journals such as *International Studio* and *Deutsche Kunst und Dekoration*,[43] filled with articles, photographs, and drawings showcasing work with Roycroftie qualities; hammer marks, cabochons, and geometric motifs were common elements in published work of enthusiastic amateurs and renowned professionals alike.[44] *Studio*-sponsored competitions fueled interest in production of new designs, while in America, as early as 1896, *House Beautiful* magazine featured work by C. R. Ashbee, a distinguished metalsmith, architect, designer, and founder of the Guild and School of Handicraft at Toynbee Hall, well-known for its metalwork.[45] The publishing

Information about the Copper Shop's employees, dates, and design influences remains, in many cases, spotty and speculative, but analysis of the objects themselves suggests that Roycroft metalwork, like products of the other shops, strongly resembles that of other craft schools and communities of the same period. There is little doubt that the Viennese and Glaswegian arts communities influenced Roycroft artisans.[41] However, the Arts and Crafts style was such

Plate 116: *Roycroft Fire Company Pin.* Manufactured by The Whitehead & Hoag Co., Newark, NJ. Paper and iron, 1¼ in. diam. *Collection of Charles F. Hamilton.*

Roycroft Fire Company Badge. Manufactured by The Whitehead & Hoag Co., Newark, NJ. Copper and enamel, 3⅜ × 2⅜ in. *Collection of Bruce A. Austin.*

THE ROYCROFT MARK

Elbert Hubbard claimed he had taken the Roycroft mark from a book printed in Venice in 1472, and explained that "the circle stands for eternity; the upright device means progenity; the bar across the circle symbols prohibition; and the double cross is a Dagonic device."[1] An identical symbol (save that the *R* has been replaced with the letters *O*, *S*, and *M* arranged clockwise in the sections of the circle) was, in fact, used by the Venetian printer Octavianus Scotus in 1493.[2] The dictionary reveals that Dagon was the god of agriculture among the people of the ancient Mediterranean country of Philistia, however, so it may be wise to take Hubbard's dissection of the symbol's meaning with the grain of salt so many of his stories require.[3]

Hubbard copyrighted his version of the mark in 1906. At that time, the Roycrofters apparently were not using it on metalwork, as the description of goods to which it applied was limited to "Chairs, Settees, Bookcases, Tables, Cabinets, Music-Cabinets, Desks, Couches, Sideboards, Stools, Beds, Dressers, Cradles, Stands, Taborets, Pillows, and Picture Frames."[4]

Several variants of the familiar cross-and-orb emblem appear on Roycroft copper; attempts to date objects on the basis of these alone cannot be completely successful. Even though the mark continued to evolve, old dies were kept until they broke, and every workman had access to all the dies.[5]

Nonetheless, a general chronology among the principal marks can be established. The earliest (Fig. 52), predictably the most unrefined, resembles a typewriter *R*. Next came a mark distinguished by the curling top and tail of the *R* (Fig. 53). Subsequently, the serifs were dropped from the *R* (Fig. 54). The latest pieces bore the word *Roycroft* below the cross and orb (Fig. 55). An extremely tiny cross and orb enclosed within a box (Fig. 56), almost undiscernible to the naked eye, has been detected on so few objects that its place within the chronology has not yet been established.

Sheffield (silver-plated) pieces were stamped *Sheffield* directly below the word *Roycroft* (Fig. 57). The word *Sample* has also been found on some pieces, possibly those that were part of a showroom display.

Artisans occasionally signed their work with their own marks in addition to the Roycroft symbol. Karl Kipp's familiar back-to-back *K*s are sometimes freestanding (Fig. 58), sometimes enclosed within a box.[6] Ernest A. Fuchs's conjoined initials (Fig. 59) identify his pieces; similarly, *LV* denotes the work of Leon Varley. At least one piece is known to bear the initials *WR*, the long tail of the latter descending gracefully (Fig. 60); the identity of the maker is not known. The boxed Viennese-style initials *ER* (Fig. 61) may be those of E. R. Case, the craftsman who purchased the Tookay Shop from Kipp in 1917.

Fig. 52

Subtle alterations to the cross and orb itself may also distinguish the work of particular metalsmiths. A single dot placed on the dividing line between the two upper sections of the circle (Fig. 62) is believed to indicate a piece executed by Walter U. Jennings.[7] The craftsman who added a dot within each of the two upper sections of the circle (Fig. 63) is yet to be identified.

Fig. 53

Fig. 54

Fig. 55

Fig. 56

Fig. 57

Fig. 58

Fig. 59

Fig. 60

Fig. 61

Fig. 62

Fig. 63

Many other "signatures" are no doubt waiting to be discovered and credited. They are interesting, above all else, as testament to a pride in craftsmanship that triumphed over the anonymity generally imposed upon Roycroft artisans.

MV

world's nascent version of the information superhighway permitted Roycrofters in East Aurora to keep abreast of design trends which were unfolding in Europe.

These magazines reveal the proliferation of exhibitions, expositions, Arts and Crafts societies and guilds, art museums, and arts communities in the twenty-five years between 1880 and 1915.[46] While the Arts and Crafts movement originated in Great Britain, the style was quickly adopted by other Europeans whose work was displayed at such venues as the 1904 St. Louis Louisiana Purchase Exposition,[47] which Elbert Hubbard visited in June.[48] Like hundreds of thousands of other Americans, Roycrofters must have attended many of the events and had the opportunity to see a good deal of metalwork for themselves. Public interest in these objects, as well as public demand for ones like them, was heightened when Hubbard's friend, Philadelphia merchant John Wanamaker, purchased from the Exposition "its German display of interior architecture, comprising various rooms, fittings and furniture" and installed it in his store, removing the display from the realm of the exotic exposition to the more familiar mercantile environment.[49]

While Hubbard credited his personal conversion to the Arts and Crafts brotherhood to his visit to William Morris's Kelmscott Press, his interest in and awareness of other craft communities was keen. In his travels for the Larkin Company and on lecture tours after the

Plate 117: *Side-Wall Lamp*, ca. 1910. Designed by Dard Hunter. Copper and leaded glass, 14½ × 5¾ × 6 in. *Roycroft Arts Museum, Boice Lydell.*

founding of the Roycroft, he had many opportunities to broaden his own horizons and to bring new ideas home to the Roycrofters. In an endorsement for Wanamaker's German rooms, he referred to his own visit to Darmstadt, an artist's colony near Frankfurt established in the 1890s by Grand Duke Ernst Ludwig of Hesse.[50] An important center where leading artists and artisans worked together, the colony had as its goal "influencing public taste, carrying the artistic expression of the German spirit into the homes of the populace."[51]

It is impossible to say definitively to what extent Hubbard's travels influenced developments in Roycroft metalwork, yet his concern for the market share must have encouraged the Copper Shop to produce an up-to-date line.

C. R. Ashbee's American lecture tour of 1900 indirectly brought Hubbard even closer to parallel activities in Britain. Ashbee, an influential speaker whose reformist philosophy articulated many of Hubbard's own concerns, spoke in many cities on behalf of the British National Trust. Accompanied by his wife Janet, he included Chicago on his itinerary, where he spoke to the Architectural Club and visited Hull-House.[52] After Christmas, while her husband was in New York City, Janet Ashbee visited the Roycroft campus.[53] She was sure to have recognized that the work of the Roycroft, while perhaps less polished than that of British Arts and Crafts communities, expressed a shared respect for the hand-made object. Her visit prompted some correspondence as well as Hubbard's reciprocal visit (sometime between 1902 and 1907[54]) to the Ashbees at the Guild's Cotswold community in Chipping Campden, where he could not have been unaware of the parallels with his own enterprise. Ashbee believed, as did Hubbard, in the healthful value of rural living, where skilled artisans could work side by side with untrained locals. "Life skills" were taught as well as crafts, and distinguished lecturers shared a stage with amateur theatrical productions. Like the Roycrofters, the Guild relied on catalogues to promote its distinctive line of hand-crafted metalwork (this despite Ashbee's dislike of advertising, an important exception to parallels with Hubbard); a 1905 catalog illustrated over one hundred examples of metalwork and jewelry.[55] The stunning work produced by Ashbee's Guild may have been an impetus for Hubbard to establish a more comprehensive metalwork operation at the Roycroft.

Local competition from the active community of metalsmiths in Buffalo, just a short train ride away from East Aurora, may have provided Hubbard with an even more compelling incentive to expand the metal line. A look at the work of the Heintz Art Metal shop in Buffalo suggests how Roycroft metalworkers may have expanded their repertoire of design and technique without traveling very far. An internationally-recognized source of handcrafted jewelry and decorative house-hold accessories, the Heintz facility linked commercial enterprise with local education through its designer, Bernard V. Carpenter, who also supervised the design department of the Buffalo Fine Arts Academy at the Albright Art Gallery. As the Roycroft Copper Shop was becoming more firmly established, the nearby Heintz shop was exhibiting its wares at the St. Louis Exposition (1904), advertising in the *Craftsman* and the *International Studio*, and receiving recognition in the German magazine *Kunst und Kunsthandwerk*.[56] Carpenter and Manley Blakeslee taught metalsmithing at the Buffalo Fine Arts Academy, where the 1908 catalogue described its "decorative design" course as "a thorough study of the principles of design and their application to book covers, wall papers, jewelry, metal work, enamel, wood carving, furniture, leather, stained glass, etc. . . . In connection with this course, classes under competent instructors furnish opportunity for the making of jewelry and artistic objects in metals, leather, and wood."[57]

Perhaps these courses helped lift Copper Shop goods from the domain of functional household accessories to the realm of aesthetic objects.

The fluid interchange of ideas during the Roycroft years was like the process of metalworking itself: philosophies, techniques, and designs from many sources were heated, combined, and hammered to yield a new and original form. The Roycroft community's best work pays homage to seminal influences while remaining distinctively Roycroftie. Kipp, Hunter, Jennings, and the other Roycroft alchemists collaborated and learned from outside experts, at home and abroad, as they helped the Roycroft Copper Shop develop its own formula for transforming ideas into a solid and shapely reality.

The authors are grateful to Jennifer Goyette, Rochester Institute of Technology intern at the Memorial Art Gallery, for assisting with research for this essay.

ENDNOTES

[1] Elbert Hubbard, foreword to *An American Bible*, ed. Alice Hubbard (East Aurora: The Roycrofters, 1911).

[2] Lindsey Denison, "Elbert Hubbard's Shop: An American William Morris at Work in East Aurora," *New York Sun*, 29 October 1899.

[3] For a full discussion of Connor's background and subsequent achievements, see Laurene Buckley's accompanying essay.

[4] Interview with Rixford Jennings, son of Walter U. Jennings, by Robert Rust, 21 June 1991.

[5] *A Catalog of Some Specimens of Art & Handicraft Done by Roycroft Workers* (East Aurora: The Roycrofters, [1900]). Item 40 describes a chandelier "made at the forge by Peter Robarge and Ernest Standeven."

[6] Information about the development of major campus buildings may be gleaned from the *East Aurora Advertiser* but, inexplicably, no mention has been found regarding the construction of the wooden Blacksmith Shop or the stone Copper Shop (and its subsequent additions). The dates included herein are based largely upon examination of period photographs and may be subject to revision as other documentation comes to light.

[7] "At the Roycroft," *East Aurora Advertiser*, 14 March 1907.

[8] Andirons were still being offered in the catalogue titled *Roycroft Furniture and Other Things* (ca. 1906), although these could have been left from previous stock, or Peter Robarge could have continued making them from his own blacksmith shop on Cazenovia Street. That catalogue also offered customers the choice of either iron or copper hardware on a fireplace wood box.

[9] See Laurene Buckley's accompanying essay.

[10] *Little Journeys to the Homes of Great Scientists: Tyndall*, 17, no. 4: facing page 84.

[11] Payroll records, Elbert Hubbard-Roycroft Museum.

[12] *Roycrofter* 1, no. 1 (June 1926): 12.

[13] Dard Hunter II, *The Life Work of Dard Hunter*, vol. 1 (Chillicothe: Mountain House Press, 1981), 177.

[14] Jennings interview, 21 June 1991.

[15] *The Society of Arts and Crafts, Boston: Exhibition Record 1897–1927*, ed. Karen Evans Ulehla (Boston: Boston Public Library, 1981), 121. Initially a member in the craftsman class (1914–1918), Jennings eventually achieved master craftsman status (1919–1927).

[16] These sketches have been preserved in the collection of Robert Rust and Kitty Turgeon-Rust.

[17] The Buffalo Art Students' League was a descendent of the Students Art Club, of which two founding members were Emma Johnson, later a Roycroft illuminator, and Harriet Taber, probably the daughter of Harry Taber, first owner of the Roycroft Press. Classes at the Buffalo Fine Arts Academy during the heyday of the Roycroft included decorative design, metalwork, woodcarving, bookbinding, and leather embossing. (Joyce Woelfle Lehmann, *The "Albright Art School" of the Buffalo Fine Arts Academy: 1887–1954* [Ph.D. diss., State University of New York at Buffalo, 1984], 32–68) A number of East Aurora residents (who may or may not have been affiliated with the Roycroft) are listed among the students enrolled in these classes between 1905 and 1918, including master bookbinder John Grabau, whose work for the Roycroft is well known. (Buffalo Fine Arts Academy, Art School Catalogues, Albright-Knox Art Gallery Library)

[18] The Copper Shop also served as the headquarters of Elbert Hubbard, Banker, beginning in May of 1912.

[19] Muriel Jennings Case, the daughter of Walter U. Jennings, recalled seeing the largest of the Grove Park lighting fixtures being assembled on the lawn in front of the Copper Shop because they would not fit through the door. (Interview with Robert Rust and Kitty Turgeon-Rust, November 1982) Fixtures identical to some of those made for the Grove Park Inn, with modifications to the length of the chains, were retained for use in Roycroft buildings, including the Copper Shop itself. The Roycrofters also produced over 400 pieces of furniture for the Grove Park Inn's public rooms. The GPI is still in operation and, appropriately, is the site of an annual conference devoted to the study of the Arts and Crafts movement. For a detailed history of the Inn's development, see Bruce Johnson, *A History of the Grove Park Inn* (Asheville: The Grove Park Inn and Country Club, 1991).

[20] A paper knife illustrated in an advertisement for Roycroft copper wares in the November 1911 issue of the *Fra* displays Kipp's own back-to-back "double K" mark, suggesting that he was producing work on his own, perhaps interchangeably with objects he was making for Hubbard.

[21] An advertisement in the *East Aurora Advertiser* of 16 May 1912 announced the 21 May opening of the Tookay Shop at 636 Main Street in East Aurora, just a few blocks east of the Roycroft campus. It is possible that Kipp continued to do some contractual work for Hubbard, including a portion of the Grove Park commission.

[22] Jennings interview, 21 June 1991.

[23] Bruce E. Johnson, "The Roycroft Copper Shop & the Grove Park Inn: A New Discovery," *Arts & Crafts Conference Catalog* (1992), 30.

[24] 1910 Census (microfilm), Aurora Historian's Office. Likewise, Toothaker's departure date is unknown, but it was sometime prior to 1927. The "Local and Personal" column of the *East Aurora Advertiser* of 25 August of that year notes that "Mr. Toothaker visited his friends during his stay in East Aurora and fully maintained his position as a raconteur."

[25] The authors thank Warren Moffett, Aurora Town Historian, for this piece of information, supplied to him by Belle Knights, Hubbard's personal secretary and Toothaker's sister-in-law.

[26] *The Roycrofter* 5, no. 4 (February 1931): 112.

[27] The last ad for the Karl Kipp Shop (formerly the Tookay Shop) appeared in the *East Aurora Advertiser* on 19 April 1917. The following week it was replaced by an ad for a new shop operated by Ralph Case, who had purchased Kipp's business and moved it two doors down.

[28] Although there were "Roycroft Branches" selling Roycroft products in both the Fine Arts Building on Michigan Avenue in Chicago and Carnegie Hall on 56th Street in New York by late 1905, this venture appears to have been short-lived. (*Philistine* 22, no. 1 [December 1905])

[29] *Roycroft* 3, no. 2 (October 1918) listed 149 branch stores. In that issue, Bert Hubbard cautioned readers that "because so many of the Roycroft craftsmen have been called into service, there necessarily will be a shortage of Roycroft goods this Fall. We are glad to have the boys go—We will all go if necessary! However, those of us who are still at home will continue to make beautiful things by hand and fill your orders the very best we can." (xiv)

[30] A 13 May 1994 letter from Sandra Fagbemi, Pratt Institute associate registrar, confirms Cole's presence there from 15 April to 25 June 1920.

[31] A business card in the Leon Varley file in Roycroft Arts Museum archive shows him as a partner, along with Fred Marshall, in the East Aurora Realty.

[32] Unidentified and undated newsclipping, Archives, Roycroft Arts Museum. The Sloyd System, originally developed in Sweden, was a program of manual training based on experience gained in woodworking.

[33] Karl Kipp to Bert Hubbard, 25 April 1928, Archives, Roycroft Arts Museum. The memo indicates that Kipp tried to save the talented Walter Jennings by having him reassigned to the Bindery; an attached note indicates that the transfer did occur the following year.

[34] Bert wrote: "I hope you can swing the proposed purchase and take it all over . . . But if you can't, then I have to . . . cut the pay-roll down to a mere skeleton and just produce such stuff as may be on special order, and concentrate our effort on reducing stock on hand. All of this would mean that the department would need little supervision and no new designing. By the end of the year we would know definitely if we would continue the department on any basis at all. The new policy would mean that you would have to go into something else. This of course I regret . . . but . . . no matter what happens we have a lot of years of pleasant memories and association." (Copper Shop file, Archives, Roycroft Arts Museum)

[35] A note indicates that Walter Jennings, Henry Unverdorf, Edward Kingston, Maynard Hausauer, DeWitt Wood, Adolph Eble, and Howard Darling were laid off on 13 April 1929. This left Arthur Cole, George Willson, Roy Johnson, two "platers," and two "girls" on staff. (Copper Shop file, Archives, Roycroft Arts Museum)

[36] "Roycroft Activities," *East Aurora Advertiser*, 9 May 1929.

[37] Arthur H. Cole to Bert Hubbard, 1 June 1929, Archives, Roycroft Arts Museum.

[38] See Frederick Brandt's accompanying essay.

[39] Jennings interview, 21 June 1991.

[40] "East Aurora's Lights," *Time* (7 December 1931): 64.

[41] For a discussion of the relationship between the Viennese and the Glaswegians, see Peter Vergo, *Art in Vienna 1898–1918* (London: Phaidon Press Ltd., 1975).

[42] For example, a Prang textbook, *Art Education for High Schools: A Comprehensive Text Book on Art Education for High Schools Treating Pictorial, Decorative, and Constructive Art, Historic Ornament, and Art History* (New York: The Prang Educational Company, 1908), was owned by Cecil Jackson, a second-generation Roycrofter who attended the public school across the street from the Roycroft. Also, during this period, training in manual or applied arts, which included metalwork, was a standard offering in public schools. The Chautauqua Institution, located southwest of East Aurora, offered Arts and Crafts courses in metalwork as early as 1903. (W. Scott Braznell, "Metalsmithing and Jewelrymaking," in *The Ideal Home: The History of Twentieth-Century American Craft 1900–1920*, ed. Janet Kardon, [New York: Harry N. Abrams, in association with the American Craft Museum, 1993], 56) It also organized an Arts and Crafts conference in 1902. (Michael

James, "The Heintz Connection: Otto L. Heintz and His Art Metal Shops," *Arts & Crafts Quarterly* 6, no. 1 [Spring 1993]: 13) Hubbard's involvement with Chautauqua is mentioned elsewhere in this catalogue.

[43] The Aurora Historical Society owns a bound volume of *Deutsche Kunst und Dekoration* from 1906 with a printed label stating: "Property of the Roycroft Library. Do Not Remove from the Inn."

[44] A review of the Home Arts and Industries Exhibition at the Albert Hall states: "Wrought and hammered metal is always one of the most prolific and popular branches of the [Home Arts and Industries] Association's work." (*International Studio* 11 [1900]: 85)

[45] Alan Crawford, *C. R. Ashbee: Architect, Designer & Romantic Socialist* (New Haven: Yale University Press, 1985), 407.

[46] See Braznell, "Metalsmithing and Jewelrymaking," for an overview of the range of expositions, schools, and other phenomena which contributed to public awareness of art metalwork.

[47] Specific mention is made of "bronze jardinieres" and "figures of hand hammered copper" which were included in a German arts and crafts display in the Varied Industries department. (*Louisiana and the Fair*, vol. 3, ed. James W. Buel [St. Louis: World's Progress Publishing Company, 1904–05], 3425)

[48] "Local and Personal," *East Aurora Advertiser*, 30 June 1904.

[49] *Golden Book of the Wanamaker Stores, Jubilee Year 1861–1911* (Philadelphia: John Wanamaker, 1911), 242.

[50] Ibid.

[51] John Heskett, *German Design 1870–1918* (New York: Taplinger Publishing Company, 1986), 48.

[52] Crawford, *C. R. Ashbee*, 97.

[53] See Frederick Brandt's accompanying essay.

[54] Robert W. Winter, "American Sheaves from 'C. R. A.' and Janet Ashbee," *Journal of the Society of Architectural Historians* 30 (1971): 321. The visit would have occurred sometime between the Guild's move to Chipping Campden in 1902 and Ashbee's replacement as manager of the Guild by J. T. Webster in 1907.

[55] Crawford, *C. R. Ashbee*, 340.

[56] Michael James, "The Heintz Connection," 12.

[57] Lehmann, *The "Albright Art School"*, 47.

The Roycroft Mark

[1] Elbert Hubbard, "Roycroft Trademark," *The Feather Duster* 1, no. 2 (21 October 1907).

[2] Ernst Lehner, *Symbols, Signs & Signets* (Cleveland and New York: The World Publishing Company, 1950), 194, 197. The cross and orb is also an ancient Christian symbol, as well as a British monarchial sign. For an entertaining discussion of the many possible origins of this mark, including its purported use in the Great Pyramid at Gizah, see "Owner of Roycroft Inn Seeks Origin of Hubbard Symbol," *East Aurora Advertiser*, 13 May 1948.

[3] Alternatively, a printed Roycroft gift tag traces the mark to Cassiodorus, a monk who supposedly lived in the Middle Ages and used the the cross and circle to represent Unity and Infinity. The writer explained that they had divided the circle into three parts, signifying Faith, Hope, and Love, adding the *R* to stand for the Roycrofters.

[4] *The Official Gazette* 125, part 2 (December 1906): 1680. Michael James has kindly provided this piece of information.

[5] Interview with Rixford Jennings by Robert Rust, 21 June 1991. Jennings, the son of Roycroft master metal craftsman Walter U. Jennings, visited the Copper Shop regularly from childhood, and hence became thoroughly familiar with its workings.

[6] This should not be confused with Kipp's Tookay shopmark, which also consisted of back-to-back *K*s and the legend *Hand Wrought* bisecting a hammer, with the words *Karl Kipp East Aurora* encircling the whole.

[7] Jennings's later work, designed and made in his own studio, is marked in three known ways: with his signature, *Walter U. Jennings*, in script; with his initials, the *J* bisecting the *W*; and with a circle trisected by horizontal lines, the outer two being longer than the inner.

The Roycroft Modeled Leather Department:
Its Evolution and History

CHARLES F. HAMILTON

The historical roots of the Roycroft Modeled Leather Department, formed in 1905, may be traced back to the origin of the Roycroft Bookbinding Department. Early on, books printed at the Roycroft Print Shop had been bound by an independent bindery in nearby Buffalo. Not happy with the outside work, Hubbard decided to set up a bindery at his own Print Shop. In explaining that decision, he wrote that "the man in Buffalo could not bind books any more than the 'Blizzard' man could print and the fact was faced that the Roycrofters must bind their books; but to bind books is an art. Then it was after much searching that a Leipsic bookbinder was found."[1]

The bookbinder was Louis Kinder, an expert who had learned the craft at Leipsic, Germany, where he served seven years as apprentice to a master.[2] He was thoroughly familiar with leather modeling, incising and skiving.[3] Hubbard appreciated and collected well-crafted works of art, including paintings, pottery, fine examples of leather modeling, and exquisitely bound books. For his own pleasure, he acquired specimens of the work of great binders, including Riviere, Zahn, Cobden-Sanderson, and Zaensdorf.[4] It was natural that he should seek out Kinder in 1896 and encourage him to lead Roycrofters-in-training to aim for equal excellence.

In addition to doing much of the special binding work himself, Kinder immediately found himself training new employees as well as Roycrofters wishing to transfer from other departments. In the beginning, his only helpers were "two girls working at illuminating who found the work difficult, so they were allowed to help the bookbinder," Hubbard told his first biographer, Albert Lane, in 1901. Hubbard further explained that "it is against Roycroft ideas to send anyone away who really wants to work, so if they cannot do one thing well we let them try their hands at something else."[5]

It was common practice to "send over" employees from one department to another, depending upon the workloads of the various departments. Some were multi-skilled and others were temporarily transferred to help out in some manner to the extent of their capabilities. But whenever possible, the loaned employees were those who had expressed a desire to learn an additional craft or line of work.[6] In retrospect, this was an early example of a far-sighted employee training practice, set in motion by Hubbard as soon as his employee roster and number of departments had grown sizeable. The practice was beneficial to employee and employer alike and ambitious workers jumped at the opportunities presented.[7]

Lane wrote: "People liked Roycroft work . . . and the Little Man from Leipsic began to work miracles in levant . . . More girls were hired, and to supply them with materials, more boys too."[8] By 1901 Kinder's department employed sixty persons[9] and a new wing to house the Bindery was eventually added to the original Print Shop.[10] Kinder's staff represented almost a third of the 175 Roycroft employees reported in 1900.[11] Frederick C. Kranz, skilled in leather modeling, soon joined Kinder's staff. It was said that he too had studied the craft in Germany.[12]

As the production of leather-bound books grew (using both limp and fine leathers), leftover material accumulated. Some of this was sold as scrap and

Plate 118: *Armchair Ashtray*, ca. 1926. Leather and copper, $7/8 \times 13\frac{3}{4} \times 1\frac{3}{8}$ in. *The Charles Rand Penney Collection of Works by Roycroft Artists at the Burchfield-Penney Art Center, Buffalo State College.*

Plate 119: *Elbert Hubbard Portrait Bookends*, ca. 1915. Leather and fabric over iron and cardboard, 5⅞ × 4⅝ in. (each).
Collection of Richard Blacher.

Fig. 64: *The Roycroft Leather Book* of 1909, featuring a cover designed by Dard Hunter.
(Courtesy Turgeon-Rust Collection)

some, particularly goat and sheep skin, was used to fashion stuffed pillows to sell to out-of-town visitors as well as to local residents. The pillows, measuring twenty by twenty inches and bearing the Roycroft mark in one corner, sold for four and five dollars, according to quality.

Enterprising as they were, the Roycrofters soon struck upon the idea of making and merchandising other gift items made of leather, first from scrap and then from larger pieces ordered specifically for that purpose. As an increasing number of visitors to the Roycroft campus returned home with attractive souvenirs, the sale of leather products grew significant enough to warrant the creation of a department separate from Kinder's ever more busy Bindery.

Kranz was sent over from his position as Kinder's assistant to head that new department.

Prior to 1905, promotion of leather goods was done strictly by word of mouth, and Hubbard probably lost no

Plate 120: *Fragment of Frieze from Alice Hubbard's Office.* Design attributed to Frederick Kranz.
Leather, 13 × 91 in.
Roycroft Arts Museum, Boice Lydell.

opportunity to mention this new venture on his lecture circuit. But the 1905-06 *Roycroft Catalog of Some Things Made by The Roycrofters at Their Shop Opposite the School House in East Aurora* (a typically Hubbard-esque title, long and folksy) heralded in print the creation of the new department: "Our Modeled Leather Department is under the immediate direction of our Mr. Frederick Kranz who is thoroughly familiar with all kinds of repoussé, modeled and incised stained and illumined leather work that is produced in this country and in Europe." This introduction was followed by a modest list of leather product offerings, in addition to the pillows that had started it all: single-and three-panel screens at $25 to $250, chairs at $25 to $125, a desk pad and blotter wiper at $2, and music rolls at $4 to $5. Addition-

ally, guest books bound and decorated with monograms, coats-of-arms, and other special marks could be ordered from the Modeled Leather Department.

Initially, the department's offerings were advertised supplementally in the annual Roycroft book catalogues and the studios were located in the Bindery building. But in 1907 the Leather Department moved to separate quarters on the second floor of the Furniture Shop[13] and by 1909 rated a catalogue of its own, *The Roycroft Leather Book*. In the introduction, Hubbard wrote: "The Germans lead the world in craftsmanship, just as they have in musical composition. The Roycrofters imported the Germans—the Teutons did the rest!" He was, of course, referring to Kinder and Kranz and went on to say, "They have taught this wonderful Art to a

Plate 121: *Alice Hubbard's Portfolio*, ca. 1910. Design attributed to Frederick Kranz.
Leather, 11½ × 8½ in. (closed).
Roycroft Arts Museum, Boice Lydell.

five cents for children's styles to ten dollars for five-pocket ladies' purses. There were also design variations. The same was true for the many other items listed, utilitarian as well as ornamental.

Kranz now had administrative duties but, having been a leather modeler in the Bindery, very likely still performed some production work in the new department he headed.[14] He was listed on the Roycroft payroll through April of 1915, at which point he was earning thirty dollars per week,[15] but as early as 1913 he was preparing to leave, for he had also opened his own leather business, the Cordova Shop, in nearby Buffalo.

Two others who figured prominently in the Leather Department were Charles Youngers and George ScheideMantel. As a teenager, Youngers was first employed at the Roycroft Print Shop in 1898 to feed the presses at three dollars per week (the same amount paid to Elbert Hubbard II, the founder's son). In due course, Youngers was sent over to Kinder to learn bookbinding and leather modeling. When Kinder left the Roycroft in

Plate 122: *Standing Picture Frame*, ca. 1915. Design attributed to Frederick Kranz. Leather and silk, 11¼ × 6¾ in.
Private collection.

score or more of Roycroft boys and girls, so now we believe we are producing the best work in this line in America." The product range had expanded considerably in just four years. Listed in that catalogue were twenty-six basic leather lines and many variations within them. For example, purses alone included children's purses, saddle purses, men's purses, women's purses, and change purses. These ranged in price from seventy-

Plate 124: *Jewel Box*, ca. 1910. Design attributed to Frederick Kranz. Leather, 1¾ × 4½ in. diam.
Collection of Kitty Turgeon Rust and Robert Rust, Roycroft Shops.

1912, Youngers succeeded him as head of the Bindery. He rose to the post of Secretary of the Roycroft Corporation and remained with the Roycroft until it declared bankruptcy in 1938.[16]

ScheideMantel had worked briefly as a bellboy at the Roycroft Inn (fall of 1905 to spring of 1906) before taking a higher-paying position with the railroad. In 1913, he secured a job at the Cordova Shop and was tutored by Kranz, who was by then dividing his time between working at the Roycroft and operating Cordova. When Kranz resigned from the Roycroft in 1915 to devote all his time to his own shop, ScheideMantel was offered, and quickly accepted, the vacated department head position, with supervisory responsibility for eight to ten people. In 1918 he resigned to open his

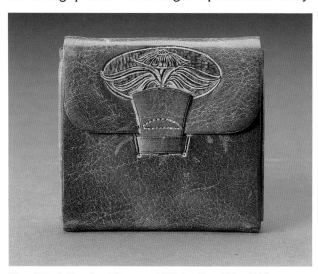

Plate 123: *Calling Card Case*, ca. 1917. Leather, 3½ × 3¼ in.
Private collection.

Plate 125: *Mantel Clock*, ca. 1919. Leather with standard clock works, 4⅝ × 6⅛ × 2 in. *Elbert Hubbard-Roycroft Museum.*

own design studio at his Oakwood Avenue home in East Aurora.[17] His work with leather inlay, an aspect of leathercrafting little pursued by the Roycroft, is especially beautiful.

After Kranz's departure in 1915, the Roycroft catalogues still touted the beauty and fine craftsmanship of the modeled leather items but no longer made mention of the department head by name. It seems clear that ScheideMantel's tenure was not deemed sufficient to warrant proclaiming him another Kranz, despite the fact that he was a superb craftsman. In *The Book of the Roycrofters*, a combination history and advertisement issued in 1921, three years after ScheideMantel's departure, a section on the book-binding and leather modeling operations included separate group photographs of their respective staffs. The Bindery photograph showed twenty-five workers; there were eleven in the leather modeling group.[18] A separate portrait of Charles Youngers provided the focal point of the picture pages. The caption gave his title as Superintendent of Bindery and Modeled Leather, indicating there were no longer separate heads for each function, as had been the case from 1905 through 1918.

The early to mid-1920s were productive and profitable years for most facets of the Roycroft operation under the leadership of Bert Hubbard, who headed the community following his father's death in the 1915 sinking of the *Lusitania*. By 1923, Helen Willson Ess and Edith Cole were the only two leather modelers still employed at the Roycroft, working under the direction of Karl Kipp in the Copper Shop, and by 1925 the Leather Department had been phased out of existence.[19]

From 1924 through 1927, the catalogues and other mailers indicated a shift from leather products to finely-bound Roycroft books and custom-binding work, along with art metal and other non-leather gift items. A thin catalogue produced in 1931, *Roycroft Modern Gift Wares*, was largely devoted to metal products. Some leather-bound books were offered, but the only other mention of leather was in reference to the corner trim of the blotter pads on two of nine styles of art metal desk sets.

Much of the success of the Roycroft Leather Department was due to Elbert Hubbard's exceptional talent as a "can do" motivator. In a series of interviews conducted in 1963, eleven of Hubbard's former employees spoke highly of him and praised Roycroft as a place to work.[20] Perhaps even more importantly, Hubbard was a skillful marketer. Through the *Philistine*, the *Fra*, and appearances on the national lecture circuit, he focused wide attention on the whole range of the Roycrofters' Arts and Crafts output.

Ralph Waldo Emerson once asserted that every institution is the lengthening shadow of one person. Elbert Hubbard's shadow was broadened and lengthened by the skilled craftspeople, artists, and writers he hired. They, with the unskilled workers they trained, gave meaning to his motto: "Head, Heart and Hand."

MAKING A MODELED LEATHER ARTICLE

Helen Willson Ess, who worked in the Roycroft Modeled Leather Department during George ScheideMantel's tenure as director, recalled the process by which the leather objects were made:

The girls would model leather by wetting the surface to make it soft and pliable. Then a paper pattern would be laid over it and traced out with a dull knife. Or, if a lot were needed at once, a heavy patterned cardboard was placed on top of the leather and a light pattern would be stamped on it. When the pattern was removed, the outline was scored with a sharp knife. The lines were then opened from the front with a modeling tool.

The areas to be raised were molded out by holding a zinc bar on the front while modeling from the back, to raise the desired designs into relief. Next, the back indentations were filled with a glucose-sawdust mixture. The designs were then smoothed out from the front and backgrounds were pounded and stamped, using metal tools with designs on the ends and a leather-headed hammer. As the glucose-sawdust mixture dried, the high area would remain in relief.

Next, the leather had to be stained. This was done in a small room in a corner of the Leather Department by Jerry Youngers, Carl Ewald and Otto Wagner. Days later, the almost-finished products would go back to the girls for lacing the seams. An awl would be used to punch holes around the edges of the article, and the leather lacing, with a paste-hardened end, was woven in and out of the holes. That finished the product.

Each girl had her own marble slab to work on and her own tools. We usually turned out two or three pieces a day, and would do different designs and articles each time, if possible.

(From notes of an undated interview with Helen Willson Ess, Roycroft Arts Museum archive)

The author wishes to thank Bruce Bland, Co-Curator of the Elbert Hubbard-Roycroft Museum, for his special cooperation in the preparation of this manuscript.

ENDNOTES

[1] *Some Books for Sale at Our Shop* (East Aurora: The Roycrofters, 1900), 14. Before acquiring his own printing press in 1895, Hubbard had briefly tried the printing services of a local newspaper, referred to in jest as the *Blizzard*.

[2] *The Roycroft Shop: Being a History* (East Aurora: The Roycrofters, 1908), 12. This oft-repeated fact, like many gleaned from Hubbard's own accounts, has yet to be corroborated by other sources.

[3] Skiving is the technique of splitting leather into thin pieces when more flexibility is desired for making wallets, purses, and so on.

[4] *The Roycroft Shop: Being a History*, 12.

[5] Albert Lane, *Elbert Hubbard and His Work* (Worcester: The Blanchard Press, 1901), 40.

[6] Copies of Roycroft payroll records (incomplete) in the Charles F. Hamilton Collection. For example, Anna Green, listed in a payroll sheet as a "detailer" in the Leather Department at four dollars per week, was transferred to the office at five dollars per week in December of 1909 and returned to the Leather Department in March of 1910.

[7] See Irene Gardner, "A Little Journey to the Home of Elbert Hubbard," *Toledo Sunday Times-Bee*, 26 July 1903. She describes the Roycroft campus and activities and addresses the "fair wage" question at some length: "Elbert Hubbard has often been accused of paying low wages. The wages paid are probably in many cases not so high as similar work might bring elsewhere. But wages alone, it must be said, in all fairness, do not represent the pay of a Roycrofter. In the first place, with but very few exceptions, the workers have been taught all they know in regard to the work in that establishment. And then, aside from the many educational advantages offered them and also aside from the almost inestimable benefit derived from the atmosphere of mutual equality that permeates the place, there is much done for the Roycrofter individually by Elbert Hubbard that is known only to those who have been closely in touch with them."

[8] Lane, *Elbert Hubbard and His Work*, 41.

[9] Ibid., 44.

[10] Ibid., 41.

[11] *Some Books for Sale at Our Shop*, 14.

[12] *A Catalog of Some Books and Things* (East Aurora: The Roycrofters, 1906), 27. See also Tran Turner's accompanying essay.

[13] "Better Facilities," *East Aurora Advertiser*, 24 January 1907.

[14] It is difficult to determine from the few existing payroll records just how many workers Kranz had solely under his direction. One extant roster of key Roycroft employees from all departments during the 1903 period listed Frederick Kranz, Katherine Comstock, and Cordelia Comstock, among others, as leather modelers. John Comstock was listed as a designer. Bookbinders included Miss Burns, Peter Franck, Louis Kinder, Sterling Lord, and Charles Youngers. (Payroll records, Charles F. Hamilton Collection)

[15] Ibid.

[16] Charles F. Hamilton, *Little Journeys to the Homes of Roycrofters* (East Aurora: S-G Press, 1963), 4, 5, 13.

[17] Ibid., 30–34. The ScheideMantel home is now the Elbert Hubbard-Roycroft Museum.

[18] Of those pictured, nine in the Bindery and six in the Leather Department were women.

[19] Undated interview with Helen Willson Ess by Boice Lydell, Roycroft Arts Museum archive.

[20] See Hamilton, *Little Journeys to the Homes of Roycrofters*.

Charles F. Hamilton is the author of *As Bees in Honey Drown*, *Roycroft Collectibles*, *Alice Hubbard: A Feminist Recalled*, and many other books and articles about Elbert Hubbard and the Roycroft. A founding member of the Roycrofters-at-Large Association, Mr. Hamilton is now a public relations consultant and free-lance writer in Florida.

"Like a Portrait by Rembrandt"
Design Ideals in Roycroft Leather

TRAN TURNER

Both before and after the death of Elbert and Alice Hubbard in 1915, the Roycrofters mounted an advertising campaign designed to make their products seem rare and artistically significant. Whether the advertisements appeared in the *Fra*, the *Philistine*, *Little Journeys*, or one of the numerous Roycroft sales catalogues, it was often a matter of indirectly linking their artistic output to famous artists such as Hans Holbein or Albrecht Dürer.[1] One ad for modeled leather stated that "it [was] all done by hand, like a portrait by Rembrandt."[2] Other advertisements created histories for the objects to intensify the European connection. In the case of leather, readers were reminded that the Moors had brought the art form to Venice, or that during the ninth century, towns along the Rhine had used a similar technique developed by the Egyptians.[3]

Although Hubbard saw the Roycroft community as an "exponent of the American philosophy," the European relationships he established forged an ideological bond with William Morris, John Ruskin, and Thomas Carlyle, early exponents of the Arts and Crafts philosophy and antagonists of industrialism. What the advertisements sold, then, in addition to Roycroft books, metalwork, furniture, and leather items, was a romanticized image of the centuries-old tradition of native craftsmen using superior skills to create beauty with their own hands. The consumer was encouraged to view the progressive design qualities of contemporary Roycroft products as the extension of a tradition well worth preserving.

Beyond suggesting links to objects of historical and artistic significance, the advertisements also claimed support from museums and from the highest pillars of worship. The Roycrofters pointed out, for example, that specimens of their fine bindings could be seen at the Vatican.[4] This proselytizing was offered to persuade consumers that their purchases were investments— that they were art objects, with significant lineage and a "divine" testimonial, which ultimately could bring a return on the money.

Additionally, certain advertisements for Roycroft leather likened the technique of modeling to the creation of bas-relief sculpture, establishing a link with three-dimensional art.[5] References to Rembrandt, the Vatican, and sculpture all created powerful images, whether or not they were relevant to the object at hand.

Discussions of the Roycroft's aesthetic achievements remained understated in its advertising. Other than using a few atmospheric words and phrases, such as "inspirational," "rare," "strikingly original," and "distinctly representative of the Roycroft standard," Hubbard did not make meaningful public statements about design principles. Technique, on the other hand, was addressed quite often, especially for bookbinding and leatherwork. For example, Frederick C. Kranz, the Leather Department's first director, wrote two full pages in the *Fra* combining history, education, and information about the process of leather crafting at the Roycroft.[6]

The aesthetic merits of the Roycroft's various products, however, are clearly discernible and the beauty of the designs was certainly among the factors that attracted potential buyers. An examination of the sources of their design concepts suggests that the Roycrofters' real contribution was as tastemakers

Plate 126: *Handbag*, ca. 1918. Leather with metal frame, 9 × 7⅛ in. *Collection of Debbie and David Dalton Rudd.*

Plate 127: *Tooled Leather Arm Chair*, ca. 1906. Oak and leather with brass tacks, 37⅝ × 24 × 25¾ in. Stamped with "R 019" inventory code. *Elbert Hubbard-Roycroft Museum.*

rather than as innovators. They synthesized contemporary European trends and successfully introduced them to a large American audience.

As Charles F. Hamilton points out in his accompanying essay, the Roycroft had begun a separate, full-time department for the production of leather items other than book bindings by 1905. Twenty years later, the Roycrofters laid claim to pioneering the "revival of [this] beautiful and distinctive art."[7] Sometimes their forms exhibit direct interaction with the surface designs, as does the architectonic sewing basket, but these examples are few. Overall, the aesthetic emphasis is on decoration rather than the integration of surface and form to produce a uniquely Arts and Crafts profile. This distinction is central to an understanding of how the designers of Roycroft leather approached the expression of their ideas.

Prior to 1910, during the formative period of the Leather Department with Kranz and his "pupils" at the helm, the design impetus came from the Print Shop and the Bindery, both of which had been established as necessary complements to Hubbard's publishing interests. Kranz, when employed by Hubbard as his "Master Leather Modeler," initially directed his talents to the design of book covers. As he and his colleagues

Plate 128: *Prototype for Book Cover.*
Leather over cardboard, 8¾ × 6 in.
Collection of Jean-François Vilain and Roger S. Wieck.

developed the Roycroft's other leather products, including purses, cases, portfolios, and a myriad of items for the home, they continued to treat them, at least formally, as flat surfaces. The style was expressed by the ornamentation of the two-dimensional plane.

Plate 129: *Sewing Basket*, ca. 1911. Designed by Frederick Kranz.
Leather, 2¾ × 8½ in. diam.
Private collection.

Jean-François Vilain shows in his accompanying essay that the artists at the Roycroft assimilated many design interests of the time. The Leather Department, however, showed a clear tendency toward Art Nouveau, a style that originated in Europe and encompassed the Jugendstil in Munich, L'Art Nouveau in Paris, the Sezession in Vienna, Stile Liberty in Italy, plus a host of similarly developed interests throughout Scandinavia, Russia, and other European countries.[8] Kranz had received his training in Germany, possibly with Professor Brinkmann at the School of Industrial Arts in Hamburg.[9] His education was probably rooted in this aesthetic ideology and he was certainly sensitive to the design principles involved. The German influence on the Roycroft's leather artists was underscored by advertisements that made reference to parallel activities in Germany, specifically those at the Darmstadt Art Colony.[10]

Even prior to the establishment of the Roycroft Leather Department, "Master Binder" Louis Kinder and his staff of bookbinders were able to keep abreast of Europe's contemporary aesthetic activities. The Roycroft library contained a complete run of *International Studio*, a magazine devoted to new schools of thought in the fine and applied arts, and received monthly issues of the German periodicals *Dekorative Kunst, Deutsches Kunst Und Dekoration*, and *Dekorative Vorbilder.*[11] These magazines were filled with articles and images representing the architecture, decorative arts, and graphic designs of Europe's progressive artists.

The magazines also introduced the "modern tendency in design" to the young Dard Hunter, who arrived at the Roycroft about the same time as Kranz and became perhaps the leading proponent of Art Nouveau design ideals among the artists in that community. Hunter wrote that "these magazines were a monthly inspiration, and many of the commercial designs I made during my early years at the [Roycroft printing] shop show this influence."[12] In fact, Hunter was so taken with

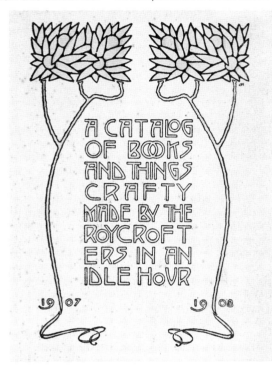

Fig. 65: Dard Hunter's design for the cover of the Roycrofters' 1907–1908 sales catalog.
(Courtesy Tran Turner)

the character of German Jugendstil and the Viennese Sezession that he went to Vienna in 1908, as part of a honeymoon trip. While there, he visited the Wiener Werkstätte (Vienna Workshop), met several influential artists, and studied contemporary architectural projects. He enthusiastically imparted the modernist aesthetic he had absorbed to his fellow Roycrofters upon his return to East Aurora later that year.[13]

During his six years at the Roycroft, Hunter made two pivotal contributions to the new aesthetic standard that developed as a collective consciousness among the various departments. He applied to Roycroft graphics, metalwork, and leaded glass the rectilinear motifs made popular by artists at the Wiener Werkstätte (including Koloman Moser and Josef Hoffmann) and the Glasgow School (specifically Charles Rennie Mackintosh and Margaret Macdonald). Secondly, he encouraged the use of the organic whiplash attributes of French, Belgian, and Italian Art Nouveau in Roycroft leatherwork.

One stellar example of Roycroft leather worked in the manner of organic Art Nouveau is a wastebasket depicting a fully-developed *fleur-de-lis*. The floral theme

Plate 130: *Wastebasket*, ca. 1910. Design attributed to Frederick Kranz. Leather over cardboard, 15 × 9 in. diam.
Collection of Charles F. Hamilton.

alternates three times with a curvilinear structure that both encapsulates the flora-form and creates a series of three open planes of rational space. These open areas are not unlike "negative space" given to three-dimensional objects, but here establish a decorative void on a two-dimensional surface, calling to mind, for example, the graphic designs of Henry van de Velde in turn-of-the-century Belgium.

Fig. 66 Henry Van de Velde, *Tropon*, 1898. Color lithograph.
(Courtesy Norwest Corporation)

The wastebasket's decoration possesses an un-bridled vitality seldom equaled in other Roycroft leather designs. (It also bears an intriguing resemblance to the flora-form pattern on a modeled leather armchair designed by the Italian Liberty Movement architect Ernesto Basile in 1903 for the firm of Ducrot and Company.[14])

Fig. 67: Ernesto Basile (for Ducrot and Company), *Armchair*, 1903. Wood and leather.
(Courtesy Dr. Prof. Rossana Bossaglia)

There is no question that Kranz, or one of his more advanced students, would have executed the modeling of the leather for such an impressive piece. Kranz, who is credited with the design of this wastebasket, could certainly have been aware of both van de Velde's and Basile's work and was no doubt stimulated by Hunter's ideas as well.

The legacy of Hunter's design ideas can also be detected in an autograph book decorated with his signature squared-rose motif. Although it was executed by Walter Jennings after Hunter's departure from the Roycroft, the configuration of linear patterns made up of squares, rectangles, and light and dark contrasts is a direct link with Hunter's fine graphic work.

The Roycroft's leather objects were not signed with an artist's monogram and were seldom credited to a specific designer in the advertising. When a particular Roycroft artist was identified with an item, it was usually to tout the singular nature of a piece and justify its price.

Plate 131: *Autograph Book*, ca. 1913. Designed and executed by Walter Jennings. Leather, German silver, and paper, 10⅝ × 6¾ in. *Collection of Mr. and Mrs. Rixford Jennings.*

One notable example is a three-panel screen, decorated with a modeled landscape in which a flock of ducks takes flight from a lake, credited to Frederick C. Kranz.[15] More often than not, however, the leather designers were as anonymous during their Roycroft careers as they remain today.

Periodicals and trade publications of the time reveal that the Roycrofters were not alone in their attraction to European Art Nouveau. Two published in nearby Syracuse, New York, were Gustav Stickley's *Craftsman* and Adelaide Alsop Robineau's *Keramic Studio*. Stickley's widely circulated magazine, in particular, was America's most accessible source of written and photographic accounts of the international design expositions.

Robineau's *Keramic Studio* was devoted to the interests of amateur and professional china painters. With page after page of designs, many of which were reprints taken directly from European magazines, it too became an index of sorts for international aesthetic developments. Because of Robineau's personal interest in French high-fire ceramics (especially contemporary work drawing upon Asian ceramic traditions) as models for her own work in porcelain, many of the designs published in her magazine were associated with French Art Nouveau. Between 1899 and 1909, *Keramic Studio* offered designs for plate borders with names like *Lotus*,

Cigale d'Afrique

papiers de Garde Guipure Ombrelle Flacon Vignette

Mr. Dufrene.

THE CICADA

From Art et Decoration

Fig. 68: Cicada motifs from *Art et Decoration*. (As published in *Keramic Studio*, November 1904)

Dragonfly, Moth, and *Ivy.* These and many related patterns were clearly responsive to the design character of Art Nouveau, with its naturalistic subjects and fervently organic presence. When the Roycrofters initiated their independent Leather Department in 1905, they began to produce circular mats for the dining table using designs strikingly similar to those presented in Robineau's journal, some even bearing the same names.

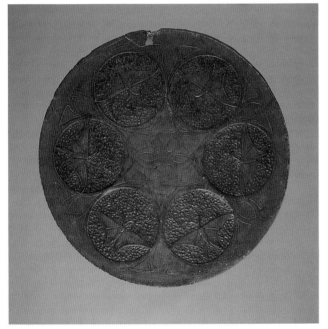

Plate 132: *Table Mat,* ca. 1911. Designed by Frederick Kranz.
Leather, 22¼ in. diam.
Aurora Historical Society.

Toward the back of each issue of *Keramic Studio* was a regular article titled "The Crafts," which provided historical overviews of a variety of media, answered questions about technique, offered spirited debate on philosophical issues, delivered statements on contemporary design concerns, and reviewed exhibitions.[16] The topic of leather found its way into those pages quite frequently, where the emphasis generally was on the review of work produced by artists throughout the country. A 1907 issue of *Keramic Studio* advertised an art leather gathering in Chicago, the second annual event of its type. Artists who worked in leather were invited to take advantage of the opportunity to exhibit their work at "the largest and most comprehensive display of leather work ever held in this country."[17] While there is no evidence that Roycrofters participated in the event, it is clear there were many opportunities for them to become familiar with aesthetic trends both here and abroad. It is also likely that they were influenced by ceramic art to a greater degree than might previously have been suspected.

Ultimately, Roycroft leather designers drew their inspiration from European sources and those American magazines that brought them to national attention, and Elbert Hubbard promoted and legitimized the objects through favorable comparisons with masterpieces of both European and American art. An advertisement in a 1911 issue of the *Fra* articulated the Roycrofters' inclusive and democratic aesthetic, one that mirrored the eclectic nature of their community: "Roycroft Modeled Leather is like Rookwood Pottery or Tiffany Glass . . . Beauty knows no rival. There is simply other beauty."[18]

Plate 133: *Hand Mirror,* ca. 1915.
Designed by Frederick Kranz.
Leather and glass, 11⅝ × 6⅜ in.
Aurora Historical Society.

The author wishes to extend special thanks for assistance provided by David Ryan, Curator of Collections at the Norwest Corporation; Kenneth R. Trapp, Curator of Decorative Arts at the Oakland Museum, and the staff of the Department of Rare Books & Special Collections, Rush Rhees Library, University of Rochester.

ENDNOTES

[1] *Fra* 6, no. 5 (February 1911): lii.

[2] *Fra* 1, no. 6 (September 1908): xx.

[3] *Fra* 1, no. 6; *Fra* 6, no. 5.

[4] *Fra* 7, no. 5 (August 1911): inside back cover.

[5] *Little Journeys to the Homes of Great Lovers: Ferdinand Lassalle and Helene Von Donniges* 19, no. 4 (October 1906): xi.

[6] *Fra* 6, no. 5 (February 1911): lii–liii.

[7] *A Little Journey Through the Roycrofter Copper and Leather Shop* (East Aurora: The Roycrofters, 1925).

[8] The term *Art Nouveau* here describes a widespread aesthetic movement in Europe during the period of the 1890s through about 1910. For further reading see: Kathryn B. Hiesinger, ed., *Art Nouveau in Munich: Masters of Jugendstil* (Munich: Prestel-Verlag, 1988, in association with the Philadelphia Museum of Art); Bernard Champigneulle, *Art Nouveau: Art 1900, Modern Style, Jugendstil*, trans. Benita Eisler (Woodbury: Barron's Educational Series, Inc., 1976); Laurence Buffet-Challie, *The Art Nouveau Style* (London: Academy Editions, 1982); Lara-Vinca Masini, *Art Nouveau*, trans. Linda Fairborn (Secaucus: Chartwell Books, Inc., 1976).

[9] *Fra* 6, no. 5 (February 1911): lii–liii. Frederick C. Kranz was presented as the author of this promotional piece. He wrote: "It was not until Professor Brinkmann, from the Hamburg School of Industrial Art, called attention of some friends to the lost art, that a few craftsmen took up anew the study, and today Leather-Modeling has reached a standard of perfection never before attained." Kranz probably would not have mentioned Professor Brinkmann by name if he had not been a personal mentor.

[10] *Fra* 1, no. 6.

[11] Dard Hunter, *My Life with Paper: An Autobiography* (New York: Alfred A. Knopf, 1958), 35, 43.

[12] Ibid., 43-44.

[13] See Cathleen A. Baker, "Sleuthing for Dard Hunter in Vienna," *Craftsman Homeowner* 6, no. 1. When Hunter returned to the Roycroft after his visit to Vienna, he opened the Dard Hunter School of Handicraft, emphasizing the production of hand-made jewelry and leaded glass. Hunter advertised his school in Gustav Stickley's *Craftsman*, in which he was stated to be "devoting his life to Arts and Crafts and . . . [working] in the leading art shops in Vienna, Munich and Darmstadt." See advertisement for Dard Hunter School of Handicraft, *Craftsman* 21, no. 1 (1911): 8a.

[14] Rossana Bossaglia, "The Protagonists of the Italian Liberty Movement," *Journal of Decorative and Propaganda Arts* 13 (Summer 1989): 32-51.

[15] Mary Roelofs Stott, *Elbert Hubbard—Rebel with Reverence: A Grand-daughter's Tribute* (Watkins Glen: Century House Americana Publishers, 1975), 79.

[16] The monthly feature was authored by Miss Emily Peacock of Brooklyn, who wrote about wood carving, pyrography, leather, metal, basketry, and other crafts.

[17] *Keramic Studio* (June 1907): 50.

[18] *Fra* 6, no. 6 (1911): iv–v.

Tran Turner is an art historian specializing in the design movements of the nineteenth and twentieth centuries. Formerly with the Minneapolis Institute of Arts and the Everson Museum of Art (Syracuse), he is now a free-lance curator and artists' representative in Rochester, New York.

Fig. 69: Alta Fattey and Bertha Hubbard painting china.
(Courtesy Roycroft Arts Museum)

Industry *with* Art:
The Painters, Graphic Artists, Sculptors, and Photographers Affiliated with the Roycroft

LAURENE BUCKLEY

*Life without industry is guilt;
industry without art is brutality.*[1]

From its very inception, the Roycroft community recognized the arts as a major factor in its livelihood, not only as a leisure activity but as a crucial element in each member's enjoyment of his or her production in the workplace. When Samuel Warner (1872–1947) arrived in East Aurora in 1895, the first of a long line of painters, graphic artists, and sculptors to work at the colony, he would have encountered a staff that included Elbert Hubbard, his wife Bertha, and four other adults, including the handyman, Ali Baba (Anson Blackman).[2] Bertha was the ad hoc illuminator for the first books off the Roycroft press— reprints of the *Song of Songs* (1896) and *The Journal of Koheleth* (1897)—but with Warner's arrival, the shop realized the beginnings of a genuine art department.

Born in Scranton, Pennsylvania, and only recently a student at New York City's National Academy of Design,[3] Warner was said to be a protegé of Hubbard's friend Bill Spear in Quincy, Massachusetts, when he was recruited to East Aurora.[4] According to Hubbard's later recollections, however, the artist "blew in on the way to nowhere . . . He stayed with the Roycrofters for a night, and before he knew it he was a Roycrofter himself."[5] Warner was immediately put to work creating title pages, initials, bookplates, and borders, while at the same time training local women, including Bertha, to hand color his printed designs. Five years into Warner's tenure, there were seventy or more illuminators at work,[6] among them Clara Schlegel, a painter of china, and Alta Fattey, who also taught others in the shop and who later married Hubbard's son Bert. Numerous other illuminators toiled long hours embellishing Roycroft books and have remained unheralded to this day, among them Minnie Gardner, Fannie Stiles, Mae Johnston, Maud Baker, Blanche Lewis, Ida Metcalf,

Fig. 70: Samuel Warner, with one of his designs behind him, instructing illuminators at the first Print Shop, ca. 1900. *(Courtesy Turgeon-Rust Collection)*

Margaret E. Pierce, Julia Hawthorne, Harriet Robarge, and Anna Knights.

Warner also found time to display his own work in watercolor and charcoal. His contributions to an exhibition entitled *Some Specimens of Art & Handicraft Done By Roycroft Workers,* held in 1900, principally included studies of children, but he also displayed original designs for Roycroft publications, works which he obviously felt were exhibitable on their own.[7] His style during this period evolved from one emulating the Pre-Raphaelite manner of William Morris's Kelmscott Press to a more fluid approach, utilizing the interwoven

Plate 134: Samuel Warner, *Design for Elbert Hubbard's Bookplate*, ca. 1899. Pen and ink on paper, 19⅜ × 15½ in. *Roycroft Arts Museum, Boice Lydell.*

lines of Art Nouveau. The latter style was characteristic of his work at the time of his departure from East Aurora in 1903.[8]

Warner had been at the Roycroft only a short time when another professional artist, William Wallace Denslow (1856–1915), was recruited. Hubbard might

Plate 135: Samuel Warner, *Illuminated Border*, ca. 1903. Watercolor on paper, 12⅞ × 14½ in. *Roycroft Arts Museum, Boice Lydell.*

have sought him out as an artist trained in wood engraving who could produce bookplates in a medieval manner.[9] Denslow, a well-known Chicago book illustrator, caricaturist, and designer of posters and theater costumes, was one of the most popular graphic artists in America at this time. A dedicated bibliophile, he had filled his Lake Michigan home (dubbed "Hippocampus" after his sea horse logo) with "editions *de luxe* of the choicest English, French and American fiction and *belles lettres.*"[10] A handmade book produced in America probably appealed to him, and in 1896 he wrote to Hubbard for a copy of *Song of Songs,* his letter enclosed, he later recalled, "in a low-comedy envelope done in water-color."[11] After receiving the book, Denslow sent a second note, suggesting that Hubbard use illustrations in the *Philistine* "as then," he said, "I might hope to some day become a contributor."[12] Hubbard lost no time in sending the artist twelve copies of the reprinted *Art and Life* (1896) by Vernon Lee to be illumined in Denslow's bold, decorative style.

Hubbard's collaboration with the artist continued. An announcement in the May *Philistine* of 1898 proclaimed that "Col. W. W. Denslow, Honest Roycrofter

WHY I AM A PHILISTINE

Plate 136: W. W. Denslow, illumination in Elbert Hubbard's *As It Seems To Me*, 1898. 9 × 5⅝ in. *Collection of Richard Blacher.*

... has evolved from his inner consciousness a series of poems without words that will be reproduced successfully on back of the Philistine during the next six months."[13] These comic pieces began with that issue and continued well beyond the six months—regularly, through December 1901, and then sporadically, in 1902 and 1903. A later, political cartoon entitled "Belgium's Burden," appears on the back cover of an issue of 1915, the year of the *Lusitania* tragedy.

Fig. 71: William Wallace Denslow, designer of the Roycroft's sea horse emblem. (As published in *As It Seems To Me*, 1898)

Denslow, with his distinctive walrus mustache, was remembered by Felix Shay, general manager at Roycroft, as having a "fog horn voice" and a strange sense of humor, "always grumbling about nothing, always carping, always censorious, and laughing uproariously when he secured his effects."[14] Hubbard dubbed him the "Growler" at times and, at others, "Deacon Denslow."[15] The artist began to spend a portion of almost every year in East Aurora in 1898, regularly contributing designs for the publications but also, according to an early biographer, "designing the Roycrofter library building . . . and a set of seahorse andirons," the latter based on his personal emblem, which was subsequently adopted as one of the emblems of the press.[16]

The second year that Denslow visited, in 1899, he stayed for five weeks. He brought with him a young artist named Lawrence Mazzanovich (1871–1959) who had been working for him in Chicago and living at Hippocampus.[17] A contemporary description of the Roycroft art department noted that there were "several artists of reputation, chief among them being W. W. Denslow, the Chicago caricaturist; Samuel Warner and Lawrence Mazzanovich, a lithographic designer." While "most of the page embellishments," the author continued, were designed by Denslow and Warner, "Mazzanovich does special illumination in water color on the best editions."[18] "Mazzy," as he was called, produced the highly intricate illustrations for the reprints of Oliver Goldsmith's *Deserted Village* (1898) and Ralph Waldo Emerson's *Essay on Friendship* while in East Aurora and also helped Warner conduct a summer sketching class in watercolor and charcoal as part of the Roycroft School of Applied Art.[19] Mazzanovich's affiliation with the East Aurora community and with the world of illustration in general was short-lived, however, replaced by a more compelling interest in landscape painting. He subsequently spent time abroad, mostly at Fontainebleau but also in Moret-sur-Loing, Paris, and Giverny, the home of Claude Monet.[20] Upon his return to America, his style evolved from that of Tonalism, in the years between 1905 and 1910, into full-blown Impressionism.[21]

Denslow also went on to greater fame. The same year that he first visited East Aurora, he met L. Frank Baum, the author of *The Wonderful Wizard of Oz,* which, with Denslow's illustrations, catapulted both men into the national arena of children's book production. The artist moved to New York in 1902 and, with the proceeds from his prolific output both as author and illustrator, purchased an island off Bermuda where he held court as Denslow I, with his cook as his "prime minister" and a "fleet" that included a sailboat and a yacht.[22]

Another early arrival at the Roycroft was the sculptor Jerome Connor (1874–1943), who also was lured to East Aurora from Quincy, Massachusetts, where he and Warner apparently had worked for Hubbard's friend Spear.[23] Connor had immigrated to America in 1888 from Annascaul, Ireland, at the age of fourteen.[24]

Fig. 72: Jerome Connor at work in his studio, ca. 1900. *(Courtesy Turgeon-Rust Collection)*

First trained by his father, a carpenter and stone mason, the young man was equipped to take on a number of jobs leading up to his work in sculpture. In New York City, where his career actually began, he was at various times a sign painter, mechanic, stonecutter, foundryman, and prize fighter, the last, under the name Patrick O'Connor.[25] In late 1896, he assisted the French-trained sculptor Roland Hinton Perry in the casting of Perry's multi-figured *Fountain of Neptune* for the Library of Congress in Washington, D.C.[26]

Connor is first mentioned at the Roycroft in an 1899 advertisement in the *Philistine,* as the blacksmith for a set of sea horse andirons designed by Denslow and available for sale.[27] That same year, a Roycroft catalogue announced a full line of Connor's ("Saint Gerome's") terra cotta sculptures,[28] including three bas-reliefs, a paperweight, and a bust of Fra Elbertus,

Plate 137: Jerome Connor, *Bust of Elbert Hubbard*, 1899. Bronze, 14½ × 7½ × 9 in.
Elbert Hubbard-Roycroft Museum.

later cast in bronze and which, in its quick, gestural style, fully represents the artist's approach to his craft at this time. He also was said to have produced pottery "on the wheel" during his brief stay at East Aurora and apparently built his own kiln to fire the results.[29] In the Roycroft tradition of artists teaching other artists, he was also conducting a class in clay modeling as of March 1899, according to the *East Aurora Advertiser,* which introduced him as "an all 'round artist" having skills as a wood carver, sculptor and "draughtsman."[30]

Connor's superb draftsmanship, in fact, can be seen in his designs for several Roycroft publications, including the title page for *Dreams* (1901) by Olive Schreiner, a highly complex web of stylized lettering, birds, and figure, and the overall scheme for *The Story of a Passion* (1901) by Irving Bacheller.

In January of 1902, it was announced in the local paper that Connor and his new wife, also a Roycrofter,[31] would be attending the annual exhibition of the Pennsylvania Academy of the Fine Arts, where five of the artist's works were being shown.[32] This group included the *Head of Dr. Silas Hubbard,* a highly realistic bas-relief of

Plate 138: Jerome Connor, *Head of Dr. Silas Hubbard*, 1903. Bronze, 18 × 12½ in.
Aurora Historical Society.

the aged physician. At the Philadelphia exhibition, Connor would have seen works by Augustus Saint-Gaudens, George Grey Barnard, and others who exemplified the late nineteenth-century return to naturalism in American sculpture after a long period of neoclassicism. Connor's sculpture follows in this tradition, especially as the scale of the work becomes increasingly larger. One such heroic piece, entitled *The Marriage of Art and Industry,* destined for the Roycroft lawn, was nearing completion after a year of work, when the

THE ROYCROFT POTTERY

Roycroft pottery remains one of the great puzzles in any serious study of craft production in East Aurora. Published hints of its existence are tantalizingly vague, and none include detailed descriptions of its physical appearance. As early as September 1899, the *Brooklyn Eagle* described the Roycroft as "a place where one industry has led into another—pottery is a recent addition."[1] By February 1900, Jerome Connor was reported to have produced some pottery, fired in a kiln of his own building.[2] A small catalogue produced in the autumn of that year directed Roycroft visitors to the "Potter Shop . . . just across the road from the Printery. Miss Douglass will be glad to show her wares."[3] Included in a 1902 exhibition of Douglass's paintings were "a few pieces of Roycroft pottery on sale. The pottery was very beautiful in design."[4] And in 1904, a reporter mentioned that the Phalanstery dining room was decorated with ceramics made on the campus.[5]

A few more shreds of evidence emerge in notes and correspondence that chronicle a dispute between Elbert Hubbard and Carl Ahrens over ownership of paintings that Hubbard claimed the artist had placed with him as security against a $200 loan in March 1900. Hubbard noted that during the summer of that year, Ahrens "also rigged up a pottery wheel, with the help of our blacksmith [probably Connor], and experimented in pottery. His sister-in-law, Miss Douglas, used the wheel and kept the pottery she made and sold it for herself. So did Mr. Ahrens's boys. As Ahrens was not strong, I let one of our boys help him at the pottery and supplied the kiln and fuel for burning the pottery. It was not a success and no pottery was sold. The stuff had no value. Of the hundred or so pieces he made we divided them between us."[6]

Ahrens's understanding of the transaction was wholly different; he contended that the $200 was a down payment for paintings that Hubbard purchased, with the balance due as they were sold from exhibitions at the Roycroft. On stationery bearing a "Roycroft Potter-Shop" logo, Ahrens reminded Hubbard that he came out to East Aurora to "start the pottery putting in far more time than I agreed in order to get it started for which I received the sum of seven dollars per week then after making an entire success this was taken out of my hands without explanation."[7]

Ahrens's contribution to the production of pottery was short-lived. Hubbard noted that by August or September of 1900 the artist "quit painting and got discouraged at his repeated failures in pottery . . . In October he moved away."[8] Of the hundred ceramics supposedly produced, none has been identified. Ahrens and Douglass were both landscape painters, suggesting the possibility that some of the ceramics were painted, in the manner of the very popular Rookwood ware of the same period. A clue to Ahrens's finishing technique appears in a note Hubbard scribbled to himself about the artist's shortcomings: "Ahrens refused to teach Conner [sic] how to glaze—kept secrets to himself when he had agreed to teach."[9] The simple glazed pitcher that held paintbrushes in Ahrens's studio may have been one of his own pieces.

Given the strength of the art pottery movement in America at the turn of the century, it seems odd that the production of ceramics was never fully exploited at the Roycroft. However, the three principals involved in the Roycroft Pottery (Connor, Ahrens, and Douglass) had all severed their ties with the Roycroft by 1904. The expense of running the kiln, the departure of the artisans who could have taught the skill to others, and the residue of combative relations the Pottery had engendered may simply have made it unfeasible to persevere on a commercial scale.[10]

Fig. 73: Carl Ahrens, painter and head of the Roycroft Pottery, ca. 1900. *Courtesy Roycroft Shops.*

supporting beams holding the piece collapsed, leaving the immense sculpture in total ruin.[33]

Whether or not this disappointment led to Connor's leaving Roycroft is not known, but in July of 1902 the *East Aurora Advertiser* announced that, "after a stay of nearly four years," the artist was about to leave for Syracuse to "direct the Arts and Crafts in that city. In addition to some important commissions in bronze," the reporter added, "Mr. Conner [*sic*] is to . . . also direct the Fine Arts in the well-known Strickley [*sic*] establishment of Eastwood."[34] By 1903 Connor was working on the first of these Syracuse commissions, a memorial to Walt Whitman, which did not see completion beyond the stage of its full-scale plaster studies. It was the casts of the attendant figures for the monument, however, that, when shown at the 1903 annual of the Pennsylvania Academy of the Fine Arts, gave Connor his first taste of national recognition. After seeing the paired figures representing skilled and unskilled labor, Lorado Taft applauded the sculptor's "interpretation of the life of the workingman," and, in an extensive article on Connor's work in *Booklovers Magazine,* a Philadelphia journal, he was proclaimed "a sculptor of the people."[35]

Connor went on to produce two major fountains for Union Park in Syracuse, both representations of the Onondaga people of that region. One, a figure of a Native American boy with a parrot, was erected in 1903, but because of vandalism, is now housed in the city's zoo. The other, of two Onondaga warriors, was also placed in Union Park, but has since disappeared. A third fountain apparently never went beyond the design stage.[36] After moving to Washington, D.C., in 1910, Connor was asked by the United States government to design a memorial for the Irish-born general and senator James Shields and, through this work, came to the attention of a host of Irish-American patrons. Two later commissions relate to Roycroft: the heroic figure of Elbert Hubbard, which was completed after Connor moved back to Ireland in 1925 and finally unveiled at the Roycroft campus in 1930, and the *Lusitania* memorial monument for which the artist was named sculptor in 1925 by a committee that included Franklin Delano Roosevelt, Gertrude Vanderbilt Whitney (whose brother was lost in the tragedy), and Mrs. J. Borden Harriman, who alone gave $30,000 for the project. At Connor's death eighteen years later, the memorial was still not finished, owing to his gradual downward slide towards poverty and eventual bankruptcy.[37]

The same 1900 exhibition catalogue in which Warner's and Connor's art appeared, *Some Specimens of Art & Handicraft Done by Roycroft Workers,* introduced two new names to the Roycroft roster.[38] Thirteen paintings, all landscapes, are listed by the Canadian Carl Ahrens (1862–1936), who was invited to East Aurora in 1900 to head the newly formed Ceramics Department.

His cousin, Eleanor Douglas [born Eleanor Douglass] (1873–1914)[39] is mentioned as a member of the "Potter Shop . . . just across the road from the Printery. Miss Douglass," the notation reads, "will be glad to show her wares."[40] Neither artist was noted for this specialty before or after a brief Roycroft employment, although Ahrens had worked in New York under the sculptor F. Edwin Elwell.[41] His major interests were painting and printmaking, especially etching and monotypes, having studied with Toronto's J. W. L. Forster, a portraitist, and George A. Reid, one of the founders of the Canadian Group of Seven, and later, with William Merritt Chase and Elwell in Manhattan.[42] His greatest inspiration, however, was George Inness, whom he met in Montclair, New Jersey, in 1892.[43] By the mid-to-late 1890s, no doubt under Inness's guidance, Ahrens had shifted his subject matter from genre subjects[44] to dreamy landscapes, seasonal views captured at the most poetic times of day and often in a dominant hue of yellow, grey, or green.

It was at this time that Ahrens met Hubbard at one of the Roycroft leader's lecture tours in Toronto. According to Jennifer C. Watson, author of *Carl Ahrens as Printmaker,* the artist "had been successful in a Chautauqua pottery," and Hubbard asked him to introduce that skill to the Roycrofters.[45] In May of 1900, he and his family moved to East Aurora,[46] but within two years, the arrangement had soured. "We finally parted," Ahrens later said, "but I always admired him. He was the most interesting man I have ever met."[47] Ahrens stayed in Willink, the tiny settlement adjacent to East Aurora, until 1905, not wishing to have any "connection whatever with 'the shop,'" before moving on to New York City and California.[48] Thereafter, except for brief stays in Rockport, Massachusetts, Woodstock, New York, and England, he lived at "Big Trees," his home in the woods near Toronto, where he authored short stories and poetry and became known as a painter of trees— "trees at dawn, trees at sunset, trees at noon, trees at dusk, trees of infinite variety."[49]

Eleanor Douglas came to the Roycroft at about the same time as Ahrens to help in the Pottery Shop, but she, too, was far better known as a painter, especially of Barbizon-inspired woodland scenes. Like her cousin, she had grown up among the Ojibway people north of Toronto, her grandfather being the proprietor of the store and post office on the Saugeen reservation.[50] She was named Phpense ("Laughing Girl") by the Ojibway and learned the ways of nature so well that she could sustain long periods in the woods—camping, canoeing, and producing sketches for works to be finished in the studio.[51] She, too, left the employ of Hubbard soon after her arrival, but, unlike Ahrens, stayed at Willink the rest of her life and was friendly with several of the Roycroft artists.[52] Known as the "Lady of the Forest,"[53] Douglas was also a regular exhibitor, as was Ahrens, at the Royal

Plate 139: Carl Ahrens, *The Path*. Oil on artist's board, 12 × 10 in.
Private collection.

Plate 140: Jules Gaspard, *A Group of Etchings: Burns, Byron, Tennyson, Coleridge, Disraeli, and Morris.* Etchings in Roycroft oak frame, 11 × 37½ in.
Collection of Bruce A. Austin.

Canadian Academy, Toronto, the Ontario Society of Artists, and, occasionally, at the Buffalo Society of Artists.

When Hubbard began to be successful with his *Little Journeys* series, which featured mostly fictional visits to the homes of noted writers, statesmen, and painters, among others, he needed artists who could produce good likenesses of these personalities. Jules Maurice Gaspard (1862–1919) began working for Roycroft in 1899, when the first of his delicate crayon drawings was lithographed for the frontispiece of *Little Journeys to the Homes of English Authors, Book II.* The insightful portrait renderings of Thomas Babington Macauley, Lord Byron, Joseph Addison, Robert Southey, Samuel Taylor Coleridge, and Benjamin Disraeli are just a few of his many enhancements to Roycroft publications.[54]

Parisian-born, Gaspard came to this country when he was seventeen years old, settling first in Chicago, where he is said to have studied at the Chicago Art Institute.[55] Between 1886 and 1890 he was in New York City, registered for brief periods of study at the Art Students' League, including a class in drawing from antique casts in 1889 and 1890 under the Impressionist John Henry Twachtman.[56] Back in Chicago by 1898, he was the art critic for the Chicago *Inter-Ocean*[57] when he was asked to illustrate for the Roycroft. One story about Gaspard, who was a devout Christian Scientist, is told by Felix Shay in his memoir *Elbert Hubbard of East Aurora.* The artist had just completed a portrait of the church's founder, Mary Baker Eddy, and had shown it to her at her home in Boston. When he returned to East Aurora, he read the essay that was to accompany the portrait in the series, *Little Journeys to the Homes of Great Teachers,* and objected to its content so strongly that Hubbard, who

usually resisted such criticism, agreed to turn the drawing over to the artist, without reproducing it in the publication.[58] Although Gaspard is reported to have left East Aurora around 1901[59] and, according to the *American Art Annual,* became a resident of Chicago between 1903 and 1905,[60] he may have subsequently returned to the Roycroft, as indicated by an *East Aurora Advertiser* article of 1909 announcing his departure at that later date for the Windy City.[61] Gaspard's contributions to Roycroft publications, whether or not they were recycled in later years, continued to 1914, five years before his death.

The other artist who created portraits for Roycroft books, beginning with the *Little Journeys to the Homes of the Great Philosophers* series of 1903 and 1904, was Otto J. Schneider (1875–1946). A painter-etcher, he also produced likenesses for the *Fra,* starting with the July issue of 1909, the year of Gaspard's departure. Schneider's spritely linear technique, emboldened with rich, shadowy areas, as in the portraits of Robert Louis Stevenson, Mary Wollstonecraft, Charles Wesley Emerson, Joaquin Miller, and Voltaire, offered a distinct contrast to the softer approach used by Gaspard. A dashing image of Hubbard and a companion rendering of Alice were executed in 1905.

Born in Atlanta, Illinois, Schneider had moved with his family to Chicago by the age of twelve.[62] He spent a short time at the Art Institute of Chicago during the school season of 1892–93[63] before illustrating for a number of newspapers in that city. By 1900 he was proficient enough in printmaking, his new field, to have a one-man show of drypoints at the Albert Roullier Gallery in Chicago.[64] The years between 1900 and 1910 appear to have been divided between East Aurora, New York City, and Chicago.[65] Except for at least one sojourn in Europe,[66] the remainder of his life was

Plate 141: Jules Gaspard, *Alice Hubbard*. Conté crayon on paper, 18 × 13 in.
Collection of Mark and Sarah Roelofs.

Plate 142: Jules Gaspard, *Elbert Hubbard*. Conté crayon on paper, 19⅞ × 14 in.
Elbert Hubbard-Roycroft Museum.

Plate 143: Otto Schneider, *Elbert and Alice Hubbard*, 1905. Etchings, lithographed motto, in Roycroft oak frame, 15½ × 33 in. *Elbert Hubbard-Roycroft Museum.*

spent in the Midwest, where he regularly exhibited his etchings and was an active member of the Chicago Society of Artists.[67]

A major event for the Roycroft took place in 1901 with the opening of the Pan-American Exposition in nearby Buffalo. One of its main thrusts was to highlight the Arts and Crafts movement in America, with examples of workmanship by Charles Rohlfs of Buffalo and Gustav Stickley of Syracuse. Thousands of visitors to the fair also flocked to see the regional crafts center at East Aurora, and the Roycrofters welcomed them with open arms.[68] The exposition, in turn, offered East Aurorans a golden opportunity to see the best art being produced in America at the time. Paul Bartlett's (1865–1925) model for his bronze statue of Michelangelo (ca. 1895, Library of Congress, Washington, D.C.) was a gold medal winner at the fair. It may have inspired Hubbard to seek a version of the work for the Roycroft campus, a request that was fulfilled in 1908.[69] Louis Rhead (1857–1926), the nationally known poster artist, whose drawing of Walt Whitman had appeared in Hubbard's *Essay on Walt Whitman by Robert Louis Stevenson* in 1900, was represented at the exposition by several works, including illustrations for reprints of John Bunyan's *Pilgrim's Progress* and Alfred, Lord Tennyson's *The Idylls of the King*. Rhead's Whitman design had been used by Hubbard without permission, leading to a complete halt in their relations.[70] Also on display was a painting by Sandor Landeau, an artist who was living in Paris at the time but who would later be associated with the Roycroft, beginning in 1916. His *Annunciation to the Shepherd* received an honorable mention at the fair and had earlier won the Second Wanamaker Prize at the American Art Association of Paris in 1900.

A close friend of Landeau and Bartlett in Paris was

Fig. 74: Paul Bartlett with his bronze sculpture of *Michelangelo* on the Roycroft lawn. (As published in the *Fra*, September 1909)

Alexis Jean Fournier (1865–1948), who was represented at the exposition with a single painting, *Moonrise, Normandy.* Fournier would soon replace all others as the "court painter of the Roycroft."[71] Hubbard had met him on a lecture stop in Minneapolis in 1896,[72] but it was in 1902 that serious recruitment began. That year Hubbard accompanied the artist on a visit to the Art Institute of Chicago to see a major show of Fournier's work and to purchase two European subjects out of the exhibition, *Silvery Moonlight* and *The Shepherd's Return.* Fournier's landscapes by this time had evolved from an earlier pristine realism that he used for his urban views of Minneapolis to a Tonalist style based on a deep-seated admiration for the French Barbizon painters. He had just returned from his fourth trip to France, where he studied with the academics Jean-Paul Laurens and Benjamin Constant at the Académie Julian in Paris. He and Nicholas Brewer (1857–1949), a portrait and landscape artist who would visit Fournier often in East Aurora, dominated the landscape school in Minneapolis, then on the rise.[73] Fournier had also designed murals for Craftshouse, an Arts and Crafts center in Minneapolis run by John Scott Bradstreet, and this may have been another reason that Hubbard desired his presence at the Roycroft.

Two months after Hubbard and Fournier renewed their acquaintance in Chicago, the artist was in East Aurora supervising the reinstallation of the Roycroft art gallery.[74] By the first of June, 1903, Fournier had moved to the village, at least on a part-time basis,

bringing with him enough canvases to present a midsummer exhibition.[75] The selection included Hubbard's two previous purchases and a more recent one, *Auvers-sur-Oise.* Also shown were *L'Angelus,* a painting undoubtedly owing its origins to the work of Jean-François Millet, and *Crepuscule,* a picture of an old shepherd and his flock of sheep, the work that had been accepted at the Paris Salon of 1901.[76] At the end of that summer, the *Minnesota Journal* announced that "the Philistine man is making him [Fournier] known to his patrons and has offered him tempting inducements to remain."[77] One of these inducements was a gift of land adjacent to the Roycroft campus, on Walnut Street. Fournier lost no time in constructing a home on the property, where he summered regularly the rest of his life.

The painter's first duties as "artist-in-residence," a title he preferred to art director, involved conducting a summer class[78] and lecturing twice a month to the Roycrofters, a task he performed with some verve. One such lecture was described by Hubbard's daughter Miriam in 1979. Asked to "spark up" the Roycroft convention of 1908, Fournier instigated a "duet of the arts," matching his colors on canvas to the accompanying pianist's interpretations of "Dawn, Noon and Night."[79] A major part of Fournier's early period in East Aurora, however, was spent in the production of murals for the Roycroft Inn, a project said to have taken a full year.[80] "Alexis J. Fournier is shut up in his studio in East Aurora," a reporter noted in March of 1905, "giving

Fig. 75: The Roycroft Inn Salon and Music Room, showing Alex Fournier's murals of the great cities of the world, ca. 1910.
(Courtesy Elbert Hubbard-Roycroft Museum)

the last touches to a beautiful piece of mural decoration. The various countries of Europe are represented by exquisite landscape views."[81] The series included a Greek temple in ruins, scenes of London, Venice, and Paris, and one section "showing American art in the summertime of its progress."[82] In a room of dark walls and solid oak furnishings, these murals must have added a lively backdrop to the lectures, concerts, and regular meetings that were held there.

In 1906, Hubbard sent Fournier to France, specifically to sketch the region of the Fontainebleau forest where Millet, Jean-Baptiste-Camille Corot, Charles-François Daubigny, Théodore Rousseau, Charles-Émile Jacque, and other members of the Barbizon community lived and worked. The series that evolved, twenty paintings in all, was entitled "The Homes of the Men of 1830," and was shown, in total or as a selected group, in New York City, Detroit, Chicago, St. Paul, Toledo, Buffalo, Boston, and Rochester, New York.[83] It would secure for the artist a national reputation as the "last American Barbizon."[84] In fact, what held Fournier in East Aurora every summer for so many years was the village's similarity in coloration and light to the French countryside. The Cazenovia Creek Valley was a particular favorite. "If ever you erect a monument to me," he wrote, "place it somewhere along the creek, where I have spent twenty-five such happy summers."[85] Fourteen years earlier, he had pined, "I love that valley as much, if not more than I did Normandy . . . It

possesses all the brightness of Normandy and it is so near home."[86] Just as the Barbizon artists had earlier escaped the hustle of Parisian life, Fournier delighted in East Aurora's quietude. He loved the poetic times of day—dawn and dusk—and much preferred the softer tones of spring and autumn to the more intense light of winter and summer. Many of his works around 1910 use the word "peace" in the titles, as is the case in a bucolic view of the Roycroft chapel and herd of sheep, bathed in a warm late afternoon haze.

Yet even in East Aurora, Fournier could not be assured of complete solitude. The *Minnesotan* reported

Fig. 76: Sheep grazing on the lawn outside the Roycroft Chapel. *(Courtesy Town of Aurora Historian's Office)*

Plate 144: Alexis Jean Fournier, *Peace*, 1913. Oil on canvas, 30 × 41¼ in. *Meibohm Fine Arts, Grace Meibohm Demme.*

Plate 145: Alexis Jean Fournier, *The Camp,*
Aurora, New York. Oil on canvas,
17¼ × 21¼ in.
Frederick-Waters Fine Art.

in 1916 that Hubbard was sending so many visitors to the painter's studio that "Mr. Fournier was obliged to lock his door, and carry the only key safely concealed in his pocket."[87] Apparently, the artist did not always stay on Hubbard's good side. With his friends Brewer, and the writer Richard Le Gallienne, both frequent visitors to the Roycroft, he formed the "Tommyrotters' Club,"[88] a group which, according to Brewer, would often "retreat some distance from the Inn and sing comic ballads," calling down a "severe reprimand from His Majesty, Fra Elbertus." Momentarily expelled from the colony, they would then charter a boat and "sail down the river on moonlight nights."[89] Fournier's sketching excursions took him far afield of the campus, as shown by his painting, *The Camp,* which portrays one of the many outlying cabins used by the Roycrofters.[90] Executed in the deep, rich tones of late summer or early autumn, the scene might have recalled for Fournier one of his earliest experiences at East Aurora. According to Felix Shay, Fournier was invited one day to the Ten Mile Camp, located near the village of South Wales. Hubbard

selected an axe for the artist and asked him to cut down an ironwood tree. Knowing that it took three strong men to accomplish this feat, the other members of the group watched for the "dude" to falter. Fournier cleverly chose instead a soft chestnut tree and, within five minutes, "dropped the trunk in the grove."[91]

Around 1913, Fournier started associating with a group of artists in Brown County, Indiana, where a regional school of Impressionism was developing.[92] When he married Cora Ball, his second wife and a prominent art patron in South Bend, in 1922, Fournier continued his summers in East Aurora but began to spend winters in Indiana. His own Impressionism, a third style for the artist, can be seen in *The Garden at Evening.* The color is high-keyed, in greens and yellows, and the pigment is applied in loose, feathery brushstrokes, yet the objects remain intact, not diffused, as in classic French Impressionism. The view is of the nearly obscured Roycroft Furniture Shop through the trees of the former orchard on which Fournier's house was built. His focus, however, is the garden itself, seen in its full glory and overflowing with

Plate 146: Alexis Jean Fournier, *The Garden*
at Evening, 1938. Oil on canvas, 24 × 30 in.
Collection of Kitty Turgeon-Rust and Robert
Rust, Roycroft Shops.

Fig. 77: Alex Fournier (left) in the garden outside his "bungle house."
Photograph by Charles Kingsbury.
(Courtesy Turgeon-Rust Collection)

wildflowers and hollyhocks. The artist had long since moved to a nearby cottage he named the "bungle house," because, he said, "it didn't deserve to be called a bungalow."[93] Even when he moved to East Aurora permanently in 1938, this smaller house, with an obstinate apple tree growing up through the roof, apparently suited his modest needs.[94]

Fournier's presence at the Roycroft clearly added the stature of a professional painter to the community, yet it didn't alleviate the ongoing need for designers of the publications. A number of graphic artists found their way to East Aurora in the ensuing years, contributing

a variety of styles and sensibilities. Richard Kruger, a painter known later for his landscapes of the Southwest, was briefly at the Roycroft in 1902. That year he produced an elaborate figural title page for Hubbard's book *Contemplations.* The next year, "Dickie" Kruger is mentioned in an advertisement for the *Philistine* as instructor of painting and drawing at the Roycroft Shop,[95] but by 1906 he had moved on, first to Los Angeles, until 1918, and, from 1920 to 1924, at least, he was living in San Francisco.[96]

With the arrival of Dard Hunter at the Roycroft in 1904, a new energy was added to the community in nearly every endeavor to which he applied his skills: furniture, copperwork, stained glass, pottery, ironwork, and book production. Hunter was from a family of Ohio newspapermen, printers, and craftsmen. (His father was co-founder of the Lonhuda Pottery workshop.) Dard began his career as an artist for his father's newspaper, the *News-Advertiser,* and later was the "chalk artist" in his brother's traveling magic act.[97] While on tour, he became enamored of mission-style furniture at a California hotel and determined to do some furniture designs of his own.[98] After enrolling at Ohio State University, he developed an even greater appreciation for the books produced at the Kelmscott Press by William Morris and for the Arts and Crafts movement in general. He was also familiar with the *Philistine,*

Fig. 78: Dard Hunter, ca. 1906.
(Courtesy Dard Hunter III)

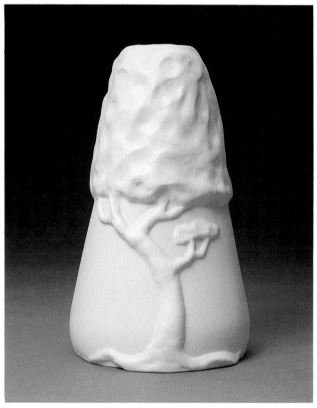

Plate 147: Dard Hunter, *Tree-Form Vase*, ca. 1905. Ceramic, 9½ x 6 in.
Roycroft Arts Museum, Boice Lydell.

having seen his brother's copies of the periodical.[99] About this time, he wrote to Hubbard asking for a job at the Roycroft, receiving a rather cool response on June 21, 1904: "I will have to explain," Hubbard said, "that we only employ people who live right around here in our immediate vicinity, and as it is just now we have more workers in our shop than we can well make room for with our limited facilities."[100] The young man persisted and, after his arrival in East Aurora in July, he was put to work designing "one or two pieces of furniture . . . a little wood-carving . . . and several objects in iron and copper."[101] He was given free room and board at the Roycroft Inn and a weekly wage. At the end of the summer, he was sent to New York City to study stained glass design at the J. & R. Lamb Company, specialists in church interiors. In a few months, he was back in East Aurora, working on a set of eight windows for the Inn in a former carriage house that he transformed into a studio.[102] After six months of effort, the windows were installed, but Hunter soon became dissatisfied with the "clumsy glass tulips,"[103] and, taking a hammer in hand, smashed them to bits. His second set, in a more conventionalized design executed in less garish colors, is still in place at the Roycroft Inn.

Meanwhile, Hunter's first book designs were making their appearance. His ornamentations for Hubbard's *Man of Sorrows* (1904) and the reprints of Washington Irving's *Rip Van Winkle* (1905) and Ralph Waldo

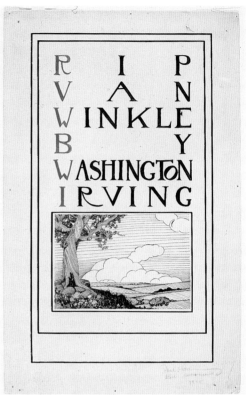

Plate 149: Dard Hunter, *Title Page for Rip Van Winkle*, 1905. Pen and ink on paper, 14¾ × 9⁵⁄₁₆ in.
Collection of Jean-François Vilain and Roger S. Wieck.

Emerson's *Essay on Nature* (1905) all demonstrate Hunter's early leanings toward stylization in their patterned linework, especially in the treatment of trees and foliage. After a six-month stay in Mexico, Hunter returned to East Aurora in 1907 and was immediately asked to design a new monthly publication called the *Fra,* which showed a marked improvement aesthetically over the *Philistine.* A turning point in Hunter's art came about this time, due to his absorption in the Viennese Sezession designs he saw in several publications at the Roycroft library, including *Dekorative Kunst, Deutsche Kunst und Dekoration,* and *Dekorative Vorbilder.*[104] Nature was now seen in more geometricized shapes— squares and rectangles—as evidenced by a squared-rose motif that became Hunter's mainstay during this time. A trip to Vienna in 1908 only served to heighten his admiration for the Sezessionists and their work.

Back in East Aurora in October, Hunter was promoted to art director at the Roycroft and, with Karl Kipp, organized the Dard Hunter School of Handicraft, a do-it-yourself correspondence course in making jewelry and stained glass.[105] Hunter's woodblock rendering of the Roycroft Print Shop shows the clean lines and color of his post-Vienna period. By the end of the summer of 1910, Hunter had left Roycroft for good and was once again in Europe, this time enrolled at the K. K. Graphische Lehr und Versuchsanstalt in Vienna, in the

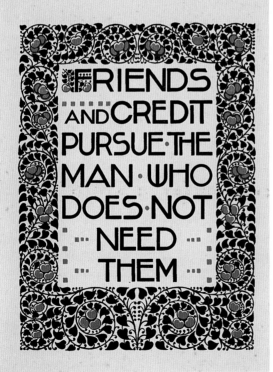

Plate 148: *Motto: Friends and Credit Pursue the Man Who Does Not Need Them.* Designed by Dard Hunter. Paper with ink and colours, 15½ × 11½ in.
Collection of Kitty Turgeon-Rust and Robert Rust, Roycroft Shops.

Plate 150: Dard Hunter, *The Print Shop*, 1910. Woodcut,
10¼ × 13¾ in.
Collection of Mr. and Mrs. Christopher Forbes.

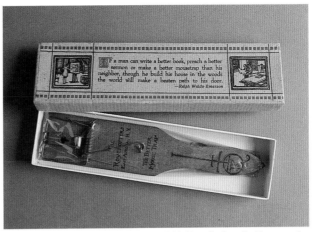

Plate 152: *Roycroft Mousetrap*, ca. 1912. Box designs by Raymond
Nott. Wood, metal, cellophane, and cardboard, 2⅜ × 9¼ in.
Elbert Hubbard-Roycroft Museum.

study of lithography and letter form design. The next year
he was in London, working at the Norfolk Studio and
studying at the Royal Technical College of Finsbury.[106]
Thereafter, Hunter's new-found interest in papermaking
dominated his career. He set up his own papermill at
Marlborough-on-Hudson, New York, where he produced the first books made entirely by the hand of one
person, and, later, a commercial mill in Lime Rock, Connecticut. In 1939, he established the Dard Hunter Paper
Museum at the Massachusetts Institute of Technology,
which was subsequently transferred to the Institute of
Paper Chemistry in Appleton, Wisconsin (now the
American Museum of Papermaking, Atlanta, Georgia).

Hunter's departure in 1910 left an opening for

Plate 151: Raymond Nott, *Tea House Announcement*, 1910.
Gouache on artist's board, 14⅞ × 10¼ in.
Roycroft Arts Museum, Boice Lydell.

another talented graphic artist, Raymond Nott, who
may have been at the Roycroft as early as 1904.[107] His
work began to appear in the publications in 1906 and
1907, with illustrations for the back covers of the
Philistine. Nott was made acting art director in 1908,[108]
perhaps when Hunter was in Vienna, but it was between
1910 and 1912 that he made the deepest impact on
Roycroft productions. In those years he designed book
covers, motto cards, bookplates, and stationery in a style
fairly similar to that employed by Hunter. At least one
show of Nott's original work is known, a group of pastels
shown in a 1912 joint exhibition with Fournier at East
Aurora's Tookay Shop.[109] By 1916, Nott was no longer
the art director at Roycroft, that role soon to be taken by
Merle James (1890–1963), who designed for the *Fra*
and other Roycroft publications during a period that
began in 1917 and ended in 1924, when he became the
Rotogravure Editor for the Buffalo *Courier-Express.*[110]

A few other artists who were associated with book and
magazine design at the Roycroft deserve mention. Burt
Barnes (1872–1947), who advertised his New York City
art classes in both the *Fra* and the *Philistine* in 1908,[111]
was producing in 1909 the first of many illustrations he
would do for both periodicals. Trained at the Art Institute
of Chicago and having worked for commercial firms in
Chicago and New York City, his style varied from
cartoon-like, figural work to a more naturalistic
approach, especially in his later years.[112] Albert W. Miller
(active at the Roycroft 1915–16), was another cartoon-
ist, whose drawings were used for the *Fra* and the
Philistine. Sweden's Axel Sahlin (1877–1956) was invited to East Aurora by Charles "Cy" Rosen, the head of
the printery, after seeing the younger artist's work in
Swedish trade journals.[113] Sahlin came to the community in 1911 an accomplished artisan, having
apprenticed at his father's printing shop in Lund, Sweden, and with several other printers in that country. He
worked his way up at the Roycroft from typographer to

Plate 153: Burt Barnes, *Parish Work*, 1910 (as reproduced on back cover of the March 1910 *Philistine*), 6 × 4⅝ in.
Private collection.

Plate 154: Axel Sahlin, *Ali Baba with Gardening Tools*, 1926. Pen and ink on paper, 14½ × 9⅞ in.
Roycroft Arts Museum, Boice Lydell.

foreman to superintendent of typesetting by 1915,[114] and on occasion would produce handmade greeting cards and finely detailed drawings, as in the pen and ink sketch of Ali Baba. John Septimus (Jack) Sears (1875–1969), a native of Salt Lake City, had studied at the Mark Hopkins Art Institute in San Francisco, and with William Merritt Chase, George de Forest Brush, and Robert Henri before working as a newspaper artist in New York City, Rochester, New York, and Chattanooga, Tennessee. Apparently he was at the Roycroft in 1914 and 1915 when he executed back covers for the *Philistine*. From 1919 to 1943 he was at the University of Utah in Salt Lake City teaching drafting, printmaking, and graphic design.[115]

A latecomer to the Roycroft colony was the painter Sandor Landeau, who joined in 1916 at the request of Bert Hubbard,[116] but probably also because of his friendship with Fournier. A native of Hungary, Landeau had studied in this country and had become a naturalized citizen[117] before going to Paris around 1896. He and Fournier became close associates while they were studying at the Académie Julian.[118] Landeau's early works were large religious and genre subjects intended for the Paris Salon. His *Remorse of Judas, Samson and Delilah, The Village Story Teller,* and *Christ Casting Out the Evil Spirit* (all unlocated) were probably similar in style and technique to the enormous canvas, *For the Sailors Lost at Sea*, a gold medal winner in the 1907 Paris Salon.[119] Like other Americans who painted abroad during this period, among them Gari Melchers, George Hitchcock, Elizabeth Nourse, Daniel Ridgway Knight, and Charles Sprague Pearce, Landeau was struck by the simple dignity of the peasantfolk of Europe. The painting, now owned by the Aurora Historical Society, recreates a humble candlelight vigil for the missing fishermen of a Normandy village, a common enough occurence in the lives of coastal peoples. The darkly clad figures, their sober faces softly illuminated

Fig. 79: Sandor Landeau's oil on canvas *For the Sailors Lost at Sea*, ca. 1907, which now hangs in the Aurora Town Hall.
(As published in Catalog of the Salon of 1907)

ALI BABA

The illustrious Ali Baba began life in 1839 as Anson Alonzo Blackman. He worked for C. J. Hawlin, a prominent breeder of race horses, until 1884, when he became Elbert Hubbard's general handyman, tending horses, chickens, gardens, and small children with equal aplomb.[1] Despite a more colorful story to the contrary (invoking the name of the famous thief from *The Arabian Nights* after Blackman allegedly filched some tobacco from W. W. Denslow's humidor), Elbert Hubbard II claims to have bestowed the celebrated nickname as a young boy, when "Baba" was as close as he could come to pronouncing "Blackman."[2]

When Elbert Hubbard adopted him as an alter ego and promoted him to titular head of the Motto Department, the grizzled Ali Baba assumed almost mythic proportions for readers of the *Fra* and the *Philistine*.

Plate 155: Sandor Landeau, *Ali Baba (Anson Alonzo Blackman)*. Oil on canvas, 30 × 25 in. *Roycroft Arts Museum, Boice Lydell.*

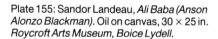
Build your art horse-high, pig-tight and bull-strong.
ALI BABA, in his great lecture,"Art As I Have Found It."

Art is largely a matter of hair-cut.
—*Ali Baba*

With characteristic good nature, the beleaguered Baba shouldered authorship of some of Hubbard's most crusty pronouncements ("Art is largely a matter of haircut"), as well as those considered too earthy to have issued from the pen of the Fra ("Two in a bush are the root of all evil").

MV

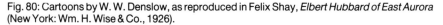
Fig. 80: Cartoons by W. W. Denslow, as reproduced in Felix Shay, *Elbert Hubbard of East Aurora* (New York: Wm. H. Wise & Co., 1926).

by the glow of the candles, starkly contrast with the powerful emotions elicited by the scene. According to Landeau's friend Henry Wack, the French government offered to purchase the painting, but Landeau chose to tour the work in the United States—first at the 1908 annual exhibition of the Pennsylvania Academy of the Fine Arts, and then in Cleveland, Detroit, Toledo, Chicago, and Buffalo.[120]

Landeau continued to live abroad for some twenty-five years after his training, except for a short period between 1904 and 1908 when he maintained a joint residency in New York City and Paris.[121] He traveled extensively—in Russia, Egypt, Palestine, Syria, Morocco—while continuing to send paintings to exhibitions in major American cities. After his early genre works, Landeau turned to classical themes, such as *The Dance of Pan* and *The Passing of Pantheism,* while still producing religious subjects as well. His *Abide in Me* and *Christ Ministering to Fallen Soldiers* were executed around the time of the outbreak of World War I, when Landeau returned to this country. By 1916, he was an active member of the Roycrofters, joining Fournier in teaching an outdoor class in figure and landscape painting that summer.[122] Fifty of his European works were shown at the Broderick Galleries in Buffalo in 1916,[123] and, that same year, another exhibition of mostly European pictures was held at Vose Galleries in Boston, where it was reviewed by the noted critic William Howe Downes. Downes described the work as mostly "religious, imaginative and symbolic" in composition, endowed "with something of the idealistic quality which removes it from the realm of stark realism. His palette," the critic continued, "is not that of an opulent colorist; in fact it is rather restricted, and decidedly cool, running largely to pale greens and blues. But he accomplishes some rather remarkable things within this narrow range of tones."[124] The Vose show included a single portrait, that of Elbert Hubbard's two grandchildren, "by way of proving," noted Downes, "that he [Landeau] can make the actualities of today appear as real as his visionary subjects."[125] Possibly a new subject for the artist after his arrival at Roycroft, portraiture may have been undertaken to alleviate Landeau's chronic need for emergency funds. Landeau's *Portrait of Nancy Hubbard with Doll* and his warm portrayal of Ali Baba were probably of a style similar to the portrait in the Vose exhibition, all displaying his perceptive gift for characterization. The subjects, although placed against a rather plain backdrop in each case, are painted with sure, thick strokes in a brighter palette than in most of Landeau's other works. In 1917 the majority of the paintings shown at Vose were hung in the Roycroft Chapel,[126] suggesting that sales may have been disappointing in Boston. Gradually, Landeau's enthusiasm for exhibiting waned, as is indicated by constant references to his reclusiveness and slow methods of working.[127] Only with sufficient prodding by Bert Hubbard did he then prepare enough paintings

Fig. 81: Nancy Hubbard breaks her pose for Sandor Landeau, as Alta Fattey Hubbard and Emma Fournier look on, 1916.
(Courtesy Turgeon-Rust Collection)

Plate 156: Sandor Landeau, *Nancy Hubbard with Doll*, 1916. Oil on canvas, 24 × 20 in.
Private collection.

for a new show.[128] Landeau, however, held to his own point of view. "It would be better for art," he said to an interviewer not long before his death, "if quantity were curbed. There is jazz painting, just as there is jazz music and writing and cooking and conversation. Enduring art must have profound self-expression. Impatience, hurry, carelessness are enemies of good pictures."[129] A series of letters written by Landeau in 1923 gives some indication of his desperate situation. He had already turned over his *For the Sailors Lost at Sea* in exchange for back rent,[130] and in August of that year he wrote to a Mr. Radgers, offering to sell his *Flight of Boabdil* at two-thirds of the original cost and the *Tower of Boabdil* at half price. "It is only the imperative needs of funds that would impell [*sic*] me to part with them at such low figures," he maintained.[131] By February of 1924, the year of his death, Landeau was asking Bert to purchase his *Toilers in the Fields,* one of the works accepted for the Paris Salon, for three thousand dollars in order to cancel his debt and, with the balance, allow him to go to California for "a change of scenery and climate."[132] The news of Landeau's death, at age sixty-four, in "comparative poverty and isolation,"[133] was received with profound sadness by Fournier, who was in Indiana at the time.[134] Upon his return to East Aurora, he placed a simple, unmarked stone at the grave of his old friend.[135]

Another facet of the Roycrofters' accomplishments was in the field of photography, although it played a relatively minor role. It centered mainly around the work of Paul Fournier (1888–1961?), the son of Alexis, Ernest J. Rawleigh (1884–1954), a Buffalo artist said to have been at Roycroft between 1910 and 1915,[136] and the art and photography critic Sadakichi Hartmann, who lived in East Aurora from 1911 to 1916.

Paul Fournier was the first photographer of any distinction at the Roycroft. He came with his family in 1903 and was put to work producing lantern slides for the many lectures held in the Chapel.[137] He also did landscape photography and numerous portraits of the Hubbard group, especially of Elbert, which, when distributed nationally with Roycroft products, also promoted young Fournier as a photographer. A good example of his work is the photograph of Miriam Hubbard, daughter of Elbert and Alice. The artist's use of a soft focus, with diffusion of line and extraneous detail into a unified whole, produces less of an individual's portrait than a subjective notion of that person, true to the precepts of Photo-Pictorialism, a movement to which Fournier's work belongs. Originated in England, the style blossomed in this country through Alfred Stieglitz's Photo-Secession group, established in New York City in 1902, and, at about the same time, within the "Buffalo School" of photography as represented by the work of its founders: Wilbur H. Porterfield, Oscar C. Anthony, Will A. Hatch, Samuel S. Lloyd, John M. Schreck, Charles

Plate 157: Paul Fournier, *Miriam Hubbard*, ca. 1904. Platinum print, 19 × 14 in.
Collection of Kitty Turgeon-Rust and Robert Rust, Roycroft Shops.

A. Booz, G. Edwin Keller, and Edward B. Sides. Choosing a halfway approach between photography and painting, hence "Photo-Pictorialism," these artists were not above manipulating the negative to achieve a desired, often romantic, effect. Fournier's aim was "to make a picture look as beautiful as possible."[138]

In 1906 the *East Aurora Advertiser* announced that Fournier had gone to Philadelphia "for a new job with one of the leading photography studios in that city."[139] In the following years, he received a number of national awards, but by 1910 his photography career apparently was at an end, possibly with the general demise of the Photo-Pictorial movement around the time of World War I.

In 1907, the year after Fournier left for Philadelphia, the noted critic Sadakichi Hartmann was asked to lecture at the annual Roycroft convention. Hartmann was already nationally known for his pioneering essays on Modernism, especially in promoting photography as a fine art, and was also part of the Stieglitz circle in New York City. He and Stieglitz had a brief falling out when Hartmann sold his prose poem, "White Chrysanthemums," to Hubbard for the *Fra* (April 1909), having previously been paid by Stieglitz for its appearance in *Camera Work*, the main organ for the Photo-Secessionists.[140] Hartmann later wrote about his 1907 "vacation" in East Aurora: "I thought I would indulge for a change in Elbert Hubbard's philosophy of sunshine, get interested in flowers, trees and Roycroft products, and forget for a while all about art and photography."[141] Instead, he was greeted by a hoard of camera buffs and "was inveigled into dissertations on art in photography at all hours of the day and night."[142]

One admirer was Lillian Bonham, a freelance artist who at times did caricatures and other work for the Roycroft.[143] She and Hartmann later met again in New York City and, by the time Hartmann came to stay at East Aurora in 1911, they were married. They settled in a rented cottage named "Dreamhaven," on Grove Street. Hartmann was often away from the village on lecture tours, but he did manage to contribute some writings to the *Fra* and the *Philistine,* as well as ad copy for the products. Hubbard's letter requesting him to try his hand at writing advertisements—"one on the subject of Roycroft Modeled Leather, another on the subject of Roycroft Copper and another on Roycroft Books"—also implies that Hartmann's preference had been to write poetry for the publication.[144] "Poetry is strictly on the bum," Hubbard stated, but added, "I think that you would make a very able ad writer. Poetry usually advertises nothing but a man's own futilities."[145] Hartmann continued his critical writings while at Roycroft, as in his book *Landscape and Figure Composition* (1910), in which he reproduced seven of Paul Fournier's works as excellent examples of the principles of good photography.[146] The critic left East Aurora in 1916, after submitting a memorial piece about Hubbard that was not published.[147] Hartmann's later writings never quite matched the brilliancy of his early work, and by 1923, he had moved to southern

California, where he reviewed Hollywood films and even tried his hand at acting. His last years were spent on an Indian reservation near Banning, California.[148]

Any attempt to characterize the forty-year history of artistic endeavor at the Roycroft as a single stylistic voice, as we are somewhat able to do with other artists' colonies in America, such as those at Woodstock, New York, or Cos Cob and Old Lyme, Connecticut,[149] would be fruitless, considering the many viewpoints taken by the East Aurora artisans. Perhaps the closest semblance to a general style preference at the Roycroft, aside from the Art Nouveau tendencies in the graphic work, would be the monochromatic, Tonalist approach in the work of Ahrens, Douglas, Brewer, Landeau, and both Fourniers. Certainly, Elbert Hubbard's taste ran in that direction, given his writings on the Barbizons and his recruitment of artists steeped in that aesthetic. Impressionism to him was merely an extension of the same school of thought—the sentimental subject seen through Tonalist eyes,[150] and early Modernism, which was beginning to take hold in the urban centers of the country, especially after the Armory Show of 1913, was nowhere to be seen at the Roycroft. Suffice it to say that the community's ideal offers instead a legacy of another kind, a belief that art should be a part of one's daily life—and work. "Beauty is a gratification, a peace and solace to every normal man and woman," Hubbard wrote in 1902. "Beautiful sounds, beautiful colors, beautiful proportions, beautiful thoughts, how our souls hunger for them! Matter is only mind in an opaque condition, and all beauty is but a symbol of spirit."[151]

Fig. 82: Lillian Bonham's bookplate for her husband,
Sadakichi Hartmann, 1912. (As published in the *Fra,* August 1912)

The author wishes to acknowledge the valuable assistance of Beverly Waller, Mary Myers, Wendy Smith, and Kim Liddle, interns at the Memorial Art Gallery of the University of Rochester, New York; M. Elizabeth Boone and Rebecca Stamm, independent researchers in New York City and Buffalo, respectively; William H. Loos, Head Librarian, Rare Book Room, Buffalo and Erie County Public Library, Buffalo; Catherine Mason, Assistant Librarian, Buffalo and Erie County Historical Society, Buffalo; Kathy Ritter and Kari Horowicz of the Albright-Knox Art Gallery

Library, Buffalo; Kitty Turgeon and Robert Rust, Director and Curator of the Foundation for the Study of the Arts and Crafts Movement, East Aurora; Bruce Bland, Co-Curator of the Elbert Hubbard-Roycroft Museum, East Aurora; and Evelyn Walker, Librarian, Department of Rare Books & Special Collections, Rush Rhees Library, University of Rochester, New York. The author is also indebted to William H. Gerdts for the use of his extensive reference library.

ENDNOTES

[1] Quoted in Roycroft motto card, reproduced in Mary Roelofs Stott, *Rebel with Reverence, Elbert Hubbard: A Granddaughter's Tribute*, 2nd ed. (Watkins Glen: American Life Foundation, 1984), 57.

[2] Bonnie Baker Thorne, "Elbert Hubbard and the Publications of the Roycroft Shop 1893–1915" (Ph.D. diss., Texas Woman's University, 1975), 49.

[3] School Records, National Academy of Design, New York City. Warner was registered at the National Academy of Design for the season of 1893 and 1894. He was given an honorable mention for his work in the Life School in May of 1894.

[4] In a letter from Bert Hubbard, East Aurora, to Máirín Allen, Dublin, Ireland, undated (quoted in Máirín Allen, "Jerome Connor-One," *Capuchin Annual* 13 [1963]: 358), Bert says that his father knew a man in Quincy, Massachusetts, named Bill Spear who had taken both Warner and Jerome Connor, a sculptor later at the Roycroft, "under his wing and was helping them with their economic and other struggles." An undated, unpublished manuscript in the Roycroft Arts Museum archives, written by Warner, describes in the first chapter (pp. 1–3) the artist's introduction to Hubbard via their mutual friend Spear in West Quincy, Massachusetts; in the next chapter (pp. 6–7) Warner mentions the invitation from Hubbard to join the Roycroft community. Spear was the caretaker of the Old John Adams House and the Quincy Historical Society, according to the manuscript.

[5] "Another Account of the Roycroft Shop," *American Printer and Lithographer* 29 (February 1900): 332.

[6] See A. R. Andrews, "The Roycroft Printing Shop," *American Printer & Bookmaker* (29 February 1900): 329. The author describes a visit to the Roycroft where he observed "young girls and ladies of the village, some seventy or more" filling in initials "which were printed in outline in the forms," applying colors with a brush and "the gold work with a pen." Elbert Hubbard, Jr., in a letter to George Farrel, 26 March 1963 (Roycroft File D.77, 2:2, Department of Rare Books & Special Collections, Rush Rhees Library, University of Rochester), remembered that his wife, Alta Fattey, an artist in her own right, worked under Warner beginning around 1900. He "would lay out color schemes for whatever work was in line. At one time there were seventy-five girls in his department."

[7] *A Catalog of Some Specimens of Art & Handicraft Done By Roycroft Workers* (East Aurora: The Roycrofters, [1900]), 4. One other early exhibition is mentioned in the literature on Warner, a joint show with W. H. Levitt held in 1902 at the Orchard Studio in East Aurora. ("Roycroft Artist Samuel Warner's 'History' Rediscovered," *East Aurora Advertiser,* 10 December 1982)

[8] Information on Warner's years immediately after the Roycroft is still relatively sparse. About the period 1903 to 1913 little is known, but from 1913 until his death in 1947 he was involved in the school system of Pembroke, Massachusetts, and the surrounding towns, developing art programs for some fifty-three schools. He married the artist Mary Ward in 1919, divorced in 1926, and settled permanently in Duxbury, Massachusetts, where he occasionally exhibited his work in oil, watercolor,

pastel, and charcoal. ("Roycroft Artist Samuel Warner's 'History' Rediscovered")

[9] Even after Denslow was working for the Roycroft, Hubbard was apparently still looking for an artist with wood engraving skills. A 1900 article on the Roycroft Shop mentions that engravings were still being done by a "zinc process," but the author quotes the Roycrofters as saying "with supreme optimism, a wood engraver will blow in and their bookplates will be printed just as were the bookplates of centuries ago." ("Another Account of the Roycroft Shop," 332) Denslow had mastered the difficult art of woodcut engraving by the age of seventeen, when he illustrated for the magazine *Hearth and Home* in New York. His drawing skills were also finely tuned by this time as the result of coursework taken at the Cooper Institute for the Advancement of Science and Art, New York, in 1870 and 1871 (Douglas G. Greene and Michael Patrick Hearn, *W. W. Denslow* [Mt. Pleasant: Clarke Historical Library, Central Michigan University, 1976], 4); and classes in the antique (1872–75) and a life drawing class (1874–75) at the National Academy of Design, New York City. (School Records, National Academy of Design, New York City)

[10] Forrest Crissey, "William Wallace Denslow," *Carter's Monthly* 13 (March 1898): 274.

[11] Albert Lane, *Elbert Hubbard and His Work* (Worcester, Mass.: Blanchard Press, 1901), 83.

[12] W. W. Denslow, Highwood, Ill., to Elbert Hubbard, 20 July 1896, quoted in Paul McKenna, *A History and Bibliography of the Roycroft Printing Shop* (North Tonawanda, N.Y.: Tona Graphics, 1986), 27.

[13] "Announcement," *Philistine* 6, no. 6 (May 1898): 190.

[14] Felix Shay, *Elbert Hubbard of East Aurora* (New York: William H. Wise & Co., 1926), 149.

[15] Greene and Hearn, *W. W. Denslow,* 77.

[16] Douglas G. Greene, "W. W. Denslow, Illustrator," *Journal Of Popular Culture* 7 (Summer 1973): 90.

[17] Ibid., 92. Denslow's wife, who accompanied the two men to East Aurora, fell in love with Mazzanovich and eventually married him.

[18] Andrews, "The Roycroft Printing Shop," 329.

[19] *The Roycroft School of Applied Art* (East Aurora: The Roycrofters, [ca. 1900–01]), 1.

[20] See William H. Gerdts, *Monet's Giverny: An Impressionist Colony* (New York: Abbeville Press, 1993), 241, n. 82.

[21] Charles Teaze Clark, *Lawrence Mazzanovich, 1871–1958: Tryon Paintings* (Tryon, N.C.: Tryon Fine Arts Center, 1991), 2.

[22] "Hippocampus Den," *Baum Bugle* 2 (Autumn 1963): 7. Denslow seems to have kept in touch with his Roycroft friends. A reporter for the *East Aurora Advertiser* made mention of "nothing but original pictures by Denslow" on the walls of the new Bindery in March of 1907 ("Among the Roycrofters, *East Aurora Advertiser,* 7 March 1907); and in 1909 the same paper noted that Denslow was in town, reminiscing about his "former times as a Roycrofter." ("Former Roycrofters," *East Aurora Advertiser,* 25 November 1909)

[23] B. Hubbard to M. Allen. Connor's address in the *American Art Annual* for 1899 is listed as Quincy, Massachusetts (Florence N. Levy,

ed., *American Art Annual*, vol. 1 [New York: MacMillan Co., 1899], 435), although there is no evidence in the Quincy city directories for 1899–1900 that he was a resident that year.

24 R.S.W., "Distinguished Irishmen—XIV. A Moulder of Marble in an Irish Bohemia," *Daily Express* (London), 10 August 1929.

25 Giollamuire Ó Murchú, *Jerome Connor, Irish-American Sculptor: 1874–1943* (Dublin: National Gallery of Ireland), 74.

26 Ibid.

27 Elbert Hubbard, "Heart to Heart Talks," *Philistine* 8, no. 3 (February 1899): 82–84.

28 *A Few Bits of Sculpture in Terra Cotta as Made by Saint Gerome, at the Roycroft Shop, East Aurora, New York, U.S.A.* (East Aurora: The Roycrofters, 1899).

29 "Another Account of the Roycroft Shop," 332.

30 "Local and Personal," *East Aurora Advertiser,* 9 March 1899.

31 Anne Donohoe Connor had previously worked two years in the Roycroft Bindery. (Ó Murchú, *Jerome Connor*, 74)

32 "Local and Personal," *East Aurora Advertiser,* 16 January 1902.

33 Felix Shay, *Elbert Hubbard of East Aurora*, 148.

34 "Local and Personal," *East Aurora Advertiser,* 10 July 1902.

35 Lorado Taft, *The History of American Sculpture* (New York: MacMillan Co., 1903), 448; and Frances B. Sheafer, "A Sculptor of the People," *Booklovers Magazine* 1 (June 1903), 622–28.

36 I am grateful to Valerie Balint, Project Coordinator for Save Outdoor Sculpture (SOS), Troy, New York, for this information.

37 For a complete history of the Lusitania commission and other facets of Connor's post-Roycroft career, see Ó Murchú, *Jerome Connor*. The memorial was finally completed in 1966–68 for a waterfront location in Cobh, Ireland.

38 *A Catalog of Some Specimens of Art & Handicraft,* 3.

39 Douglas apparently dropped the final s when she began to exhibit her work. Her birth date, according to the East Aurora town census of 1900, was 1873, but the 1910 census gives her age as 36, which would make it 1874. Other sources give the birth year as 1872.

40 Ibid., 1.

41 Jennifer C. Watson, *Carl Ahrens as Printmaker: A Catalogue Raisonné* (Kitchener, Ontario: Kitchener-Waterloo Art Gallery, 1984), 7–8.

42 Ibid., 7.

43 In filling out the biographical form for the National Gallery of Canada (date unknown), Ahrens stated, "I studied for a short time with the above men [Wm. Chase, N.Y., F. Edwin Elwell, Sculp., N.Y.] but George Inness who was my friend advised me to work out my problems alone which I have done thanks to his good advice." (Carl Ahrens File, Library Archives, National Gallery of Canada, Ottawa)

44 Early works include *The Fisherman's Child,* exhibited at the Royal Canadian Academy in 1893, *Cradled in the Net,* shown at the 1893 World's Columbian Exposition in Chicago, and *The Goose Girl,* which was included in the 1894 Palette Club exhibition in Toronto.

45 Watson, *Carl Ahrens as Printmaker*, 10.

46 Ibid., 7.

47 R. C. Reade, "Hermits of Art," *Star Weekly,* 4 May 1929.

48 Edwina Spencer, "Carl Ahrens and His Work," *Brush and Pencil* 14 (April 1904), 18.

49 Vee See, "In a Garden Behind No. 278," *National Life* (August 1922): 2.

50 Newton A. Fuessle, "Eleanor Douglas and Her Studio," *The Claxton* 1 (September 1910): 27–31.

51 Ibid., 30–31.

52 Douglas taught the poet and author Richard Le Gallienne, a frequent visitor to the Roycroft, the names of local birds, trees, and flowers (Fuessle, "Eleanor Douglas and Her Studio," 31); she allowed Sandor Landeau, an artist who came to East Aurora in 1915, the use of her studio in the winter of 1920 (S. L. Landeau to the Board of Water Commissioners, East Aurora, 21 November 1921, private archive, East Aurora); and she shared with Alexis Fournier, a Roycrofter from 1902 on, favorite sketching haunts along the banks of the Cazenovia Creek in East Aurora. ("A Lover of the Woods," *Buffalo Illustrated Express*, 29 March 1908)

53 Rachelle Francis, "The West End School: A Magnet for Creative Minds," *Roycroft Review* 1 (1991): 53.

54 Gaspard's list of portraits for Roycroft publications included such notables as Dante Gabriel Rossetti, Rosa Bonheur, George Washington, Thomas Jefferson, Abraham Lincoln, Sandro Botticelli, Peter Paul Rubens, Jean-Baptiste-Camille Corot, Jean-François Millet, Diego Velázquez, Victor Hugo, Walt Whitman, George Eliot, Samuel Johnson, and Clara Barton.

55 Florence N. Levy, ed., *American Art Annual,* vol. 1, 447. The school records of the Art Institute of Chicago contain no mention of Gaspard having studied there; documentation in the 1880s, however, was extremely poor.

56 School Records, Art Students' League, New York City.

57 Peter Hastings Falk, *Who Was Who in American Art* (Madison, Conn.: Sound View Press, 1985), 225.

58 Shay, *Elbert Hubbard of East Aurora,* 150–51.

59 Rena Neumann Coen, *In the Mainstream: The Art of Alexis Jean Fournier, 1865–1948* (St. Cloud, Minn.: North Star Press, 1985), 48. Coen states that Fournier took over for Gaspard as art director in 1901.

60 Florence N. Levy, ed., *American Art Annual,* vol. 4 (New York: American Art Annual, 1903), 29.

61 "Personal Pointers," *East Aurora Advertiser,* 29 April 1909.

62 Lena M. McCauley, "Otto J. Schneider: Painter-Etcher," in *The Print Collector's Bulletin: An Illustrated Catalogue of Painter-Etchings* (Chicago: Albert Roullier, n.d.), Pamphlet Files, Ryerson Library, Art Institute of Chicago.

63 School Records, Art Institute of Chicago. Schneider received a mark of 64 in the Academic Department of the school.

64 *Catalogue of an Exhibition and Sale of Dry-Points by Otto J. Schneider* (Chicago: Albert Roullier, 1900), 1.

65 Ibid.; and Macauley, "Otto J. Schneider: Painter-Etcher." Two letters to Schneider, one from Alice Hubbard dated 22 December 1905, and another from Elbert dated 23 December, thanking him for his work on their portraits, were addressed to Carnegie Hall in New York, a popular building for artists' studios, even today.

66 *Exhibition of Original Drawings and Etchings by Otto J. Schneider* (Chicago: Albert Roullier's Art Galleries, 1915), 1. The architectural scenes of Paris reproduced in the catalogue, in extremely fine detail, are presented as the "fruit of Mr. Schneider's recent European travels." The author notes that the artist had just returned from Paris where he had been "working for several years."

67 Levy, *American Art Annual,* p. 65, lists Schneider in Chicago in 1903; volumes 5 and 6 list him in New York City from 1905 to 1908 (Florence N. Levy, ed., *American Art Annual,* vol. 5 [New York: American Federation of Arts, 1905–06], 416; and vol. 6, [New York: American Federation of Arts, 1907–08], 410); there is no listing between 1910 and 1912, but by 1913 he is in Chicago (Florence N. Levy, ed., *American Art Annual* [New York: American Federation of Arts, 1913], 343). There is one notice of Schneider in the New York City directories for 1905 and 1906, when his address is given as 883 7th Avenue, the Carnegie Hall artists' studios. He apparently was still at the Roycroft in 1907 since he signed Warner's autograph book "To Sammy – with apologies – Otto J. Schneider, E. A., July 6, 1907." (Schneider file, Archives, Roycroft Arts Museum, East Aurora)

[68] H. Kenneth Dirlam and Ernest E. Simmons, *Sinners, This is East Aurora* (New York: Vantage Press, 1964), 136.

[69] Bartlett came to East Aurora in April of 1908 to make "preparations to erect in front of the Roycroft Shop a replica in bronze of his 'Michael Angelo.'" ("Paul Bartlett," *Fra* 1 [April 1908]: 7) The *East Aurora Advertiser* announced on 5 May 1909 the erection of the statue; and the minutes of the Annual Meeting of Stockholders of the Roycroft Corporation, 25 May 1909, record the $1500 casting by Gorham Company, as a "gift of Paul Bartlett." (Archives, Elbert Hubbard-Roycroft Museum, East Aurora)

[70] Portrait painter, lithographer, ceramic designer, and illustrator, English-born Rhead would have been a valuable asset to the Roycroft. According to Lynn Scholz, whose manuscript on the artist is soon to be published, Rhead was not commissioned by Hubbard for the Whitman portrait drawing. This information, according to Ms. Scholz, is contained in a letter from Rhead to Hubbard dated 2 September 1900 (Archives, Harry Ransom Humanities Research Center, University of Texas, Austin).

[71] Lynette I. Rhodes, *The Roycroft Shops, 1894–1915* (Erie: Erie Art Center, 1975).

[72] *Minnesotan* 1 (January 1916): 15, cited in Coen, *In the Mainstream*, 48.

[73] According to William H. Gerdts (*Art Across America: Two Centuries of Regional Painting, 1710 – 1920*, vol. 3 [New York: Abbeville Press, 1990], 14), Brewer and Fournier dominated the rising art establishment in Minneapolis about this time—Fournier, especially, with his showing of 193 works at the Minneapolis Industrial Exposition of 1892. Many of these works were drawings of cliff dwellings he produced as the official artist of the 1891 H. Jay Smith Expedition to Colorado and New Mexico, which were incorporated into a giant panoramic mural at the World's Columbian Exposition in Chicago the next year. Fournier also did a four-season mural for the home of Dr. Arthur Strachauer (Coen, *In the Mainstream*, 45). He would repeat this seasonal concept for murals at his home in East Aurora.

[74] Coen, *In the Mainstream*, 48.

[75] *Oils by Fournier – "Roycrofter-at-large"* (East Aurora: The Roycrofters, 1903), Archives, Roycroft Arts Museum.

[76] Fournier was accepted in the 1894, 1895, 1899, 1900, and 1901 Paris salons.

[77] *Minneapolis Journal*, 29 August 1903: 16.

[78] Documented summer classes are those in 1904 and a later one in 1916 with his friend Sandor Landeau, who had joined the colony that year.

[79] Miriam Hubbard Roelofs, "Tribute to Alexis Jean Fournier," in *Alexis Jean Fournier: A Barbizon in East Aurora* (Buffalo: Burchfield Art Center, 1979), 6; and "New Thought Convention," *East Aurora Advertiser*, 8 August 1913.

[80] "Roycroft Convention," *East Aurora Advertiser*, 1 June 1905.

[81] "The World on Canvas," unidentified clipping, ca. March 1905, Hauenstein Scrapbooks, vol. 3, p. 119, Library Archives, Albright Knox Art Gallery. Other murals were done for the homes of Mr. and Mrs. William C. Carr and Mr. S. C. Pratt, both of Buffalo.

[82] Ibid.

[83] The complete series, alternately titled "The Homes and Haunts of the Barbizon Masters," was shown at the Schaus Art Galleries, New York City, in 1910; at the Detroit Art Institute, the Art Institute of Chicago, the Minneapolis Society of Fine Arts, and the St. Paul Gallery and School of Art in 1911; and at the Albright Art Gallery, Buffalo, in 1913. Part of the series was shown at Vose Gallery, Boston, and the Memorial Art Gallery, Rochester, in 1919. Hubbard's 1911 and 1912 second series of *Little Journeys to the Homes of Eminent Artists and Painters* included many of the Barbizon artists.

[84] "Alexis J. Fournier, Landscapist, Dead," *New York Times*, 21 January 1948.

[85] "Can You Capture Sunsets? One East Auroran Who Can Host to Advertiser Writer," *East Aurora Advertiser*, 18 October 1934.

[86] "Fournier Funeral Rites Being Held Friday Afternoon," *East Aurora Advertiser*, 22 January 1948.

[87] "Who is Who in Minnesota Art Annuals: A Little Journey to the Home of a Well Known Artist in East Aurora, New York," *Minnesotan* 1 (January 1916): 15.

[88] Coen, *In the Mainstream*, 15. Another longtime friend of Fournier's who visited the Roycroft was the Minnesotan painter Herbjørn Gausta (1854–1924). A portrait of Fournier by Gausta hangs in the Elbert Hubbard-Roycroft Museum, East Aurora.

[89] Nicholas R. Brewer, *Trails of a Paintbrush* (Boston: The Christopher Publishing House, 1938), 168–69. Le Gallienne described his and Fournier's adventures on a hiking trip from East Aurora to New York City in his 1910 book *October Vagabonds* (New York: Mitchell Kennerley, 1910).

[90] Some of the other camps built by the Roycrofters include the "Three-Mile Camp," built around 1895 and located four miles from the village; the "Log House," on North Grove Street; the "Brushken," a shack built on top of a landfill located at the foot of Hubbard Hill; and the "Camp on Hubbard Road" where department heads would go to exercise and have steak dinners. (Archives, Roycroft Arts Museum) There was also the "Little Journeys Camp," described by Bert Hubbard in the *Fra* 16, no. 1 (October 1915): 1–2.

[91] Shay, *Elbert Hubbard of East Aurora*, 267–68.

[92] Coen, *In the Mainstream*, 77–84. Two of the Indiana colony, Adolph Robert Shulz and George Ames Aldrich, were students at the Académie Julian when Fournier was there. He also knew Adam Emory Albright, a fellow member of the Society of Western Artists. Another artist in the Brown County Impressionist group was J. Otis Adams, who exhibited twenty-four paintings at the Roycroft Chapel art gallery in 1905. ("Local and Personal," *East Aurora Advertiser*, 26 January 1905)

[93] "A. J. Fournier, Famed Artist, Dies of Injury," *Buffalo Courier-Express*, 21 January 1948.

[94] "Can You Capture Sunsets?"

[95] *Philistine* 17, no. 2 (July 1903): 3.

[96] Los Angeles city directories, 1906–18; and San Francisco city directories, 1920–24.

[97] Cathleen Baker, "Dard Hunter—Roycroft Artist," *Arts & Crafts Quarterly* 6 (January-April 1993): 6–7. Ms. Baker is presently working on a definitive biography of the artist.

[98] Dard Hunter, Riverside, Calif., to Phil Hunter, Chillicothe, Ohio, 25 November 1903, quoted in Baker, "Dard Hunter—Roycroft Artist," 7.

[99] Dard Hunter, *My Life with Paper* (New York: Alfred A. Knopf, 1958), 29.

[100] Baker, "Dard Hunter—Roycroft Artist," 7.

[101] Hunter, *My Life with Paper*, 31.

[102] Ibid., 31.

[103] Ibid., 34.

[104] Ibid., 43.

[105] Baker, "Dard Hunter—Roycroft Artist," 10.

[106] Ibid., 10; and "Author Makes Paper and Prints Own Books," *Popular Mechanics* 43 (April 1925): 557–58.

[107] Paul McKenna, *A History and Bibliography*, 34.

[108] Anne McIlhenney, "Important Art Colony Flourishes in Suburb," *Buffalo Courier-Express*, 11 November 1934.

[109] "Local Brevities," *East Aurora Advertiser*, 11 July 1912.

[110] "Merle D. James, Painter and Retired Editor, Dies," *Buffalo Courier-Express*, 12 November 1963. James subsequently left East Aurora for Cushing, Maine, to be near his daughter and son-in-law Andrew Wyeth. James's watercolors, having supplanted his work in oil around 1943, bear much resemblance in technique and freshness to Wyeth's work.

[111] *East Aurora Advertiser*, 23 July 1908.

[112] For more information on Barnes, see Cleta H. Downey, *Burt*

Barnes (Albuquerque: University Art Museum, 1974); and the Burt Barnes papers, Archives of American Art, Smithsonian Institution, Washington, D.C.

[113] Thorne, "Elbert Hubbard and the Publishing of the Roycroft Shop," 70.

[114] "Artist in Printer's Type," *Buffalo Business* 20 (October 1945): 15.

[115] Doris O. Dawdy, *Artists of the American West*, vol. 3 (Athens, Ohio: Ohio University Press, 1985), 395.

[116] "Grave of Artist in Local Cemetery Remains Unmarked," *East Aurora Advertiser*, 30 March 1961. According to the Minutes of the Roycroft Annual Shareholders/Directors meeting of 1909, a Landeau painting was purchased for $500, seven years before he came to the community.

[117] "Sandor Landeau," *Literary Digest* 86 (15 August 1925): 27.

[118] "Grave of Artist in Local Cemetery Remains Unmarked." Like Fournier, Landeau studied with Jean Paul Laurens and Benjamin Constant, artists associated with the academic point of view.

[119] *La Dame a l'Echarpe* won an honorable mention at the same salon.

[120] Henry Wellington Wack, "A Painter of the Spiritual Life," *Current Opinion* 72 (June 1922): 806.

[121] Landeau gave a New York City address with his entry in the National Academy of Design annual of 1904. (Peter Hastings Falk, *Annual Exhibition Record of the National Academy of Design, 1901– 1950* [Madison, Conn.: Sound View Press, 1990], 314) The same year he gave a Paris address to the editors of the *American Art Annual* (Florence N. Levy, ed., American Art Annual, vol. 4 [New York: American Art Annual, 1903], 44; and dual New York City and Paris addresses in the same publication for 1905–08. (Florence N. Levy, ed., *American Art Annual*, vol. 5, 6 [New York: American Art Annual, 1904–06, 1907–08], 382, 375, respectively)

[122] "Fournier-Landeau Outdoor Summer School of Art," *Fra* 17 (June 1916): xiii.

[123] Charles F. Hamilton, *Roycroft Collectibles* (Tavares, Fla.: SPS Publications, 1980), 85.

[124] W[illiam] H[owe] D[ownes], "Mr. Landeau's Pictures," *Boston Evening Transcript* [ca. 1916], reprinted in *Exhibition of Oil Paintings by Sandor Landeau* (Hingham, Mass.: South Shore Country Club, 1921).

[125] Ibid.

[126] *Exhibition of Paintings by Sandor L. Landeau at the Roycroft Chapel, East Aurora* (East Aurora: The Roycrofters, [ca. 1917–18]). The catalogue states that the "majority of the paintings comprising this collection were recently exhibited in Boston." The paintings were being "offered for sale at about half the original prices," owing "to the war conditions."

[127] Wack, "A Painter of the Spiritual Life," 808; *Exhibition of Paintings by Sandor Landeau*, 1; and "Sandor Landeau," *Literary Digest*, 27.

[128] "Grave of Artist in Local Cemetery Remains Unmarked."

[129] "Sandor Landeau," *Literary Digest*, 28.

[130] Unidentified manuscript, Landeau file, Memorial Art Gallery.

[131] Sandor Landeau, East Aurora, to Mr. Radgers, 16 August 1923, Landeau file, Archives, Roycroft Arts Museum.

[132] Sandor Landeau, East Aurora, to Bert Hubbard, 20 February 1924, Landeau file, Archives, Roycroft Arts Museum.

[133] "Sandor Landeau," *Literary Digest*, 28.

[134] Alexis Fournier, South Bend, Ind., to Bert Hubbard, East Aurora, 20 June 1924. In the letter, Fournier expresses a wish that "things had been different for us all."

[135] "Grave of Artist in Local Cemetery Remains Unmarked."

[136] Anthony Bannon, *The Photo-Pictorialists of Buffalo* (Buffalo: Media Study, 1981), 96.

[137] "Local and Personal," *East Aurora Advertiser*, 6 September 1906.

[138] Paul Fournier, "Impressionistic Photography: A Conversation," *Arena* 38 (November 1907): 530.

[139] "Personal Pointers," *East Aurora Advertiser*, 11 October 1906. According to Bannon (*The Photo-Pictorialists of Buffalo*, 90–91), Fournier married a Virginia woman in 1923 and, around the same time, was a salesman and credit manager for the Encyclopedia Britannica. He died in Van Nuys, California.

[140] Sadakichi Hartmann, *The Valiant Knights of Daguerre: Selected Critical Essays on Photography and Profiles of Photographic Pioneers*, ed. Harry W. Lawton and George Knox (Berkeley: University of California Press, 1978), 12.

[141] Ibid., 278.

[142] Ibid.

[143] Charles F. Hamilton, "The Roycroft Period: Hartmann, Hubbard, and East Aurora," *Sadakichi Hartmann Newsletter* 2 (Spring 1971): 2.

[144] Elbert Hubbard to Sadakichi Hartmann, Arden, Del., 16 August 1912, quoted in ibid., 3.

[145] Ibid.

[146] See Sadakichi Hartmann, *Landscape and Figure Composition* (New York: Baker & Taylor Co., 1910).

[147] Hamilton, "The Roycroft Period," 4.

[148] Hartmann, *The Valiant Knights of Daguerre*, 26.

[149] For information on these artists' colonies, see Gerdts, *Art Across America*, vol. 1, 120–25, 168–71.

[150] Elbert Hubbard, "Realism and Impressionism," *Fra* 7, no. 3 (June 1911): 86.

[151] Elbert Hubbard, "An Interesting Personality: Elbert Hubbard," *Cosmopolitan* 32 (January 1902): 308–20.

The Roycroft Pottery

[1] Charles M. Skinner, *Brooklyn Eagle*, 3 September 1899, quoted in "East Aurora Defined," *Philistine* 9, no. 6 (November 1899).

[2] "Another Account of the Roycroft Shops," *American Printer and Lithographer* 29 (February 1900): 332.

[3] *A Catalog of Some Specimens of Art & Handicraft done by Roycroft Workers* (East Aurora: The Roycrofters, [1900]).

[4] "Art Students' League Farewell Tea and Sale," *Buffalo Express*, 22 March 1902.

[5] F. F. D. Alberry, "The Roycroft Shop," *Columbus Dispatch*, 28 August 1904, reprinted in untitled, undated Roycroft brochure of same title.

[6] Manuscript captioned "Statement of Facts for Benefit of Mr. Merritt," Elbert Hubbard-Roycroft Museum archive.

[7] Carl Ahrens to Elbert Hubbard, 1 September 1901, Elbert Hubbard Museum archive.

[8] "Statement of Facts."

[9] Ahrens file, Elbert Hubbard-Roycroft Museum archive.

[10] The multi-talented Dard Hunter did experiment with a few molded ceramic pots at some point during his stay at the Roycroft (see Plate 147); these are signed with his monogram and variations on the Roycroft mark. There is no evidence, however, that Hunter's pots were intended for commercial distribution.

Ali Baba

[1] Genealogical records, Blackman file, Archives, Roycroft Arts Museum.

[2] *Fra* 16, no. 3 (December 1917): 73–74.

Laurene Buckley, formerly Chief Curator and Assistant Director for Curatorial Affairs at the Memorial Art Gallery of the University of Rochester, is now Director of New Britain Museum of American Art.

"An Ideal Place for Tired Humanity"
Snippets from the Guest Books of the Roycroft Inn

MARIE VIA

Elbert Hubbard's biographers are numerous, his detractors many, his devotees legion. He is painted as both saint and sinner, savior and charlatan. The Roycroft itself emerges either as a community that offered manual training and cultural enrichment to young people with few other opportunities—or as a purely capitalistic enterprise that allowed Hubbard to build a small dynasty on the backs of naive country people.

Many of the standard Roycroft references were written years after Hubbard's death; while names and dates may be verified through public records, published accounts of *life* at the Roycroft were often shaped by personal motives, selective memory, and sentiment. The recent discovery of many hundreds of first-person chronicles, recorded in the pages of guest registers of the Roycroft Inn, provides an unexpectedly clear window through which the reader can gaze back through time, directly into the hearts and minds of people *as* they experienced the Roycroft.

Plate 158: *Guest Book from the Burne-Jones Room of the Roycroft Inn*, ca. 1916–1923. Suede leather, silk, and paper, 8½ × 6½ in. *Elbert Hubbard-Roycroft Museum.*

Fig. 83: The Roycroft Inn, ca. 1905. (As published in *The Roycroft Inn*, undated promotional booklet)

The *Philistine*, the first of Elbert Hubbard's widely-circulated monthly magazines, appeared in 1895, eventually exposing tens of thousands of Americans to the Roycroftie brand of folksy humor and pragmatism. When the first curious souls ventured out to East Aurora to see for themselves what was going on at the Roycroft, Hubbard took a few paying guests into his own home. Later, as growing numbers made this increasingly impractical, visitors were sent over to the Phalanstery, a frame building which had housed the original Print Shop and offices, but which had been turned into a dormitory for Roycroft workers after the presses were moved into new and roomier quarters across the street. Eventually, the guests outnumbered the workers; the Phalanstery was enlarged and improved and in 1903 became known as the Roycroft Inn.

Plate 160: *Dinner Plate from the Roycroft Inn*, ca. 1926. Design attributed to Dard Hunter, manufactured by Buffalo Pottery. Painted china, 10 in. diam.
Collection of Bruce A. Austin.

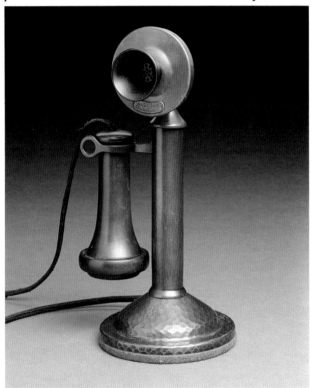

Plate 159: *Telephone from the Roycroft Inn.* Manufactured by American Telephone & Telegraph Company. Copper, molded synthetic, and cord, 11¾ × 5¼ in.
Collection of Fritz and Jane Gram.

If the shops were the heart of the Roycroft community, then surely the Inn was its soul, the spiritual center from which pulsed the raw energy that powered the community. Guests entered the hotel through a massive oaken door carved with the first of many inspirational mottoes they would encounter during their stay: "Produce great people; the rest follows." The inviting reception room, with its beamed ceilings, massive fireplace, and Navajo rugs bore no trace of its birth as a print shop. In the well-stocked library, guests could relax with a good book or write letters to those back

home, while in the dining room two hundred guests and Roycroft workers could find places at large round tables conducive to conversation. The salon was decorated with a frieze of murals by Alex Fournier depicting the great cities of the world—London, Paris, Venice, East Aurora—and from the dais Elbert Hubbard addressed guests and workers alike in a regular series of lectures. Connecting the two main wings of the building was a peristyle, opening onto a beautifully planted garden, that provided the romantic setting for many a summer evening dance.

Plate 161: *Teapot from the Roycroft Inn*, ca. 1907. Design attributed to Dard Hunter, manufactured by Buffalo Pottery. Painted china, 6 × 9 × 5¾ in.
Private collection.

Fig. 84: A simple room at the Roycroft Inn, ca. 1910.
(Courtesy Elbert Hubbard-Roycroft Museum)

The fifty guest rooms were furnished simply but comfortably with furniture and lighting produced in the Roycroft shops. The rooms were not numbered, but rather given the names of famous people; guests were escorted to the Cleopatra Room, or the Benjamin Franklin Room, or the Susan B. Anthony Room. The choice of

Plate 162: *Plaque from the Susan B. Anthony Room of the Roycroft Inn.* Oak, 3¾ × 22 in. *Roycroft Revitalization Corporation and The Landmark Society of Western New York.*

men and women so honored reveals a great deal about Hubbard's eclectic interests and knowledge of the world. Icons from the spheres of art, music, and literature were represented, as were great names in science, philosophy, politics, and social reform. The grandest chambers, predictably, were the William Morris Room and the John Ruskin Room, the latter occupying, both physically and symbolically, the loftiest setting.

Within each room a blank book, bound at the Roycroft Press, was placed at the guests' disposal. The salutation on the first page invited them to "register and if the spirit moves—make a record of their impressions and feelings, whatever they are."

Fig. 85: The Ruskin Room, ca. 1910.
(Courtesy Turgeon-Rust Collection)

The Architect

The Printer

The Artist

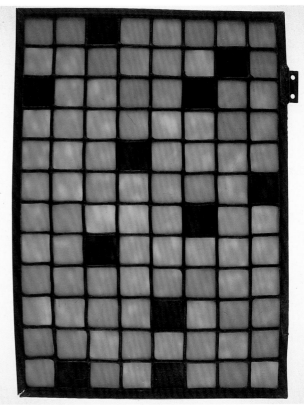

The Back Opening Panel

Plate 163: *Chandelier from the Roycroft Inn*, ca. 1909. Designed and executed by Dard Hunter. Copper and leaded glass, 20 × 32 × 42 in. *Roycroft Revitalization Corporation and The Landmark Society of Western New York.*

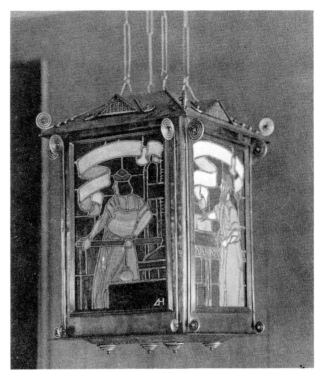

Fig. 86: The chandelier in situ. The lantern's three figural panels depict the Architect, the Artist, and the Printer. The fourth panel, providing access to the interior, is a checkerboard pattern of glass.
(Courtesy Dard Hunter III)

Hundreds did exactly that. Elbert Hubbard was a beacon for imaginative people from all walks of life and the Inn became a home-away-from-home to a veritable encyclopedia of the human experience. Even though these visitors were not historians or professional writers, there is an immediacy to their impressions that cannot be duplicated. The guest books are full of poetry and cartoons, jokes and sermonettes, even the occasional photograph of the writer. It seems the words that Hubbard inspired provide as fascinating a sampling of opinion and observation as those he wrote.[1]

Fig. 88: A photograph and accolades from prize-fighter Fred Welsh in a Roycroft Inn guest book.
(Courtesy Elbert Hubbard-Roycroft Museum)

Fig. 87: Poetry and a cartoon from a Raphael Room guest book.
(Courtesy Elbert Hubbard-Roycroft Museum)

Nestled into a gently rolling landscape, on the banks of the Cazenovia Creek, East Aurora was (and remains today) a picturesque and friendly village. At a time when the seven-day work week was standard and indoor plumbing remained a dream for many, visitors appreciated the happy marriage of beauty and comfort provided by the Roycroft Inn. One big-city refugee wrote:

> *October 6, 1921*
> *After a cordial greeting in the office we are conducted through halls and spacious rooms decorated with portraits of philosophers, artists, poets, men of letters, and with other works of art, and are ushered into sleeping apartments bearing the names of Raphael and Angelo. Naturally we wonder if the Inn caters especially to the aesthetic tastes of its guests to the partial neglect of their bodily comforts. After two happy and contented days we conclude that the Roycroft is, practically, a perfect Inn— with no suggestion of "outs."*
>
> *A. C. Baillett, Chicago, Illinois*

When the Inn first opened its doors, America was still reeling from the heady imperialism of the Spanish-American War and from the shock of President McKinley's assassination. Medical and technological advances of the day were staggering: X-rays were discovered, Sigmund Freud unleashed his theories on the interpretation of dreams, George Eastman patented the pocket Kodak, and the Wright Brothers made history at Kitty Hawk. The world was changing, rapidly, and Elbert Hubbard capitalized on East Aurora's main asset: "peace and quiet" and a certain sense of refuge. Elbert Hubbard's friendship with Henry Ford notwithstanding, the Roycroft Inn betokened relief for this resident of the auto capital of the world:

> *May 20, 1917*
> *It certainly was a pleasure to be awakened this morning by the denizens of the barnyard—instead of by the exhaust of a Ford with a blown-out muffler, or a street car with a flat wheel, and to inhale real air and not gasoline fumes.*
>
> *Albert Miller, Detroit, Michigan*

And while the Inn touted its comfortable amenities— Turkish baths, electric lights, steam heat, outdoor sleeping porches for those who wished to enjoy the fresh air, a library and a music room—it was careful to

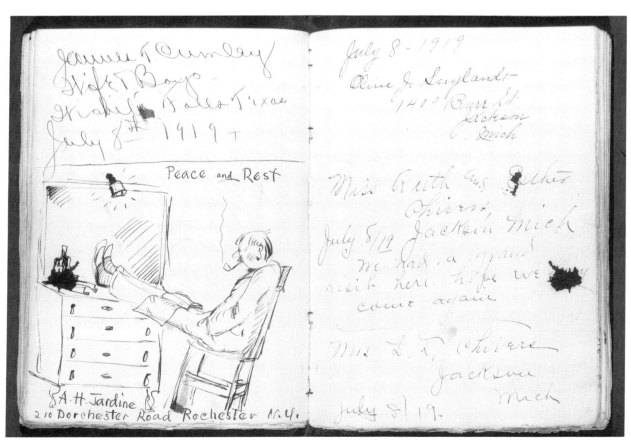

Fig. 89: A cartoon and some signatures from a Burne-Jones Room guest book.
(Courtesy Elbert Hubbard-Roycroft Museum)

Fig. 90: The kitchen of the Roycroft Inn.
(Courtesy Jack Schang)

avoid the pitfalls of modernity ticked off by a guest from the Big Apple:

[no date]
It is such a pleasing contrast to the hotel one usually finds, with accompanying kitchen odors, tip-luring waiters, elevators, stuffy bed-rooms, lobby saturated with rotten tobacco smoke.
                                W. D. Park, New York City

Part of the Inn's allure was the ease with which it became a surrogate home for those far away from their own:

June 10, 1906
The Roycroft Inn excels because it makes a house of public entertainment a near approach to a real home of peace and plenty and refinement.
                                                [unsigned]

And what better testimonial could an innkeeper offer a fastidious prospective guest than:

July 2, 1919
This place is "Bread, Beauty, Brotherhood" and it's **clean** *like* **home.**
                Elizabeth Towne, Holyoke, Massachusetts

The meals concocted in the Roycroft Inn's kitchen, under the capable direction of "Mother Grant," as she was known, were a source of great pride. Fruits, vege-

tables, and grains were grown at the Roycroft Farm, and contented Roycroft cows provided milk, cream, butter, and cottage cheese. The Roycroft even boasted its own chicken ranch. The staff canned, pickled, and otherwise preserved the bountiful harvest for the guests, and the secret recipe pecan patties were so popular that they were eventually packaged and sold by mail order. A promotional brochure claimed that "if you will name the famous places, we will produce food that matches theirs, soup for soup and entree for entree. And as for desserts, well, we have a Master Dessert Maker . . . there are not many hostelries that can hope to match Roycroft when it comes to desserts."[2] The lament of one particularly satisfied guest lends credence to that claim:

October 23, 1924
Peace Perfect Peace
But
The Wages of Peace is Fat.
Alas
I have gained three pounds in as many days.

If you are Fat and would be Thin
Then tarry not long at Roycroft Inn
But
If you are Thin and would be Fat
The Roycroft Inn will attend to that.
                                T. A. L., Toronto, Canada

The Roycroft Inn welcomed small conventions of one hundred guests or less with an atmosphere devoid of the distractions of big-city hotels. It hosted the annual gatherings of groups as diverse as Rotary Clubs and Purina Feeds, with a healthy number of traveling salesmen arriving on a regular basis as well. It was a safe haven for the growing number of women traveling on business:

June 30, 1927
Should I attempt to give my impressions of the Roycroft Inn, the account would read like a chronic invalid's description of his favorite sanatorium. Here I have found peace, quiet, an atmosphere of true culture, industry without chaos, and beauty that is never flamboyant. Truly, a Chicago business woman's idea of heaven materialized.
Grace Wittenberg, Chicago, Illinois

The Roycroft Inn was also an enormously popular stop for honeymooners. Niagara Falls was just a short distance to the north and East Aurora probably offered more privacy than was possible in that epicenter of newly-wedded bliss. Although one bride and groom reported a puzzling problem with their accommodations:

August 8–9, 1923
For a nice quiet rest, command me to the Roycroft. But why twin beds for honeymoon couples?
Dr. and Mrs. W. L. Denny, London, Ontario

in large part, newlyweds seem to have reacted with a common desire to perpetuate the lofty ideals which permeated the atmosphere at the Roycroft:

October 28, 1921
We heard of it: We read of it: We came to it: We go from it satisfied that Roycroft Inn leads one on to nobler and better ideals, gives one an incentive to carry on in the happy way in which we have started.
"On our honeymoon"
Dr. and Mrs. Gordon Murray, Toronto, Canada

It is logical to assume that many guests read the entries which had been recorded by previous occupants of the room. The florid declarations of so many lovebirds prompted a backlash of rather hard-boiled compliments:

September 22, 1920
If I couldn"t get into the Roycroft Inn except by "Honeymooning"—I would do even that.
Arthur Morrison, Wayne, Michigan

June 7, 1922
When a man and his wife have stood 11 years of married life they deserve a week at the Roycroft Inn.
[unsigned]

Romance, certainly, was not the goal of every Roycroft guest. The intellectual stimulation provided by a dizzying schedule of classes, lectures, concerts, and debates was a powerful drawing card as well. Perhaps those lured to East Aurora were simply predisposed to introspection—but the seeds of poetic self-expression may have been warmed by experiences at the Roycroft:

August 11, 1906
Roycroft supplies the soil in which the souls of men can germinate and grow.
Sverre Gulbrandson, Gloucester City, New Jersey

August 4, 1924
Like a guide post in life, Roycroft Inn bids you stop, look, and listen to the beauties and harmony around you.
Bert and Julia Mills, Akron, Ohio

June 9, 1917
We have made a "little journey" from Illinois to spend some time with the Roycrofters. We find the institution to be a solid woven fabric of deliberate purpose.
Mr. and Mrs. Peter Elbert Launer, Danville, Illinois

Another loyal Roycroft constituency was convalescents in search of a "rest cure," the Hubbards's bracing version of which included home-cooked meals, open-air sleeping compartments, and vigorous outdoor activity. And if the paying guests could be induced to help out with some of the regular chores during the course of the "cure," no one seemed the worse for it. One guest reported that "from August 13th till August 17th, we pulled weeds, hiked, canoed, danced, in fact had one great big time." Lively cardiac exercise sometimes produced the prescribed degree of relaxation and replenished the wood-pile at the same time:

December 16, 1922
After the doctor ordered a complete rest, the "Roycroft" was the choice, and it was a pleasant rest too. The tree chopping at Bert Hubbard's Saturday parties, in the woods, at his foremen's camp, was some lifesaver.
Claude King, Springfield, Massachusetts

Many came to the Roycroft for pure rest and rejuvenation and were able to draw pleasure from the simplest amusements:

[no date]
I will never forget the bath-tub party.
Earl Carroll

This cryptic entry is undated, leaving readers to speculate about whether it refers to some Prohibition-period pastime or to a randier form of entertainment involving what one guest described as the longest bathtub she had ever seen in her life.

In any case, the Roycroft offered a respite from the soul-deadening daily grind. Various permutations of an "oasis" metaphor appear frequently in the pages of the guest books: a "bright oasis in the desert of humdrum," an "oasis of spiritual content in a Sahara of material strife," or "an oasis in a Sahara of wanderings."

Of course, for every beautifully-crafted observation, there are a dozen less imaginative reports: "This is one beautiful spot" or "Having a dandy time" or "The beds in the Ingersoll Room are exceedingly comfortable" or "Dinner splendid—service ditto." It's possible these prosaic souls simply wished to avoid a blast like the one signed and dated "Alice Roosevelt, 1907":

> *I am an easygoing individual (never had a pain in my life) but these "inspired" sentiments* **make me sick**.

The Roycroft Inn enjoyed its fair share of celebrity guests; advertising copy assured that there was "no extra charge for communing with Famous Guests and filching their autographs and their Ideas."[3] Among the luminaries who stayed the night in East Aurora were Theodore Roosevelt, Carl Sandburg, the actress Ellen Terry, Booker T. Washington, Paul Tyner Post (of Postum fame), and Henry Ford. One guest book even contains an undated entry signed "Jean Harlow" that reads: "Charming places, really I quite adore them." For the most part, however, visitors were "just plain folks" who had probably learned about the Inn through the *Philistine* and the *Fra*, widely-circulated magazines published by the Roycroft's charismatic founder.

Many of the entries support the claim that "the Fra," as Hubbard called himself, was indeed a figure of almost religious importance to the devoted disciples who made the pilgrimage to East Aurora. Some alluded to their elevated regard for the Roycroft ideal in general:

> *August 1, 1909*
> *I came here a New Yorker,*
> *I go back a Roycrofter.*
> *Maida Gregg, New York City*

> *June 23, 1917*
> *We've found here an atmosphere charged with things beautiful—physical and spiritual.*
> *Mr. and Mrs. Charles Collins*
> *Dr. and Mrs. Charles Carroll*

> *August 14, 1927*
> *Two days and three nights have refreshed soul and body, given us a deeper appreciation of the beautiful and of work well done, and inspired us to better things.*
> *Mr. and Mrs. E. M. Beachley, Topeka, Kansas*

But often, a visitor's frank devotion to Elbert Hubbard himself found voice:

> *August 25, 1923*
> *For 20 years I have had two ambitions, to be a better chemist and to read and know Elbert Hubbard and his Roycrofters. The former has fed the wife and babies, but the Fra's writings have cheered many a bleak hour—Here's to you, Liberator from superstition!*
> *M. J. Rentschler, Willoughby, Ohio*

> *August 7, 1912*
> *When a man can hew out a niche like this in a community of ordinary mortals, when he can endow it with a distinctive atmosphere, when he can make everyone who comes in contact with it feel and* **do** *according to his ideals even for the time being and when he can* **maintain** *place, atmosphere and action against the inertia of things, he possesses not only genius but* **power** *of creative quality.*
> *L. B. Elliot, Rochester, New York*

Historians may reject altruism as the basic component of Hubbard's motives and actions, but the goodness he inspired remains undiminished in the tributes of many with firsthand experience of things Roycroftie:

> *July 19, 1921*
> *The late Elbert Hubbard helped me to see the wisdom of duties, righteousness and above all sincerity, which most of us lack. Cultivate it—you'd like it.*
> *Dave Sweet, Hamilton, Ontario*

Even a few cynics of Hubbard's own time were swayed in the end:

> *March 20, 1922*
> *Elbert, old Boy, I thought you were Bunk;*
> *I came here tired and thoroughly funked.*
> *After a sleep full of rest,*
> *I woke up with zest—*
> *I'm sorry, Elbert, I thinked the wrong thunk.*
> *C. D. Robling*

Sometimes the voice of admiration assumed slightly fanatical undertones, as in this posthumous homage:

> *[no date]*
> *It is with a prayer in my heart that I approach and leave thy dwelling place. For who shall say thy spirit is not here in this place of thy creation?*
> *[unsigned]*

After such adulation, assessments more gruff in nature provide a welcome relief:

[no date]
Mr. Hubbard once told me that with all his work he hadn't done much. He's a damned liar.
                                    E. H. Beach, Detroit, Michigan

Sundry declarations of esteem should not imply that Hubbard was universally loved and admired. Stout objections were sometimes expressed even (or perhaps especially) by those who had spent their money to linger in the Fra's long shadow. While relatively rare, negative comments are sprinkled in and among the devotions:

April 1920
Yes, Roycroft Inn and Roycroft Shops are wonderful and inspiring—but too "bourgeois," too expensive for ordinary folks. The whole psychology is upper class. Roycroft caters to the aristocracy of America and does not minister to the welfare of the common people, the masses.
                                    [unsigned]

[no date]
    Unique in Art
    Strange in Design
    the Meals are good
    the Beds are fine

    But just the same
    As ere you will
    It hurts like Hell
    To pay the bill.

                                    Anonymous

And Carl Ahrens, a painter and potter who fled Hubbard's employ in 1900 in the wake of bitter accusations on both sides, rendered a harsh judgment of the Roycroft ideal:

[no date]
    It's / a / lie.

The Fra's antipathy for organized religion rankled even some of his own supporters. The Roycroft Chapel was in reality a gift shop, exhibition gallery, and lecture hall, a surprise not favorably received by some visitors, including one who stayed in the Raphael Room:

[no date]
Only one jarring note on this quiet Sabbath—a "chapel" without prayer or praise to God in whom we live and move and have our being. Functioning as a salesroom the building should be renamed.
                                    [unsigned]

Hubbard's association with controversial figures of the day spawned some of the more candid comments, both for and against, set forth in the guest books. When he named one of the rooms after the late Robert

Ingersoll, an outspoken lawyer and orator who was both admired and reviled at the turn of the century, the political dichotomy in America was dramatized in the reactions of guests who found themselves in that particular sleeping apartment:

July 30–August 1, 1917
Robert J. Ingersoll and Elbert Hubbard carried the torch of reason high and were not afraid. No other two men ever did more to remove the shackles of dogmatic theology from the minds of those who think for themselves and not as they are told.
                        Walter J. Helm, wife and young son,
                                    Port Hope, Ontario

Clearly, Mr. Helm (if not his nameless wife and young son) was eager to absorb whatever psychic vibrations might emanate from the room named after an independent thinker he linked with Elbert Hubbard. More cautious is the rumination of a subsequent guest:

August 15, 1919
Ingersoll's Room! If he's where they say he is, I'd rather be here than with him.
                                    E. Dean, Gowanda, New York

And outright disapproval was registered by Dr. and Mrs. J. M. McGrady of Port Arthur, Ontario:

[no date]
Ingersoll *Room—when we came, we put him out.*

This prompted an anonymous guest to inscribe, directly below Dr. McGrady's self-righteous brush-off:

October 27, 1920
"He drew a circle and shut me out
Heretic, robber, a thing to flout
But love and I had the wit to win
We drew a circle and took him in."

McGrady should read The Gospel according to Ingersoll.

Similar written transactions between guests appear frequently, often in the form of mild rebukes or gentle jibes. When confronted with the quotation of a popular inspirational poem:

August 18–20, 1922
Two men looked out of prison bars
One saw mud—the other, stars.
                                    Marion Heysel, Olean, New York

an anonymous wit penned a bit of graffiti below:

Wonder what the second one was hit with?

Other times, visitors simply continued to build upon a theme expressed in the earlier pages of the guest book in their particular room. One of the most protracted exchanges is the ongoing lament about the resident occupant of the Socrates Room, whose snores disturb the peaceful slumbers of those in the adjoining chamber. An erudite volley, with its reference to Socrates' shrewish wife, is fired by two guests obviously well-read in the classics:

August 16–17, 1923
This is a charming place but we have discovered why Xanthippe lost her angelic disposition.
Margaret Hutchins
Margaret Stevens, Palmyra, New York

Dozens of similar complaints about this problem are registered with varying degrees of good humor, awkward rhyme, resignation, and resourcefulness:

October 20, 1922
Silence is bliss, but the snores in "Socrates" you couldn't miss.
Mr. and Mrs. H. Stratton, Owen Sound, Ontario

April 1921
The Roycroft Inn is the place I know best
For those who need comfort and rest
But the sleeper in Socrates Room
Did not modify his tune
Sorry this shortened my pleasant stay
Still it will not keep me away.
I. Steinberg, Toronto

July 31, 1921
In this place of self-expression, my neighbor snores.
H. F. Thompson, Lockport, New York

May 1–2, 1921
Yes, Socrates is a loud sleeper, but we won out by going to sleep first.
Mr. and Mrs. H. J. Carter, Toronto

A clue to the possible identity of the nocturnal offender can be gleaned from one defensive entry:

October 26, 1922
The snoring in "Socrates" was conspicuous by its absence—moreover M[onsieur] Landeau is a most pleasing and jolly person.
Mr. and Mrs. A. J. Terry Brown,
Sault Ste. Marie, Michigan

Sandor Landeau was the portly painter who spent the last several years of his life in residence at the Inn, running up a seldom-paid tab for room and board and, it now seems likely, annoying the guests.

Ultimately, the people who visited and worked at the Roycroft were just as essential to the creation of its character and to its endurance as were the beautiful objects created there or the millions of words which

flowed from the pens of Elbert and Alice Hubbard. The simplicity of their testimonials, and the sagacious understatement that marks so many of them, reveals much about the character of those attracted to the Hubbards and the community they created:

July 29, 1905
I've had a genuine Roycroft day and leave this hearty tribute to Roycroft hospitality and freedom: I haven't felt so like a happy child in years.
Stella M. Wylie, New York City

June 14, 1918
Don't take yourself too darn seriously when you come here—for these Roycrofters know men and women.
Silas Mason, Newton, Iowa

July 7, 1907
A day with the Roycrofters is worth a long journey.
Mr. and Mrs. O. O. Wagley
Valley City, North Dakota

The Roycroft Inn may be viewed as a paradigm for the symbiotic relationship that existed between Elbert Hubbard and his Roycrofters, as well as that between the Roycroft and the outside world. When the Warner House, then considered East Aurora's leading hostelry, burned to the ground in October of 1905,[4] Elbert Hubbard seized the opportunity to fill the void with his newly expanded Inn. The musical performances, the lectures by speakers of note, the classes, and the outdoor activities at the Roycroft were doubtless offered in part to attract visitors to East Aurora's newest contender for the hospitality crown. But these programs also provided a level of cultural and intellectual stimulation for Roycroft workers and townspeople that was unusual for villages of East Aurora's size. This environment of inquiry, inspiration, and tutelage in turn produced a general atmosphere of growth and enthusiasm on campus that inspired employee loyalty, good public relations, and repeat visitors.

It may be argued that the majority of those who stayed at the Inn were already among the converts to the Fra's way of thinking and that their commendations skew the perspective from which we view the Roycroft.

Be that as it may, the memories and impressions created in East Aurora seem to have had a lasting and largely positive effect on those who spent a few hours, days or weeks at the Roycroft Inn.

October 31, 1922
I've gazed, from the harbor, on Naples
And tramped o'er the Appian Way,
Climbed the Palatine Height
While the soft morning light
On the dome of St. Peter's made play.
I've been bathed in the joy of old London
Have strolled through the Bois of "Paree"
But, wherever I've been,
The Old Roycroft Inn
Went with me in sweet memory.

[unsigned]

The author wishes to thank Rita Hubbard for planting the seed of the idea for this particular research, and Bruce Bland, Co-curator of the Elbert Hubbard-Roycroft Museum, for providing the opportunity to spend many pleasant afternoons in the sun-drenched study of the ScheideMantel House, reading and transcribing guest book entries.

ENDNOTES

[1] All guest books quoted here are in the collection of the Elbert Hubbard-Roycroft Museum, East Aurora, New York. Entries within a given book do not proceed chronologically and usually span a number of years.
[2] *The Roycroft Inn* (East Aurora: The Roycrofters, n.d.), 30.
[3] *Fra 3*, no. 6 (September 1909): xi.
[4] "Large Hotel Burned," *East Aurora Advertiser*, 26 October 1905.

Marie Via is Assistant Curator at the Memorial Art Gallery of the University of Rochester.

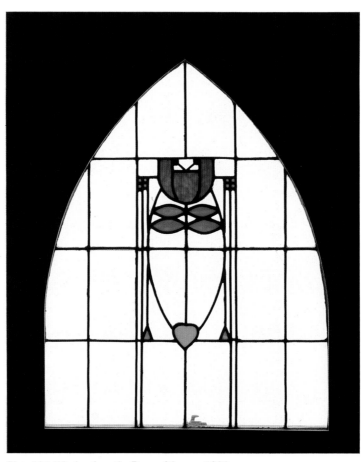

Plate 164: *Window from the Roycroft Inn*, ca. 1905.
Designed by Dard Hunter. Stained glass, 30 × 24 in.
Roycroft Arts Museum, Boice Lydell.

Product Price Structure at the Roycroft
and the Creation of Consumer Culture

BRUCE A. AUSTIN

The present exhibition on the Roycroft affords an opportunity to celebrate and examine critically the art and aesthetics of the East Aurora community. Simultaneously, it invites analysis of the broader context of consumer culture into which Elbert Hubbard sought entry for the distribution and retailing of Roycroft-manufactured goods. Although the exhibition objects embody the special Arts and Crafts ethos of the Roycroft, they were also created for commercial, cultural, and ideological purposes. While the Roycroft is justifiably lauded for important artistic achievements in several media, one additional factor must be underscored: the Roycroft can be seen most clearly and accurately as an icon of and a monument to early twentieth-century commodity and consumer capitalism. For in order to make the whole Roycroft enterprise work—that is, spread the ideology, apotheosize Hubbard, and earn a profit—the Roycroft needed to manufacture not only a product but willing customers as well.

An examination of the price structure of Roycroft products and this structure's relationship to personal economics at the turn of the century is revealing: who could afford and would have been predisposed to purchase Roycroft products, given their retail cost? And what is the "fit" between the results of this analysis and Hubbard's espoused "common man" philosophy? To contemporize the investigation, period retail prices for Roycroft goods have been adjusted for inflation to 1993 levels.

Roycroft and the Rise of Consumer Culture

The year 1900, a scant five years after the Roycroft's founding, marked not only a change in century but, more importantly, the beginning of a socio-economic era dramatically unlike that which had preceded it and with consequences both profound and cataclysmic. Hubbard and his emerging Roycroft community were caught—though certainly not trapped—in the tension of an enormous social and economic shift. Propelled by the nineteenth-century Industrial Revolution, an emerging consumer culture challenged Victorian mores of self-restraint. The new twentieth-century ethos valued spending over thrift and indulgence in place of restraint.[1]

The turn of the century saw "Victorian values of self-denial and work [give] way to ideas of self-fulfillment that sanctioned consumption as a source of identity."[2] The demise of the family firm, the development of retail "chain" stores, and the emergence of an affluent middle class of corporate bureaucrats all led to a concomitant creation of a consumer culture among middle and upper classes. In his analysis of consumer culture, Stuart Ewen writes:

> The mechanisms of mass production could not function unless markets became more dynamic, growing horizontally (nationally), vertically (into social classes not previously among consumers) and ideologically . . . It became imperative to invest the laborer with a financial power and a psychic desire to consume.[3]

For most Americans, however, the necessary "financial power" to match the instilled "psychic desire" did not fully arrive earlier than the 1920s, by which time manufacturers were quite overt about their intentions: *Printers' Ink*, for instance, boldly stated that "the future of business lay in its ability to manufacture customers as well as products."[4] One difficulty encountered by the Roycroft enterprise was that it entered the marketplace at a time when, across income classes, the notion of disposable discretionary income was just materializing and its amount was at best small. Further compounding this problem is the fact that throughout the decade and a half after 1900, inflation was nearly constant. "Even if people were not actually losing out in the struggle to keep up with inflation," Daniel Horowitz reports, "many in the middle class felt they were fighting a losing battle."[5]

Hubbard and his Roycroft were a bundle of contradictions. Outwardly, Hubbard sought to align the Roycroft in a communal-socialist and worker-oriented context. However, the modus operandi both for Hubbard and

Fig. 91: Elbert Hubbard, 1879. Photo by Fitz W. Guerin, St. Louis.
(Courtesy Roycroft Arts Museum)

the Roycroft "factories" was most decidedly that of entrepreneurial capitalism. The incongruity evidenced at the Roycroft was rooted in Hubbard's own personal history. As the Larkin Company's marketing manager, he was responsible for enhancing the firm's distribution and sales levels, which led to his building a personal fortune of such considerable size as to make possible his retirement before reaching the age of forty; Hubbard sold his interest in Larkin in 1892 for about sixty-five thousand dollars. As Anne T. Kirschmann argues convincingly, Hubbard was no socialist, certainly not in the Marx-Morris vein.[6] Despite early forays toward socialism and communism, which he was later to reject, Hubbard was quite clearly the capitalist's capitalist. More often than not he found himself aligned politically and philosophically with the era's captains of industry. Nor did Hubbard find profitability contradictory to his interest in making the Roycroft a seemingly alternative model to the corporate capitalism emerging at the time. The Hubbard/Roycroft ethos was contrary to the English Arts and Crafts ethos (especially as articulated by John Ruskin) that capitalism necessarily corrupted work.

Yet another, perhaps more profound, contradiction is noted by Cheryl Robertson, who writes that "the Arts

and Crafts movement was a multinational critique of conspicuous consumption, dehumanizing labor, and self-aggrandizement."[7] An absence of conspicuous consumption would have driven the Roycroft to bankruptcy long before that indeed occurred in 1938 at the end of the Depression. As for self-aggrandizement, the Roycroft, with its name or emblem boldly displayed at every opportunity, especially on its products, conveys and reveals all the subtlety of a billboard.

Roycroft—the place, the products, and its personification in Hubbard—represents one significant aspect of mass culture: that is, culture ostensibly for the masses as made tangible through various media including paper, leather, wood, and metal. It is axiomatic that the economics of production is necessarily tied to the economics of consumption; one without the other invalidates the idea and realization of entrepreneurial capitalism. In order to understand the Roycroft fully, one needs to understand not only Hubbard and those whom he gathered to East Aurora, but also and especially importantly, those outside of East Aurora who would financially support the enterprise. Who were the Americans who bought Roycroft products, what were they like, and how did they live? Although space constraints forbid a finely detailed discussion of the American consumer public, selected economic highlights contextualize the consumer culture into which the Roycroft entered.

The Consumers of Roycroft

Prior to the turn of the century, data on U.S. consumers are sketchy and often unreliable. Carroll D. Wright's landmark survey for the Massachusetts Bureau of Statistics of Labor, however, systematically collected information on how the population—especially working class families—spent its money. In 1875, Wright reported, a typical family spent most of its income on food, clothing, and shelter. Regardless of opportunity or desire, most working class families earned no more than what was needed to cover the bare cost of their existence.[8]

Since 1900 economic data on American families have been carefully collected and reported by the U.S. Bureau of the Census and are revealing both insofar as they paint a broadstroke portrait of consumption expenditures over time and provide snapshots of expenditures at given points in time. The average after-tax income for American families from 1917 to 1919 was $1,505. Of that number, as was true in Wright's 1875 study, nearly two-thirds was spent on day-to-day necessities: food (36.5 percent), clothing (15.8 percent), and housing (12.4 percent). In the category the Census Bureau labels "furnishing and equipment," families spent an average of $62 (4.1 percent) of their annual income. Average expenses for furnishings were exceeded only by the three categories noted above and, more modestly, by home fuel and medical care ($74 and $64 annually respectively). When families were sorted by after-tax income class, the richest and poorest classes spent the least amount of their total after-tax income on furnishings (3.8 and 3.5 percent respectively); the five income classes between these two extremes spent the most, averaging 4.0 to 4.4 percent of after-tax income spent in this category.[9] In short, family income from 1917 to 1919 averaged about $29 weekly, of which about one dollar was spent on furnishings.

Even after recognizing the inherent limitations of mathematical "averages," what the Census Bureau and related contemporaneous data clearly suggest is, at best, modest expenditure for such items as furniture and decorative accessories among Americans at this time. For instance, William F. Ogburn's 1918 study for the National War Labor Board reported that actual expenditures among shipyard workers in New York City for furnishings was $35 a year, or just 2.5 percent of their $1,386 annual income.[10] Other period budget studies of both working- and middle-class families corroborate this finding: conspicuous by its absence in the research reported from 1900 to 1916 was any substantial discussion—indeed, even mere mention— of spending on furnishings and decorative accessories. When family budgets did permit spending on such non-necessities, the money tended to be spent on automobiles, vacations, and commercial recreations, especially movies.[11] Moreover, the previously noted post-1900 inflation affected equally the working and middle classes,[12] resulting in a resurgence of traditional, pre-twentieth century attitudes in which prudence and restraint were the imperatives advocated by conservative moralists in venues ranging from the popular press to the pulpit.

We are therefore compelled to acknowledge Hubbard's Roycroft venture as bold and daring. Possessing marketing acumen is one thing; having a marketable product is another. Soap—Larkin or any other brand— is arguably a necessity, or at least a social convention resulting in a market of considerable breadth and depth. Small press operations, hammered copper objects, or oak furniture have a much more narrow and shallow market. Clearly elitist is book publishing since the market is constrained first by cost and second by literacy.[13] Less elitist are hammered copper bookends, for instance, though they too represent a marketing challenge since their necessity is questionable.

Table 1 displays the retail cost of selected exhibition objects. The data are reported for the year 1912 and are adjusted for inflation to 1993 levels.[14] Assuming the average $62 available annually for furnishings, one might have been able to purchase a single Roycroft

TABLE 1

Retail Cost of Roycroft Products in 1912 and in Inflation-Adjusted 1993 Dollars

Object	Plate number	Retail Cost in 1912 $	Adjusted Cost in 1993 $
Metalware			
Trapezoidal Vase	82	7	91
Egyptian Vase	91	5	65
Tapered Vase	106	10[a]	131
Vase	99	5	65
Bookends	100	5	65
Candlesticks	102	15 (pair)[b]	196
Candlesticks	19	7 (pair)	91
Fern Dish	85	12	156
Studded Ice Bucket	96	6	78
Jewel Box	80	10	131
Card Tray	90	2[a]	26
Humidor	77	9	117
Tray	77	5	65
Furniture			
Tooled Leather Chair	127	125	1622
Straddle Chair	60	15.50	201
Desk Chair	62	18	234
Marshall Wilder Chair	56	11	143
Child's Chair	12	8	104
High Chair	53	12.50	162
Bride's Chest	64	28	363
Tabouret	59	9	117
Magazine Pedestal	52	22	285
Lady's Writing Desk	72	35	454
Bedstead	66	42	545
Dressing Table	65	37	480
Chest of Drawers	67	56	727
Lighting & Leather			
Table Lamp	112	60[a]	778
Lamp	89	22.50[b]	292
Lamp	111	35[b]	454
Calling Card Case	123	5.50[a]	71

[a] price as listed in 1919
[b] price as listed in 1929

Sources: 1912 prices from *A Catalog of the Roycrofters: Some Things for Sale in Our Shop*, Stephen Gray, ed. (New York: Turn of the Century Editions, 1989); 1919 and 1926 prices from *The Book of the Roycrofters: Being a Catalog of Copper, Leather and Books. A Facsimile of Two Catalogs, 1919 [and] 1926* (East Aurora: House of Hubbard, 1977); furniture prices from *Roycroft Handmade Furniture: A Facsimile of a 1912 Catalog with Other Related Material Added for the Sake of Interest* (East Aurora: The House of Hubbard, 1989).

table lamp or, more generously, somewhat more than half of the metalware presented in the table, or two or three pieces of furniture. The data reported in Table 1 indicate that workers of average means most likely were not the target market nor were they going to be consumers of Roycroft goods. Perhaps such individuals would have treated themselves to a Roycroft souvenir; buying a bedroom set, though, appears to have been out of the question.

Another way of looking at the 1912 data is to ask: besides Roycroft goods, what other manufacturer's products might one purchase? Mail-order merchandising, popular since the 1880s, and phenomenally successful following the U.S. Post Office's adoption of the Rural Free Delivery (1896) and Parcel Post (1913) systems, was a reasonable and viable alternative for many consumers to the local retailer.[15] Not the least among such merchandisers, in addition to the Roycroft, were the well-known Montgomery Ward and Sears, Roebuck catalogues, each of which offered hundreds of pages displaying thousands of products. Though absent the mystic cachet of the Roycroft brand, other mail-order retailers offered consumers equally serviceable furniture and attractive decorative accessories.

Turning to the 1993 inflation-adjusted cost of Roycroft products, the price levels presented here may initially strike one—especially the contemporary collector—as "bargains." Today, collectors would certainly pay eight hundred dollars for a Roycroft table lamp. But *only* collectors would be willing to make such a purchase. The same kind of price discrimination can be seen today as was the case in 1912: to be a Roycroft collector today requires a certain level of economic comfort. While a collector will (perhaps eagerly) pay eight hundred dollars for a Roycroft table lamp, the rest of the world goes to a department (or even a discount) store and buys a table lamp for under one hundred

Plate 165: *A Catalog of Books and Things Hand Made at the Roycroft Shops*, ca. 1920.
Cover designed by Raymond Nott. 9⅛ × 6½ in.
Collection of Debbie and David Dalton Rudd.

ROYCROFT GOODS *in* COLUMBUS

READERS of *The Fra* living in Columbus, Ohio, and its environs will be pleased to learn that the beautiful Art Creations for home and fireside produced at the Roycroft in East Aurora may now be obtained direct at the store of

THE F. & R. LAZARUS & CO.

¶ The F. & R. Lazarus & Co. are exclusive agents for Columbus, and have a special department called "The Roycroft Shop," which is given over to the display of Roycroft Hand-Wrought Copper and Hand-Modeled Leather Goods, and Books.

¶ We urge you to pay an early visit to "The Roycroft Shop" in Columbus, because here you can actually *see* the useful and artistic productions of the skilled Roycroft Craftsmen, you can handle them, inspect them, caress them and appreciate the art and beauty a few of these pieces would carry into your home ⌘ ⌘

THE ROYCROFTERS, EAST AURORA, NEW YORK

Fig. 92: Advertisement for one of the Roycroft "satellite" shops. (As published in the *Fra*, November 1916)

dollars. Admittedly, furniture and accompanying decorative accessories possess symbolic as well as utilitarian value. Moreover, we must acknowledge that at times an object's symbolic value may influence purchase decisions in its favor and over that of any instrumental value the object possesses. However, with the exception of the economically privileged, more often than not the conflict "between the desire to use furniture as a status symbol and the need to use it simply as furniture"[16] is resolved in favor of the latter.

From economic and marketing standpoints, Hubbard and the Roycroft were faced with the problem of convincing the public to spend a precious portion of their furnishing "budget" on the goods produced in East Aurora. To accomplish this, Hubbard anticipated and implemented an advertising theory to be more widely developed in the mid-1920s: advertisers "recognized that in order to get people to consume and, more importantly, to keep them consuming, it was more efficient to endow them with a critical self-consciousness in tune with the 'solutions' of the marketplace than to fragmentarily argue for products on their own merit."[17] Long before the theorists and researchers

operationalized and defined it, Hubbard, through his Roycroft philosophy and product line, sought to put into action the concept of marginal utility. Marginal utility extends the notion of value beyond a given commodity's utilitarian or application function to "a notion of value which is politicized [such as its] fashion, taste, status-giving function"[18] or, for that matter, belonging however indirectly to the Roycroft fraternity.

The merchandising techniques Hubbard had innovated at the Larkin Company—a "club selling plan" and the "advertising premium"—were honed to a fine edge at Roycroft. Using his numerous publications as vehicles, Hubbard was able to sell Roycroft products directly to retail buyers, thereby avoiding both the burden and bother of wholesale distributors. With the opening of the Roycroft Inn and the attached souvenir gift shop, Hubbard clearly marked his move to entrepreneurial capitalism. The extent to which he was able to capitalize on the principle of marginal utility and other means of marketing is presently unknown, although the data presented here clearly suggest limited viability for such notions.

Conclusion

Like other Arts and Crafts movement commodities, those produced at the Roycroft ostensibly sought broad consumer appeal, thereby matching an element of the movement's ethos and providing necessary economic support for the endeavor. In fact, by virtue of price structure, they simultaneously shunned lower economic class buyers. Clearly, the Roycroft both fits and was nested within the context of the new twentieth-century ethos valuing spending and indulgence. However, despite the many changes identified by economic and cultural historians, the emerging consumer culture was, in fact, still a restrained one, its boundaries marked by consumer cognizance of a limited budget. At the turn of the century, the financial resources of most Americans were inadequate to meet any "psychic desire" to acquire such products as those made at the Roycroft. This is especially true given the hefty retail prices charged by the Roycroft as well as the ready availability of alternative products from other, lower-priced manufacturers.

As was true for the nascent movie industry,[19] the Roycroft needed to seek and seduce the patronage of aristocratic economic elites not so much for their social status and accompanying wealth per se, but as a means to legitimize and valorize the Roycroft products and, with very little stretching of the imagination, its founder as well. The Roycroft product pricing produced clear market segmentation by income rather than a democratic form of consumer art and furnishing. How, exactly, these factors of pricing and segmentation actually played out among consumers is yet to be learned.

Still unanswered are questions concerning the quantity of each object produced, absolute cost of production, and the level of sales achieved. Answers to these questions would not only help to determine Roycroft's profitability, but would further our knowledge of the period's consumer culture and could serve as confirmation of the intentionality suggested by this essay's thesis, rather than unwitting cause and effect.

MEASUREMENTS

Mr.		Elbert Hubbard	
Address		East Aurora, N.Y.	
Date		April 19th, 1915	

Neck	14½	Forearm	10¼
Shoulder	43	Waist	34½
Chest, normal	35½	Hips	
Chest, expanded	38¼	Thigh	20½
Chest, contracted	34	Calf	13¾
Bust		Weight	162
Upper arm	12⅜	Height	5–9½

(From a chart in the Roycroft archive, Department of Rare Books & Special Collections, Rush Rhees Library, University of Rochester)

ENDNOTES

[1] T. J. Jackson Lears, "From Salvation to Self-Realization: Advertising and the Therapeutic Roots of the Consumer Culture, 1880–1930," in *The Culture of Consumption: Critical Essays in American History, 1880–1930*, ed. Richard Wightman Fox and T. J. Jackson Lears (New York: Pantheon Books, 1983), 3. Lears writes that in the U.S. "the bourgeois ethos had enjoined perpetual work, compulsive saving, civic responsibility, and a rigid morality of self-denial. By the early twentieth century that outlook had begun to give way to a new set of values sanctioning periodic leisure, compulsive spending, apolitical passivity, and an apparently permissive (but subtly coercive) morality of individual fulfillment." See also Daniel Horowitz, *The Morality of Spending: Attitudes Toward the Consumer Society in America, 1875–1940* (Baltimore: Johns Hopkins University Press, 1985), xxii–xxvi for a summary of various historians who trace the onset of these fundamental changes as far back as 1830.

[2] Richard Butsch, "Introduction: Leisure and Hegemony in America," in *For Fun and Profit: The Transformation of Leisure into Consumption*, ed. Richard Butsch (Philadelphia: Temple University Press, 1990), 17. The psychological and social relationships between material possessions and the self are a fascinating subject of inquiry. An instructive literature review and summary from the perspective of consumer research may be found in Russell W. Belk, "Possessions and the Extended Self," *Journal of Consumer Research* 15 (September 1988): 139–168. Interestingly, the dimension of possession of antiques and collectibles (such as Roycroft products) in relationship to the self has been largely ignored by research.

[3] Stuart Ewen, *Captains of Consciousness: Advertising and the Social Roots of the Consumer Culture* (New York: McGraw-Hill, 1976), 24–25.

[4] Quoted in ibid., 53.

[5] Horowitz, *The Morality of Spending*, 68.

[6] See Anne T. Kirschmann, "Elbert Hubbard and the New Capitalism: The Religion of Commonsense" (unpublished manuscript, University of Rochester, 1992).

[7] Cheryl Robertson, "The Resort to the Rustic: Simple Living and the California Bungalow," in *The Arts and Crafts Movement in California: Living the Good Life*, ed. Kenneth R. Trapp (New York: Abbeville Press, 1993), 89.

[8] Horowitz, *The Morality of Spending*, 14–16.

[9] U.S. Bureau of the Census, *Historical Statistics of the United States, Colonial Times to 1970*, Bicentennial ed., Parts I and II (Washington, D.C.: U. S. Government Printing Office, 1975), 321.

[10] Horowitz, *The Morality of Spending*, 123–124.

[11] Ibid., 85–108.

[12] Ibid., 109. Horowitz writes: "From the perspective of 1918 or 1920, the inflation of 1906–16 would seem mild. Between 1914 and 1921, the cost of consumer goods doubled." On p. 89, Horowitz quotes a contemporary writer who described the salaried middle class's income as "about as elastic as New Bedford granite."

[13] I am reminded by a colleague that Mark Twain, a contemporary of Hubbard's, went bankrupt trying to operate his own book publishing company. Spending on reading materials from 1917 to 1919 averaged eleven dollars annually. In 1900, a total of 4,490 new book titles were published (U.S. Bureau of the Census, *Historical Statistics*, 321, 808).

[14] Inflation-adjusted prices were computed by using the Consumer Price Index for "House Furnishings". (Ibid., 210)

[15] See Stuart Ewen and Elizabeth Ewen, *Channels of Desire: Mass Images and the Shaping of American Consciousness* (New York: McGraw Hill, 1982), 63–68.

[16] Vincent V. Mott, *The American Consumer: A Sociological Analysis, Part Two*, 3rd ed. (Florham Park, N.J.: Florham Park Press, 1980), 202.

[17] Ewen, *Captains of Consciousness*, 38–39. For examples of this, see Vance Packard, "Selling Symbols to Upward Strivers," in *The Hidden Persuaders* (New York: Pocket Books, 1958). Neil Postman observes that with the industrial revolution "technological progress worked most efficiently when people are conceived of not as children of God or even citizens but as consumers—that is to say, as markets." (Neil Postman, *Technopoly: The Surrender of Culture to Technology* [New York: Vintage Books, 1992], 42)

[18] Ewen, *Captains of Consciousness*, 89–90.

[19] The parallel relationship suggested here between the Arts and Crafts movement and the developing movie industry has yet to be explored. Both were nested in the same politically and morally charged era characterized by enormous upheavals in social and moral customs, immigration, and leisure. For information on the early movie industry, see Lary May, *Screening Out the Past: The Birth of Mass Culture and the Motion Picture Industry* (New York: Oxford University Press, 1980).

Bruce A. Austin was curator of "The American Arts & Crafts Movement in Western New York, 1900–1920." He is a research consultant based in Rochester, New York, as well as a dealer specializing in American Arts and Crafts furnishings and decorative accessories.

Epilogue . . .

MARJORIE B. SEARL

It was a day in 1938, a sorrowful day for the King's Craftsmen, when the chattering monotype machines became silent, the giant color presses ground to a halt, and the sound of hammers on silver and copper ceased. The Roycroft Institution, founded in the mid-nineties by Elbert Hubbard, reverted to the ages.[1]

The Roycroft had survived the loss of its leader in 1915, but could not counter the downward economic spiral of the thirties combined with the "modern technology with its assembly line [which] slowly sapped the life of the institution."[2] Rumors and schemes abounded following the closing of the shops, including one unusual proposal by a local individual who recommended turning the Roycroft into "the Republican center of the nation, utilizing printing facilities of the shops for the publication of a monthly magazine and the Inn as headquarters of the club itself."[3] This vision of East Aurora as a "mecca of patriotic Americanism" took on a more religious flavor as hopes rose and were dashed again with the announcement of the Roycroft's purchase by the Federation of Churches of Infinite Science (whose members included followers of Hubbard), and the subsequent failure of that organization to come up with the second payment due to "war scare and flood conditions."[4]

By May of 1939, the weary community was relieved to learn that the roller-coaster ride of the past year had ended with the impending purchase of the shops and the Roycroft Inn by Samuel Guard of Spencer, Indiana, publisher of agricultural magazines, including the *Breeder's Gazette*.[5] Thus ended months of suspenseful speculation in the town and the nation about the fate of the place that had put East Aurora on the map.[6] Guard's proposal gained near-mythic status, since the only alternative at this eleventh hour was complete liquidation of the properties and equipment. In keeping with the wishes of the trustees and bankruptcy court judge, the new owner vowed to keep the complex intact.[7]

While reluctant to assume Hubbard's mantle, Guard fit the Roycroftie image of the self-made man, and much was made of his Hubbard/Alger success story. Invoking the idea that the hand of destiny could be seen

in Guard's leadership of the Roycroft, the *East Aurora Advertiser* quoted an unidentified Buffalo "radio man" who was an acquaintance of Hubbard as allegedly avowing, "If Hubbard were alive today and was assigned the task of choosing a successor, he would certainly choose Sam Guard."[8] The new owner's focus was commercial printing; on paper, he seemed to be successful in attracting customers. By the end of 1939, however, concern about the feasibility of his plan contrasted markedly with the ebullient confidence of the previous May, as Guard came to realize that it would not be possible to maintain the Roycroft complex under one economic or philosophical umbrella. Soon after he purchased them, Guard began to divest himself of properties that were not directly linked to printing activities.

The Inn was the first building to become a separate corporation, with Buffalo hotelier Anthony Rohrer assuming the executive position as the largest stockholder.[9] In 1940, Guard, in need of capital, sold the Inn to Edward "Jimmy" O'Brien, a Cornell graduate and former steward at the "exclusive Lake Placid Club."[10] Functioning as a hotel, restaurant, and the site of many community-based programs and activities, the Inn continued to be a backdrop to the social, recreational, and economic life of the town. A succession of owners followed O'Brien, including Lewis Fuchs and the Turgeon-Rust family, who managed the Inn until difficult economic conditions in the mid-1980s finally forced its closing. In 1987, when the future of the building was uncertain, the Landmark Society of Western New York purchased the Inn, as well as Roycroft furniture and artifacts, using funds provided by The Margaret L. Wendt Foundation of Buffalo. Through the valiant efforts of the Roycroft Revitalization Corporation, led by Burt Flickinger, Jr., additional funding was obtained from a variety of government, foundation, corporate, and private sources.[11] A new roof and fresh exterior paint marked the beginning of a major restoration project. In 1994 The Margaret L. Wendt Foundation assumed the responsibility of owner and developer of the Inn. The Foundation projects restoration and reopening of the Inn by late 1994 or early 1995.[12]

Fig. 93: The sleeping apartments of the Roycroft Inn, 1994.
(Photograph by James M. Via)

Other Roycroft buildings were sold to individual owners and have, in most cases, survived remarkably well. The Chapel, where workers and townspeople had gathered over the years, was acquired by the Baptist Church.[13] Valiant efforts by a far-sighted group which had urged the town to purchase that building for community activities and a Hubbard memorial were finally realized in 1958.[14] Today, Aurorans paying taxes or registering for recreational programs are reminded of their distinctive heritage by the Craftsman-style carved oak woodwork and leaded glass windows throughout the building, and the meeting room filled with Roycroft furniture and memorabilia.

The Print Shop, the other medieval-style building visible from Main Street, currently houses the Cornell Cooperative Extension. The Power House is a professional office building, and the former Copper Shop operates as a gift shop and the offices

Fig. 94: The Roycroft Chapel, now the Aurora Town Hall, 1994.
(Photograph by James M. Via)

of the Foundation for the Study of the Arts and Crafts Movement. Antique dealers and a pottery do an active business in the old Furniture Shop. Other buildings that still exist include the stock building, the fire company pumping station, the painters' building, and the laundry. Emerson Hall, in former times a hotel and residence for Roycroft workers, is now an apartment building. Sadly, the Roycroft Tea House has not survived, nor have the greenhouses. Through sensitive adaptive reuse, the complex remains visually coherent. While the structures are independently owned, they are linked by Arts and Crafts-style signage as well as by their National Historic Landmark Status.

The Inn and other Roycroft structures provide links to a world that now exists only in old photographs, beautifully hand-made objects, and still-fresh writings. But unlike many historic sites, the Roycroft has continued to generate interest in its philosophy and ideals as well as in its buildings. The Roycrofters-at-Large Association (RALA) was founded in 1976 to promote and perpetuate the ideals of Hubbard and the people who worked with him and were inspired by him. The Hubbardesque energy and enthusiasm of this group have helped renew the community's interest in its history. Yearly festivals on or near Hubbard's birthday in June attract crowds of people to a potpourri of talks, demonstrations, musical programs, and craft displays, in the spirit of the Annual Convention of the American Academy of Immortals in Hubbard's time. The Roycroft Renaissance, a program administered by RALA, recognizes artisans whose work reflects Hubbard's commitment to the unity of "Head, Heart and Hand" by authorizing them to use the "double R" logo, a variant of the community's original orb and cross.[15]

In 1987, the Aurora Historical Society and the Elbert Hubbard Museum moved their collections to a home given for that purpose by Gladys ScheideMantel when she turned one hundred. With her husband George, she had lived in the Roycrofter-built residence since its construction in 1910. George had started work at the Roycroft as a bellboy, and, true to Hubbard's employment philosophy, had ended his career as an award-winning leathercrafter and head of the Leather Department. Located at 363 Oakwood Avenue, only a few

Fig. 95: The ScheideMantel House, now the Elbert Hubbard-Roycroft Museum, 1994.
(Photograph by James M. Via)

blocks from the campus, the well-preserved Craftsman-style home provides a perfect setting for materials related to Hubbard's life and work.[16] The house was recently dedicated on the occasion of its inclusion on the National Register of Historic Places.[17]

The legacy of "Head, Heart and Hand"—the triad that expresses so well the ideals of the Roycroft community—has been carefully nurtured over the years by members of the Hubbard family, RALA, the Aurora Historical Society, and entrepreneurs guided by genuine commitment to a shared vision. That the Roycroft spirit has a real contribution to make, not as a relic but as an organic and vital philosophy, is evident to this day. Just as its founder survived personal difficulties and setbacks to become one of the best-known personalities of his time, the institution's history is one of struggle alternating with success. With the imminent reopening of the Inn and the launching of a national museum tour devoted to the Roycroft community, there is no better way to celebrate the one hundredth anniversary of its birth.

The author would like to thank Warren Moffett, Aurora Town Historian, for his assistance. Also, Henry McCartney, Director of the Landmark Society of Western New York, and Robert Rust, Curator of the Foundation for the Study of the Arts and Crafts Movement, provided important information regarding the recent history of the Roycroft Inn. Jennifer Goyette, a student intern from the Rochester Institute of Technology, was an indispensable organizational wizard. Eleanor Jackson Searl, daughter and granddaughter of Roycrofters, provided many memories of her life in East Aurora that have informed and inspired this writing.

ENDNOTES

[1] "Aurora Sesqui '68," *East Aurora Shopping Guide* 28, no. 38 (1 February 1968).

[2] Ibid.

[3] B. J. Hatmaker, "B. J. Hatmaker Offers Idea to Hasten Roycroft Recovery," *East Aurora Advertiser*, 27 January 1938.

[4] "Asks Roycroft Sale in 2 Weeks," *East Aurora Advertiser*, 6 October 1938.

[5] "Roycroft Apt to Be Union Shop if Guard Offer Accepted Apr. 10," *East Aurora Advertiser*, 23 March 1939.

[6] See "Nation's Leaders Laud Guard's Ownership of Roycroft in Letters," *East Aurora Advertiser*, 4 May 1939, for numerous letters from prominent people at state and national levels, including one from Guard's "personal friend" Alf Landon, Republican candidate for president in 1936.

[7] "Indiana Publisher to Make New Bid for Roycroft Property Next Monday," *East Aurora Advertiser*, 16 March 1939.

[8] Ibid.

[9] "Roycroft Inn is Made Separate Corporation," *East Aurora Advertiser*, 26 September 1940.

[10] *Historical Highlights: East Aurora and Vicinity* (East Aurora: Sons of the American Legion, 1940).

[11] Additional funding sources include New York State's Office of Parks, Recreation and Historic Preservation, through the Environmental Quality Bond Act; Erie County; the Village of East Aurora; the National Trust for Historic Preservation; the J. M. Kaplan Foundation; the Andy Warhol Foundation; Fisher-Price Corporation; Roycrofters-at-Large Association; and hundreds of gifts from individual donors.

[12] Jane Siebert, Architectural Resources, Buffalo, to the author, 24 June 1994.

[13] "Plans are Completed for Dedication of the Roycroft Chapel as New First Baptist Church Here Sunday," *East Aurora Advertiser*, 14 May 1942.

[14] This date is taken from a framed statement mounted on the wall inside the front door of the Aurora Town Hall.

[15] For a good discussion of the Roycrofters-at-Large Association and its activities, see Carol L. MacDonald, "Reviving the Roycroft Spirit," *Americana* 14, no. 3 (July/August 1986); Bruce E. Johnson, "The Riches of Roycroft," *Country Living* (June 1991); and *East Aurora Advertiser* insert for the 1994 Roycroft Summer Festival, 16 June 1994.

[16] "Home Built by Roycroft Craftsmen to Open as Museum," *Buffalo Evening News*, 30 May 1987.

[17] "Museum Dedication Slated on Saturday," *East Aurora Advertiser*, 2 June 1994.

Marjorie B. Searl is the Estelle B. Goldman Curator of Education at the Memorial Art Gallery of the University of Rochester.

MOTTOS
OF THE FRA

To escape criticism: Do Nothing, Say Nothing, Be Nothing.

To be stupid when inclined and dull when you wish is a boon that goes only with high friendship.

Conformists die, but heretics live on forever.

A thought is mental dynamite.

Weep not peeling other people's onions.

To repeat an unkind truth is just as bad as to invent a lie.

A retentive memory is a great thing, but the true token of nobility is the power to forget.

The mintage of wisdom is to know that rest is rust, and that real life is in love, laughter and work.

One ounce of loyalty is worth a pound of cleverness.

The leader of the orchestra is always a man who has played second fiddle.

To maintain order, excellence and harmony in the territory immediately under one's own hat will keep one fairly well employed.

SELECT BIBLIOGRAPHY

Allen, Frederick Lewis. "Elbert Hubbard." *Scribner's Magazine* 104, no. 3 (September 1938): 12–14.

Andrews. A. R. "The Roycroft Printing Shop." *American Printer & Bookmaker* 29 (February 1900): 328–29.

"Another Account of the Roycroft Shop." *American Printer & Bookmaker* 29 (February 1900): 330–32.

Baker, Cathleen. "Dard Hunter: Roycroft Artist." *Arts and Crafts Quarterly* 6, no. 1 (1993): 6–11.

Balch, David Arnold. *Elbert Hubbard: Genius of Roycroft.* New York: Frederick A. Stokes, 1940.

Beisner, Robert L. "'Commune' in East Aurora." *American Heritage* 22 (February 1971): 72–75, 106–11.

Bishop, Morris. "A Reporter at Large—Roycroft Revisited." *New Yorker* 14 no. 34 (8 October 1938): 48–52.

Bodhan, Carol. "The Roycrofters of East Aurora." *Connoisseur* (March 1980): 209–15.

Burchfield Center, State University College at Buffalo. *The Roycroft Movement: A Spirit for Today?* exhibition supplement. Buffalo: Buffalo State College Foundation, Inc., 1977.

Caruthers, J. Wade. "Elbert Hubbard: A Case of Re-interpretation." *Connecticut Review* 1 (October 1967): 67–77.

Cathers, David M. *Furniture of the American Arts and Crafts Movement: Stickley and Roycroft Mission Oak.* New York: New American Library, Inc., 1981.

Champney, Freeman. *Art and Glory: The Story of Elbert Hubbard.* New York: Crown Publishers, Inc., 1968.

Clark, Robert Judson. *The Arts and Crafts Movement in America, 1876–1916.* Princeton: Princeton University Press, 1972.

Coen, Rena Naumann. *Alexis Jean Fournier: The Last American Barbizon.* St. Paul: Minnesota Historical Society, 1985.

Denison, Lindsey. "Elbert Hubbard's Shop: An American William Morris at Work in East Aurora." *New York Sun*, 29 October 1899.

Dirlam, Kenneth and Ernest Simmons. *Sinners, This is East Aurora.* New York: Vanguard Press, 1968.

Edwards, Robert. "Roycrofters: Their Furniture and Crafts." *Art and Antiques* 4 (December 1981): 80–87.

Forbes, Christopher. "All's Well That Sells Well." *Art and Antiques* 6 (October 1989): 124–28, 161.

Hamilton, Charles F. *Alice Hubbard: A Feminist Recalled.* East Aurora: G. M. Hamilton and Sons, 1991.

——. *As Bees in Honey Drown.* South Brunswick, New Jersey: A. S. Barnes and Co., 1973.

——. *Little Journeys to the Homes of Roycrofters.* 2d edition. East Aurora: S-G Press, Inc., 1987.

——. *Roycroft Collectibles.* Tavares, Fla.: SPS Publications, 1992.

Hamilton, Charles F., Robert Rust, and Kitty Turgeon. *History and Renaissance of the Roycroft Movement.* Buffalo: Buffalo and Erie County Historical Society, 1984.

Hartt, Rollin Lynde. "Elbert Hubbard." *Critic* 35, no. 869 (November 1899): 1005–1008.

Heath, Horton H. "Elbert Hubbard: Salesman." *Printer's Ink Monthly* 23 (October 1931): 41–56, 73–75.

Heath, Mary Hubbard. *The Elbert Hubbard I Knew.* East Aurora: Roycroft Press, 1929.

Hopkins, John Stephens. *Elbert Hubbard and the American Business Creed.* Master's Thesis, Brown University, 1970.

Hunter, Dard. *My Life With Paper.* New York: Alfred A. Knopf, 1958.

Kaplan, Wendy. *"The Art That is Life:" The Arts and Crafts Movement in America, 1875–1920.* Boston: Little, Brown and Company, 1987.

Koch, Robert. "Elbert Hubbard's Roycrofters as Artist-Craftsmen." *Winterthur Portfolio* 3 (1966): 67–82.

Lane, Albert. *Elbert Hubbard and His Work.* Worcester, Mass.: The Blanchard Press, 1901.

Ludwig, Coy L. *The Arts and Crafts Movement in New York State.* Hamilton, N.Y.: Gallery Association of New York State, Inc., 1983.

Markham, Edwin. "Elbert Hubbard, the Practical Idealist." *Literary Digest International Book Review* 4 (August 1926): 543–44.

McConnell, Kevin. *Roycroft Art Metal.* West Chester, Pa.: Schiffer Publishing, Ltd., 1990.

McKenna, Paul. *A History and Bibliography or the Roycroft Printing Shop.* North Tonawanda, N.Y.: Tona Graphics, 1986.

Ó Murchú, Giollamuire. *Jerome Connor: Irish American Sculptor, 1874–1943.* Dublin: The National Gallery of Ireland, 1993.

Ogle, David B. *On a High Shelf: Roycroft Books and Bookmakers.* Tavares, Fla.: SPS Publishers, forthcoming.

Quinan, Jack. "Elbert Hubbard: Businessman." *Arts and Crafts Quarterly* 3, no. 2: 4–9.

Rhodes, Lynette I. *The Roycroft Shops, 1894–1915: A Propelling Force of the American Arts and Crafts Movement.* Erie, Pa.: Erie Art Center, 1974.

Shay, Felix. *Elbert Hubbard of East Aurora.* New York: Wm. H. Wise and Co., 1926.

Spargo, John. "Elbert Hubbard, Karl Marx & William Morris." *Comrade* 3, no. 5 (February 1904): 103–105.

Stott, Mary Roelofs. *Rebel With Reverence: A Granddaughter's Tribute.* 2d edition, revised. East Aurora: Century House Americana Publishers, 1984.

Thorne, Bonnie Ruth Baker. *Elbert Hubbard and the Publications of the Roycroft Shop, 1893–1915.* Dissertation, Texas Woman's University, 1975.

Vidler, Virginia, "Hubbard's Roycroft." *Antiques Journal* 24, no. 24 (July 1969): 10–12.

Vilain, Jean-François. "Printing and American Arts and Crafts." *Arts and Crafts Quarterly* 3, no. 3 (June 1990): 26–28.

Weber, Brom. "Spurious Sage: A Study of the Conspiracy Between Elbert Hubbard and His Times." Dissertation, University of Minnesota, 1957.

White, Bruce. *Elbert Hubbard's* The Philistine: A Periodical of Protest, *1895–1915: A Major American "Little Magazine".* Lanham, Md.: University Press of America, 1989.

Wolfe, Richard and Paul McKenna. *Louis Herman Kinder and Fine Bookbinding in America.* Newtown, Pa.: Bird and Bull Press, 1985.

See also the numerous Roycroft product catalogues and promotional brochures, as well as Hubbard's own writings.

Lenders to the Exhibition

Aurora Historical Society, East Aurora, New York
Bruce A. Austin
Thomas Portzline and Phyllis Bieri
Richard Blacher
Burchfield-Penney Art Center, Buffalo State College, New York
David and Susan Cathers
Cooper-Hewitt National Museum of Design, Smithsonian Institution, New York, New York
Elbert Hubbard-Roycroft Museum, East Aurora, New York
Everson Museum of Art of Syracuse and Onandaga County, New York
Mr. and Mrs. Christopher Forbes
Frederick-Waters Fine Art, Auburn, Washington
Edward and Kathryn Friedman
Fritz and Jane Gram
Rocco J. and Mary Graziano
Charles F. Hamilton

Mr. and Mrs. Rixford Jennings
Landmark Society of Western New York, Rochester, New York
Don Marek
Meibohm Fine Arts, East Aurora, New York
Memorial Art Gallery of the University of Rochester, New York
Newark Museum, New Jersey
Mark and Sarah Roelofs
Roycroft Arts Museum, East Aurora, New York
Roycroft Revitalization Corporation, East Aurora, New York
Debbie and David Dalton Rudd
Kitty Turgeon-Rust and Robert Rust
Eleanor Jackson Searl
Strong Museum, Rochester, New York
Virginia Museum of Fine Arts, Richmond, Virginia
Charles and Honna Whelley-Bowen
Jean-François Vilain and Roger S. Wieck
Private collections (7)

Photography Credits

James M. Via was project photographer for *Head, Heart and Hand: Elbert Hubbard and the Roycrofters*. Additional images of exhibition objects were provided by:

Courtenay Frisse, plate 62.
Ron Jennings, plate 52.

Dan Kushel, plate 163.
Newark Museum, plate 63.
Richard Nicol, plate 145.
Don Strand, plates 65, 66, 67 and 108.
Steve Tague, plate 88.

Additional Objects

The following Roycroft objects were included in the exhibition but are not illustrated in this catalogue:

Music Roll, ca. 1910
Leather
3¼ diam. by 15½ in.
Collection of Bruce Ader

Hanging Motto: "Life in Abundance"
Ash and iron
10½ × 42½ × 4½ in.
Collection of Richard Blacher

Motto: "Be Gentle and Keep Your Voice Low"
Ink and colors on paper
7½ × 10¼ in.
Private collection

Elbert Hubbard Stationery with Portrait Watermark
Paper
10⅞ × 8⅜ in.
Private collection

Manuscript: "William Marion Reedy" by Elbert Hubbard, 1912
Paper
10⅞ × 8⅜ in.
Private collection

Hanging Motto: "Fletcherize"
Ash
11⅜ × 46½ × ¾ in.
Roycroft Revitalization Corporation and The Landmark Society of Western New York

Vase, ca. 1925
Silver over copper
16¼ × 9¼ in.
Collection of Rocco J. and Mary Graziano

Plaque from William Morris Room of the Roycroft Inn
Oak
4 × 28⅛ × ¾ in.
Roycroft Revitalization Corporation and The Landmark Society of Western New York

Thirteen Motto Cards
Ink on paper
(various sizes)
Collection of Kitty Turgeon-Rust and Robert Rust, Roycroft Shops

Invitation to Annual Convention of the American Academy of Immortals, 1905
Designed by Dard Hunter
Ink on paper
11½ × 8¾ in.
Collection of Kitty Turgeon-Rust and Robert Rust, Roycroft Shops

Roycroft Tie
Crepe de chine
46½ × 6⅜ in.
Collection of Eleanor Jackson Searl

ROSTER OF ROYCROFTERS

The names on this list have been culled from a variety of sources, both printed and hand-written. It is a preliminary (and thus far, incomplete) listing of known Roycrofters and others believed to be connected to the community.

Adams, Adell
Adams, Harry
Ahrens, Carl
Ahrens, Pauline
Andrews, Edith
Angell, Fin
Armading, ?
Arnold, Marian
Austin, Mabel
Avery, Harry
Bagley, Walter
Bailey, Martha
Bailey, Mary
Bailey, Oliver
Baker, Maud
Bann, Freddy
Barnes, Burt
Barnhart, Clara E.
Barry, Harriet
Bartzhold, Louis
Bascom, Frank
Bean, Theodore
Becker, Gladys
Beebe, Charles
Beebe, Clayton
Beebe, George
Beebe, John
Beebe, William
Bell, Eva
Bell, Fred
Bender, Fred
Bender, Nellie
Bernhart, George
Betzler, Stacy
Biddick, Fred
Bissell, ?
Bittong, Robert
Blackman, Abbie
Blackman, Anson Alonzo
Bloecker, Bertha
Bodkin, Edward
Bodkin, Emma
Bodkin, Joseph
Bonham, Lillian
Bowen, Emmett
Bowen, F. A.
Bowen, Francis
Bowen, Gertrude
Bowen, Harlow
Bowen, Hazel
Bowen, Herbert
Bowen, Jennie
Bowen, Nellie
Bradburn, J. D.
Brewster, Myrtle
Brown, Charlotte
Brown, F. A.
Brown, Frank E.
Buffum, Ella
Buffum, Harry
Buffum, Herbert
Buffum, John H.
Buffum, Wallace
Burnap, Frank
Burns, Helen

Burns, Miss
Bushnell, Mr.
Butler, Ladson
Cadzow, James
Carini, Margaret
Carmody, Frances J.
Carmody, Mary
Carrol, Margaret
Carrol, Marjorie
Carrol, Nellie
Chandler, Lyman
Charlesworth, Alice
Chase, Dorothy
Chatman, Myrtle
Chimney, Alice
Clark, Clara
Clarke, Grace Richey
Cleaveland, George N.
Coghill, Cora
Cole, Arthur H.
Cole, Edith
Comstock, Cordelia
Comstock, John
Comstock, Katherine
Connor, Jerome
Conrad, Alfred
Conrad, Caroline
Conrad, Charles
Conrad, Gene
Conrad, May
Conrad, Sophia
Corah, Grace
Corah, Jay W.
Corah, Leslie
Cornell, Edith
Cotton, Russell
Cox, Esther
Cox, ?
Creamer, George
Creen, Miss
Cummings, Richard
Curtis, Bertha
Curtis, Millard
Dake, Orpha
Dale, Dolores
Dalzell, William
Danner, Albert
Danner, Elizabeth
Danner, Fred
Darbee, Thelma
Darling, Dee
Darling, Howard
Davis, Georgia
Dawning, Dorothy
Dearmeyer, Vera
DeCamp, Nellie
Deheck, Andrew
Denshaw, George
Denslow, W. W.
Derby, Eugene
Deuz, Terence R.
Dickman, ?
Dirlam, H. Kenneth
Dodge, Florence
Donahue, Thelma
Donnor, Gida
Donohue, Ann
Donter, Willard
Dooley, Florine
Dorsey, Sabina
Douglass, Eleanor
Dovell, Clara A.
Dreil, Harry

Dubel, Madge
Dubes, Albert
DuBois, Julia E.
Dwyer, Josephine
Eastland, Doris
Ebert, Elmer
Eckman, Rena Sarah
Edwards, William
Ehiers, Dorothy
Ehler, Dorothy
Ehrenberg, George
Ehrenberg, Leroy
Elbe, Adolf
Ensinger, Gus
Erion, Bessie M.
Ess, Andrew
Ess, Arthur
Ess, Clarence
Ess, Emma
Ess, Florence
Ess, Floyd
Ess, Helen Willson
Ess, Lillie
Ess, Maud
Ess, Nicholas
Evans, Fanny
Ewald, Carl
Faber, Charles
Faber, Maude
Faber, Nick
Fahringer, June R.
Fair, Nina
Faller, Annabelle
Fattey, Bertha
Fattey, Cecil
Fattey, Clayton
Fattey, Eleanor Farrell
Fattey, Elgie
Fay, Wilson H.
Feesley, Milton
Ferdinand, Julius
Ferguson, Emma
Field, Lille
Flanagan, Florence
Flemming, Theodore
Flynn, Richard
Forgey, Craig
Foss, Lucille
Fournier, Alexis Jean
Fournier, Emma
Fournier, Grace
Fournier, Paul
Fox, Alvina
Fox, Sylvester R.
Franck, Peter
Franz, Clara
Frischman, Hudson
Frischman, Margaret
Fuchs, Ernest A.
Fuchs, Herbert J.
Fuest, Margaret G.
Fuller, Beatta
Fuller, Lena
Gaillard, John
Garcia, Manuel
Gardner, Minnie
Garrett, Arthur T.
Garrett, Paul
Gaspard, Emmira
Gaspard, Jules Maurice
Gearhart, Lillian Hawley
Gilbert, Florence
Goeller, ?

Golligan, Edward
Goslin, Jeanette
Grabau, John
Granger, ?
Grant, Ellen
Griffin, Elizabeth
Griffin, Fanny
Guittler, Jennie
Hagard, Hugh
Hall, Charles S.
Hall, Grace
Hall, Harry
Hall, John
Hartmann, Sadakichi
Harvey, E. S.
Haskell, Violet
Hausauer, Maynard
Hawthorne, Julia
Hawthorne, Lyle
Hawthorne, Margaret
Heaps, Arthur
Hehn, ?
Heim, Florence
Heim, Kenneth
Heinaman, Arthur
Heinrich, Laura R.
Heitman, Frances
Heitman, Freda
Helin, Joyce
Heller, Lester
Henry, Grace
Hessel, Marian Beebe
Higgins, Frank J.
Hiles, Alice
Hiles, Elberta
Hiles, Harrison N.
Hill, Violet
Hilt, Otto
Hines, Mildred
Hise, James L.
Hoag, Liva
Holland, Lester Cross
Holmes, Bertha
Holmes, John
Holtzborn, Cecilia
Hood, Beulah Rudd
Hood, Lucy
Hopkins, Susan
Horton, Marian
Hour, Robert
Howe, Wilma
Hoyle, John T.
Hubbard, Alice Moore
Hubbard, Alta Fattey
Hubbard, Bertha
Hubbard, Elbert II
Hubbard, Juliana
Hubbard, Katherine
Hubbard, Miriam
Hubbard, Ralph
Hubbard, Sanford
Hubbard, Dr. Silas
Hubbs, George
Hubbs, Loretta
Hubbs, Mrs. Ray
Hudgins, Gertrude
Hunter, Dard
Ingersoll, Walter E.
Ingham, Alberto Vyrde
Jackson, Cecil
Jackson, Merritt
Jackson, Myra
Jackson, Myrtle